SECOND FRIENDS

FATHER MILTON T. WALSH

Second Friends

C. S. Lewis and Ronald Knox
in Conversation

IGNATIUS PRESS   SAN FRANCISCO

© 2008 Ignatius Press, San Francisco
All rights reserved
ISBN 978-1-58617-240-4
Library of Congress Control Number 2007938142
Printed in the United States of America ∞

To my brother priests,
first friends and second friends
in the Vineyard of the Lord,
and
with special gratitude to

Monsignor Cornelius J. Burns
(1929–1995)

who so generously shared with me
his love for the great English convert authors

*He followed the truth . . . It was a wine he thirsted for,
he was love-sick for its romance . . . a man who lived
haunted by the truth, and died desiring it.*

— Ronald Knox
"The Conversion of Newman"
Occasional Sermons

Contents

Foreword

This—to quote C. S. Lewis—"is the most noble and joyous book I've read these ten years."[1] It is also one of the most surprising. After immersing myself in the writings of Lewis for half a century I could not, when I first heard Milton Walsh talk about the book, see how C. S. Lewis and Ronald Knox could benefit from being placed together. I am now totally converted. This book had led me deeper into Lewis' own writings than any I've read.

I share Fr. Walsh's regret that Lewis and Knox did not get to know one another better. But there are reasons for this. Fr. Knox was the Catholic Chaplain to Oxford University between 1926 and 1939, shortly before Lewis was converted in 1931 and about the same time Lewis was writing his first theological book, *The Problem of Pain* (1940). Perhaps if Knox had been in Oxford during the time Lewis was writing theology they might have come to know one another well. I think Fr. Knox is one of those Lewis would have asked to advise him on the series of radio talks that became *Mere Christianity* (1952).

This is certainly suggested by the delight they took in one another on the occasion that their mutual friend Dr. Havard brought them together, and when—as Fr. Walsh tells us—Lewis greeted Knox as "possibly the wittiest man in Europe".

[1] Walter Hooper, ed. *The Collected Letters of C. S. Lewis*, vol. II (San Francisco: Harper, 2004), p. 534.

It was a promising beginning. But if Knox had remained in Oxford I expect he would have noticed that Lewis was to a large extent "trapped" by his success as an apologist. Having found himself such a successful defender of "Mere Christianity" Lewis worried about what would happen to his readers if he discussed things specifically Catholic. There is also the fact that, much as he loved "rational opposition", Lewis was shy of addressing what he called "real theologians", and this would have included Catholic priests of such eminence as Monsignor Knox.

But enough conjecture. What I most love about this book is that Milton Walsh, after admitting that it is a pity they did not get to know one another better, gets on with a job so worthwhile you end up wondering if it made much difference whether Lewis and Knox were close personal friends or not. The important thing, as the author says in the Introduction, is that both men were "apostles" who "cared passionately about what they believed". Or as Lewis pointed out in the chapter on "Friendship" in *The Four Loves* (1960), it is when two people "*see the same truth*" that Friendship is born.[2]

In that same chapter Lewis pointed out that Friendship is always "about something", and there were perhaps few people living at the time who cared more than Lewis and Knox about making the Gospel known. Milton Walsh is an encyclopedia of the ideas Knox and Lewis wrote about, and by laying their thoughts side by side like railway tracks their separate apologetics influence one another and *together* constitute a powerful case for Christianity—in some ways more powerful than if read separately. The instance which moved me most was their joint work on *Miracles* in Chap-

[2] C. S. Lewis, *The Four Loves* (London: Bles, 1960), chap. 4, p. 83.

ter Four. My debt to Lewis is so enormous that it is not easy for me even to imagine how *anyone* could improve his effectiveness in writing about that subject. But I did not know that Knox had already addressed the question in *Some Loose Stones* (1913). Lewis came along and built on an edifice Knox had prepared.

I concede that the case for Miracles, when Fr. Walsh has these like-minded contemporaries, these "Second Friends", working in tandem, is one of many instances in which the "case" for Miracles is made not twice as strong, but many times stronger. They worked in tandem, not because their thoughts were identical, but because there were no two contemporaries writing at the time who complemented one the other so perfectly.

Why did no one think of putting them together before? I think I know the answer. Milton Walsh is young enough to be the grandson of Lewis and Knox, but he is so effective in getting into the "skins" on those men that one could easily mistake him for their contemporary.

Second Friends?

On most afternoons in the 1930s, two of the most popular Christian writers in England took a daily walk through
the meadows of Oxford. They did not walk together: C. S.
Lewis ambled along Addison's Walk near Magdalen College, while Ronald Knox strolled around neighboring Christ
Church Meadow. They enjoyed talking with friends during
these outings. It was on Addison's Walk that J. R. R. Tolkien
and Hugo Dyson first suggested to Lewis the idea that Christianity could be viewed as a myth that happened to be historically true, an idea that was instrumental in his Christian conversion. As for Ronald Knox, he once confided to
his friend Dom Hubert van Zeller that his idea of a perfect
vacation would be to take his daily walk in Christ Church
Meadow discussing the nature of God with his Jesuit friend,
Father Martin D'Arcy. (Dom Hubert admitted candidly that
this was certainly not *his* idea of a jolly summer holiday!)

Late in the 1930s, Doctor Humphrey Havard invited
Knox and Lewis to lunch, and the two men had a most
enjoyable afternoon. Many years later Havard recalled the
occasion:

> Lewis started well by greeting him [Knox] as possibly the
> wittiest man in Europe. After that the party flourished, and
> both afterward expressed their delight with the other. Each
> was witty, humorous, and very widely read; each had an un-
> obtrusive but profound Christian faith. They had much to

say to each other, and it was a pity that Monsignor Knox left Oxford and that they had few further opportunities to meet. Each of them later told me of their admiration and liking for each other.[1]

Had Knox stayed in Oxford, might he and Lewis have become friends? If so, they would have been what Lewis called "Second Friends". Lewis once described Arthur Greeves as his "First Friend" and Owen Barfield as his "Second Friend". What was the difference? He said a First Friend shares all your interests and most secret delights and sees the world as you do: "he and you join like raindrops on a window."[2] And the Second Friend? He shares your interests but approaches them from a different angle: "He has read all the right books but has got the wrong thing out of every one."[3] The discussions and arguments provide a seedbed for affection. Lewis was blessed with many Second Friends, and their good-natured but deadly serious debates bore fruit in the remarkable writings of the Inklings.

Knox was not a member of this illustrious circle, but he and Lewis had much in common. They were at home in the world of Oxford and enjoyed the debates and enterprises of academic life. Neither went abroad very often, and they had a passion for trains when traveling around Britain. As young men, both Knox and Lewis had been stylish in their dress, but in later life they were deliberately unconcerned about such things. Politics did not loom large: they bought the *Times* primarily for its crossword puzzle. They were much sought after as speakers, and they each had an unaffected

---

[1] James Como, ed., *Remembering C. S. Lewis: Recollections of Those Who Knew Him* (San Francisco: Ignatius Press, 2005), p. 361.

[2] C. S. Lewis, *Surprised by Joy: The Shape of My Early Life* (New York: Harcourt, Brace and Company, 1956), p. 199.

[3] Ibid., p. 199.

delivery, reading from a typescript in a reserved yet decisive manner. They wore their accomplishments lightly, and even people who hardly knew them referred to them as "Ronnie" and "Jack" (a nickname Lewis devised for himself as a child).

On a deeper level, C. S. Lewis and Ronald Knox shared a passion for the truth and the conviction that the pursuit of truth led to faith in Jesus Christ. This conviction had been the *raison d'être* for the foundation of Oxford University, but by the twentieth century such a stance was something of an embarrassment to many of their learned colleagues. J. R. R. Tolkien once cautioned Lewis that by writing about his Christian faith he was violating an unwritten law of the academic world: a professor was free to write scholarly works in his field of expertise, and he would be forgiven for writing detective stories (as Ronald Knox did), but actually to offer one's own personal religious views—and worse, to want to convince others to embrace them—was simply not done. Of course, Tolkien was delighted Lewis did it, and millions have shared that delight.

C. S. Lewis and Ronald Knox were not theologians in an academic sense; neither of them claimed to be. They were apostles. They cared passionately about what they believed, and they wanted to share with others what had captivated their minds and hearts. In the course of this book we will explore how these two Christian apologists addressed fundamental questions of the faith.

Knox and Lewis brought to their writing a convert's zeal. Strictly speaking, neither one was a convert—they had both been baptized and raised in the Church of England. Lewis lost his faith, went through a period of atheism, and then rediscovered Christianity; Knox's spiritual pilgrimage led him into the Catholic Church. But certainly what each man experienced can be called a conversion in the sense that it marked a profound change in the values and beliefs he cherished. Since these experiences had such a powerful effect on Knox's and Lewis' understanding of the Christian faith, it will be helpful to review the stories of their conversions.

Although they were born ten years apart and in different circumstances, Ronald Knox and C. S. Lewis had a great deal in common. They both had roots in Northern Ireland, and their families leaned toward the Evangelical expression of Anglicanism. Their families were not puritanical, but there was a great emphasis on a personal relationship with Christ nourished by a devout reading of the Bible and attendance at Anglican services. Both grew up in an atmosphere in which "Papistry" was despised and High Church practices were viewed with suspicion. Each was the youngest child in his family, and each endured the tragedy of losing his mother at a young age (Lewis when he was ten, Knox at the age of four). They were very close to their siblings and were precocious children. In the family home, they were encouraged to read English literature, write stories and poetry, and study classical and modern languages.

Both attended boarding schools, but they fared differently: Knox did well at Summer Fields and loved Eton; Lewis hated Wynyard School (which he called "Belsen" in his memoir) and, after one year at another school, was allowed to leave and be instructed by a tutor. By upbringing and temperament Knox and Lewis shared a love for logical argument, romantic literature, and the classics. They were thus well equipped for Oxford, and in that city they were in their element. They seemed destined to miss each other there: Knox began undergraduate studies at Balliol in 1906 and later became a chaplain at Trinity College; he left Oxford in 1917, the same year Lewis arrived as an undergraduate. After the

First World War, Lewis returned to Oxford, where he lived until 1954; for thirteen years (1926–1939) Knox lived near him, but it appears that their paths did not cross. (For the first five years of that period, Lewis was not a Christian and would hardly have sought out the company of the chaplain to the Catholic students at Oxford; Knox for his part purposely limited his attentions to Catholic undergraduates.) They had mutual friends, however, and were aware of one another's writings. In many ways they were like other dons who enjoyed the intellectual stimulation of the common room, the atmosphere of academic pursuits, and the interest in the liberal arts that life at Oxford offered. It is when we look at their lives through the prism of their conversion experiences that we gain some understanding of how much more they had in common—and how different they were.

The pattern of C. S. Lewis' religious pilgrimage is a common one: it is the story of rediscovering the faith of one's childhood as an adult. Many people pass through a stage of questioning or even rejecting the religion of their youth; if they recover it, it is no longer simply the faith of their family and acquaintances—it becomes *their* faith. Granted that the pattern itself is common enough, Lewis' conversion was significant because it meant, not simply the recovery of the religion of his childhood, but the acceptance of a deeper and richer vision of the Christian faith. And it is remarkable for the fruit it bore: he brought the enthusiasm of a convert to his description of that faith. If he called this "mere" Christianity, it was not because it was superficial or bland; belief became a romance for Lewis, and he wanted others to share his experience of falling in love.

We are fortunate that Lewis wrote two books in which the story of his conversion is central, one soon after the event and another twenty years later. However, while both works are autobiographical, neither is autobiography as such: the first, *The Pilgrim's Regress*, relates the story of Lewis' conversion in highly allegorical terms; the other, *Surprised by Joy: The Shape of My Early Life*, leaves much unsaid—so much so that Lewis' friend Havard suggested a more appropriate title might be *Suppressed by Jack*. Fortunately, Lewis' abundant correspondence and the recollections of his friends help to fill in the picture.

Lewis describes his Welsh father as passionate, rhetorical, and emotional, his English mother as cool, rational, and ironic. These strands intertwined in their son: throughout his life Jack combined a keenness for logical argumentation with a love for the poetic and the imaginative. In *Surprised by Joy* Lewis tells us that his father had some interest in Anglican liturgy but that religion did not figure strongly in his childhood. His maternal grandfather was a minister in the Church of Ireland and came from a long line of clergymen. Given the fact that the Lewises lived in Ireland, it is not surprising that his grandfather's sermons were often laced with invective against Roman Catholicism. In spite of this passionately Protestant grandfather, in later life Lewis resented the presumption that "Puritania" referred to his own upbringing. His hostility to Puritanism was complemented by a strong distaste for Anglo-Catholicism.

In both accounts of his conversion, Lewis refers to his fundamental religious desire as "Joy", which he describes in this way: "Joy (in my sense) has indeed one characteristic, and one only, in common with them [Happiness and Pleasure]; the fact that anyone who has experienced it will want it again. Apart from that, and considered only in its quality, it might almost equally well be called a particular kind of unhappiness or grief. But then it is a kind we want."[4] Lewis

---

[4] Ibid., pp. 17-18.

believed that this sense of romantic longing lies lodged deeply in every human heart and that ultimately it is a longing for God.

The harsher realities of life blocked the way back to the "joys" of Lewis' early childhood: the death of his mother, a growing estrangement from his father, separation from his older brother when he went off to boarding school, and the brutality of Wynyard all conspired to cast a shadow over his life. A shaft of light fell upon him when, at Cherbourg School, he first encountered the works of Richard Wagner, which sparked his lifelong love for Northern mythology. But it was also here that he lost his Christian faith. A contributing factor was the way his teachers treated the religious themes in Virgil's *Aeneid* as sheer nonsense; this puzzled the thirteen-year-old Lewis, who wondered if the Christian religion might not be nonsense, too. A more significant part was played, unwittingly, by a school matron who was fascinated by Spiritualism and the occult. In order to please his father —and only to please him—Lewis received the sacraments of confirmation and the Eucharist in this state of unbelief.

For the next few years, Jack was able to nurture his passion for Norse mythology, but the rational aspect of his personality came to the fore when William Kirkpatrick became his tutor. Lewis describes him as "a purely logical entity" whose pedagogy was revealed in their first conversation: the young student casually observed that the scenery of Surrey was wilder than he expected, and Kirkpatrick ruthlessly challenged all of his presuppositions, concluding that Lewis had no right to any opinion on the subject. As regards Lewis' religion (or lack of it), Kirkpatrick provided the footnotes, the scholarly apparatus that enabled his pupil to defend his atheism rationally. By the time he went to Oxford, C. S. Lewis was not only firmly convinced that there was no God, but he was happy to live in a world that was free of the Christian

God. He recognized that Christianity made ultimate claims, that it was *the* "transcendental Interferer":

> If its picture were true then no sort of "treaty with reality" could ever be possible. There was no region even in the innermost depth of one's soul (nay, there least of all) which one could surround with a barbed wire fence and guard with a notice No Admittance. And that was what I wanted; some area, however small, of which I could say to all other beings, "This is my business and mine only."[5]

The God whom Lewis rejected was "the Landlord" described at the beginning of *The Pilgrim's Regress*—a capricious autocrat who piles rule upon rule and arbitrarily visits punishment on offenders.

Having rejected the idea of a transcendent Good, Lewis found his pessimism carrying him into a philosophy that viewed the material world as fundamentally evil. Lewis felt the need to protect some inner spiritual spark of goodness from the mire of the material world; he embraced a kind of Puritan asceticism shorn of Puritan belief. This spark was the elusive and alluring Joy, but whatever this thing might be, he was certain it was not "God". Jack's father and brother recognized that many people pass through a stage of atheism, but they worried that, given his state of mind, Oxford might ruin him.

In any event, Lewis did not spend much time at Oxford; in 1917 he enlisted in the army. He wrote little about his wartime experiences (fewer than ten pages in *Surprised by Joy*), but the suffering and destruction of that conflict served to confirm Lewis' pessimistic outlook. On the other hand, mention should be made of two authors he encountered at this stage in his life who helped to tip the balance the other

---

[5] Ibid., p. 172.

way. In 1916 he fortuitously picked up a copy of a book called *Phantastes* by George MacDonald, and he began a relationship with the man whom he would come to view as his "master". The book appealed to Lewis' love of romanticism, but it also introduced him to something humble and homey —holiness. Lewis later credited MacDonald with "baptizing" his imagination. The other author was G. K. Chesterton, whom Lewis first read while convalescing during the war. In retrospect, Lewis found it strange that Chesterton had appealed to him, since Lewis' pessimism, atheism, and dislike of sentiment were so contrary to Chesterton's views. Lewis admired Chesterton's humor and goodness, although he adds that at this time, "I did not need to accept what Chesterton said in order to enjoy it."[6] But seeds had been planted: both of these authors were to become lifelong favorites of Lewis and were to influence him significantly on his religious journey.

After the war, Jack Lewis returned to Oxford to resume his studies. Like students in every generation, he explored various avenues that promised to provide a key to the meaning of existence. The wax museum of these "isms" can be toured in the pages of *The Pilgrim's Regress*: Mr. Enlightenment (rationalism and Freudianism), Zeitgeistheim (the contemporary spirit of the age), Mr. Sensible (sophisticated worldliness), Mr. Neo-Angular and Mr. Broad (intellectual and practical forms of Christian modernism), and so on. Idealism, materialism, and Hegelianism are all judged in retrospect to be cul-de-sacs on the road to Joy. His pilgrimage was influenced by his reading of Henri Bergson, from whom he came to accept the necessary existence of the universe. Acceptance of the fact of "reality" diluted somewhat Lewis'

[6] Ibid., p. 190.

pessimism: ravings against the world implied the ability to separate oneself from it, and Lewis came to consider this position unrealistic. Of his "Stoical Monism" he writes: "It was perhaps the nearest thing to a religious experience which I had since my prep-school days. It ended (I hope forever) any idea of a treaty or compromise with reality. So much the perception of even one Divine attribute can do."[7]

Far more influential than his reading were the friends Lewis made at this time, especially A. C. Harwood and Owen Barfield. Originally it was a love of poetry that drew Lewis to the two men, but religious discussions came to figure in the friendship as well, especially when they embraced anthroposophy, for which Lewis had no use.[8] It is noteworthy that Barfield did not believe that this philosophy contradicted Christianity, and so Lewis found himself interacting with a committed—albeit somewhat unorthodox—Christian. Along with curing Lewis of "chronological snobbery" (the conviction that newer is always better), these discussions led Lewis to explore the relationship between truth and imagination, a topic whose significance will appear later in Lewis' conversion story.

Other friendships developed, and increasingly with Christians, such as Nevill Coghill, Hugo Dyson, and J. R. R. Tolkien. This last was a Roman Catholic and a philologist, which required Lewis to overcome two prejudices: since childhood he had been warned never to trust a Papist, and on joining the English faculty, never to trust a philologist. Their lifelong friendship was a source of mutual imaginative enrichment, and we are the beneficiaries through *The Lord of the Rings* and *The Chronicles of Narnia*. Dyson and Tolkien

---

[7] Ibid., p. 205.

[8] Anthroposophy was a religious philosophy developed by Rudolf Steiner (1861–1925), who sought to combine natural science, psychology, eastern religions, and Christianity.

were also to play an important part in Lewis' conversion to Christianity.

In a chapter called "Checkmate" in *Surprised by Joy*, Lewis describes the stages that led him from committed atheism to an evening in 1929, when, as "perhaps, that night, the most dejected and reluctant convert in all England,"[9] he admitted God was God and knelt down in his room to pray. He outlines the various moves that brought about his "defeat". Surveying the chessboard, Lewis notes that his books had begun to turn against him: it dawned on him that his favorite authors were religious, and most of them Christian. In retrospect, Lewis admits, "I must have been as blind as a bat not to have seen, long before, the ludicrous contradiction between my theory of life and my actual experiences as a reader."[10] Writers hostile to religion—George Bernard Shaw, H. G. Wells, John Stuart Mill, Edward Gibbon, and Voltaire—continued to be entertaining but too simple, lacking in depth; the roughness of life did not appear in their books. His favorite authors—not only contemporaries such as Chesterton and MacDonald, but Samuel Johnson, Spenser, Milton, and the classical authors Plato, Aeschylus, and Virgil—were all religious. His studies of English literature yielded the same result: precursors of the Enlightenment he found boring and pompous, while religious authors such as John Donne and George Herbert were "intoxicating". An obvious question should have been, "Are these believers perhaps right?" but Lewis did not ask himself that question. Rather, he assumed a Gnostic perspective: the Christian myths conveyed a glimmer of truth to the ignorant masses unable to scale the Olympian heights of absolute Idealism accessible to the philosophical elite. Looking back,

[9] Lewis, *Surprised by Joy*, pp. 228–29.
[10] Ibid., p. 213.

Lewis found this attitude ironic, to say the least: "The implication—that something which I and most other undergraduates could master without extraordinary pains would have been too hard for Plato, Dante, Hooker and Pascal—did not yet strike me as absurd."[11]

God's first two moves were aimed at Lewis' heart and head, respectively. First, a rereading of Euripides' *Hippolytus* yanked Lewis off the desert island of his philosophical pretensions and planted him firmly in the land of longing. "Joy" was back, and it was not content to be pigeonholed as "aesthetic experience". In the wake of this stirring of the heart, the next move was addressed to Lewis' intellect. While reading a book called *Space, Time and Deity* by Samuel Alexander, Lewis was struck by the author's descriptions of "enjoyment" and "contemplation". For Alexander, enjoyment is an inner mental experience, while contemplation involves a relationship to "the other" outside of us. Lewis gives several examples, the simplest being that when he looks at a table, he "enjoys" the act of seeing the table and "contemplates" the table itself. The corollary, for Lewis, was shocking: where formerly it had seemed obvious to him that the object of love or hate was "the other", in fact attending to one's feeling of love or hate required *ceasing* to attend to "the other". Introspection attends to ("enjoys") the mental images and physical sensations within and consequently triggers a lack of attending to ("contemplating") the other without.

What might appear to be rather abstract philosophizing had a profound impact on Lewis' whole system of values. He came to see that the images and sensations that he sought in his pursuit of Joy were "merely the mental track left by the

---

[11] Ibid., p. 215.

passage of Joy—not the wave but the wave's imprint on the sand."[12] Joy was indisputably a desire, but a desire directed to its object and not to itself. Joy's response to Lewis' longing was: "You want—I myself am your want of—something other, outside, not you nor any state of you."[13] For Lewis this was a literally awe-inspiring insight, providing a road out of even the most extreme solitude to the objective reality beyond our senses.

God's third move came when Lewis connected this insight about Joy to his idealistic philosophy. In such a system "the other" is "the Other", what Lewis called "the Absolute", and insofar as we exist at all, we exist because we are rooted in this Absolute. Joy is no deception; it is the yearning for unity with the truly real Absolute. At the time, this connection did not seem significant to Lewis; it appeared to him that he had merely lost a pawn, and he was unaware that this move portended checkmate in a few moves.

In the midst of this philosophical explanation, Lewis notes two events that took place, one right after the other. First, he read Chesterton's *The Everlasting Man* and was impressed by how sensible the Christian outline of history was; paradoxically, he found himself thinking how reasonable the Christian religion was, "apart from its Christianity".[14] Soon afterward he was shocked when an ardently atheistic friend commended the historicity of the Gospels and mused that it almost looked like all that mythological stuff about a dying God may have really happened once.

Returning to his philosophical reflections, Lewis decided

[12] Ibid., p. 219.
[13] Ibid., p. 221.
[14] Ibid., p. 223.

that if the purpose of life was to enter into unity with the Absolute, he had better give it a try. That is, he recognized that this intellectual insight demanded an ethical expression. It seemed that the ascent would require tremendous effort. But then another thought occurred to him: this "Spirit" could not be unaware of, or indifferent to, Lewis' efforts. In fact, this "Other" may in fact be approaching *him*. What might have filled him with relief in fact instilled terror: "Amiable agnostics will talk cheerfully about 'man's search for God.' To me, as I then was, they might as well have talked about the mouse's search for the cat."[15] Why was Lewis horrified? He knew that if this was true, and if the Other was in reality a personal God, then he could no longer call his soul his own. The price was unconditional surrender; this Other could demand all. It was in this frame of mind that the most reluctant convert in all England fell to his knees on that evening in 1929.

Surprised by Joy is remarkably reticent regarding the final leg of Lewis' religious journey, from belief in God to Christian faith. In the space of a few pages, we are simply told that Lewis started going to church, not out of any conviction regarding the truth of Christianity, but from a sense that he should do something concrete to manifest his newfound theism. The two viable religious alternatives for Lewis appeared to be Christianity and Hinduism; he rejected the latter because it seemed to be more of a philosophy than a religion, and he judged that it lacked the historical claims of Christianity. Lewis concludes *Surprised by Joy* by relating that one morning he took a ride to the Whipsnade Zoo, and in the course of that short journey, he came to the conviction that Jesus was the Son of God.

[15] Ibid., p. 227.

The description of Lewis' Christian conversion is disappointingly scanty on details, although it does ring true for someone to have a question resolve itself almost unconsciously after a lengthy period of intense intellectual effort. However, followers of Lewis' pilgrimage want to know more, and there are clues to the forces at work that made that trip to the zoo so memorable. One crucial incident was a prolonged conversation between Lewis, Tolkien, and Dyson on the evening of (and into the wee hours of the morning after) September 19, 1931. The subject was initially the truthfulness of myths. Lewis held that myths were lies, albeit lies "breathed through silver". Tolkien vociferously disagreed. He held that the human ability to create myths was a reflection of the creativity of the Creator in the creature: since we are made in the image of God, something of his creative power is at work, however imperfectly, in us.

This fusing of truth and myth had a profound impact on Lewis in two ways. First, it helped him find a way to connect truth and imagination. Lewis' preoccupation with this question is reflected in a poem written about this time, in which he ponders the relationship between reason (the maid) and imagination (the mother):

> Oh who will reconcile in me both maid and mother,
> Who make in me concord of the depth and the height?
> Who make imagination's dim exploring touch
> Ever report the same as intellectual sight?
> Then could I truly say, and not deceive,
> Then wholly say, that I BELIEVE.[16]

Tolkien and Dyson argued that imagination's "dim touch" and reason's "intellectual sight" did report the same truth.

[16] Quoted in Walter Hooper, *C. S. Lewis: A Companion and Guide* (San Francisco: Harper, 1996), p. 568.

Second, the truthfulness of myth presented the Christian faith in a new light: according to Tolkien and Dyson, who were both Christians, the story of Christ is the "truth myth" in a unique way—it not only conveys truth in the way other myths do, but it actually *happened*. As a story, it shares the imaginative sweep of the great myths that took place "once upon a time", but as an event, it was historically true: "He was crucified under Pontius Pilate." Writing to his Christian friend Arthur Greeves about this conversation, Lewis described it in this way:

> Now the story of Christ is simply a true myth: a myth working on us in the same way as the others, but with this tremendous difference that it *really happened*: and one must be content to accept it in the same way, remembering that it is God's myth where the others are men's myths: i.e., the Pagan stories are God expressing Himself through the minds of poets, using such images as He found there, while Christianity is God expressing Himself through what we call "real things". Therefore it is *true*, not in the sense of being a "description" of God (that no finite mind could take in) but in the sense of being the way in which God chooses to (or can) appear to our faculties.[17]

For Lewis, the union of truth and imagination gave new credence to the Christian claims. Just nine days after this discussion, the road to Whipsnade Zoo became his road to Damascus.

Another important clue to Lewis' conversion is found in *The Pilgrim's Regress*. Here we encounter a puzzling contradiction: in *Surprised by Joy* Lewis has little to say about the Church, and what he says is less than enthusiastic. And yet "Mother Kirk" is the central figure in *The Pilgrim's Regress*. Lewis recognized that conversion to Christ necessarily in-

---

[17] Walter Hooper, ed., *The Collected Letters of C. S. Lewis*, vol. I (San Francisco: Harper, 2004), p. 977.

volved the Church for at least two reasons. First, in both *Surprised by Joy* and in his conversation with Tolkien and Dyson, Lewis expressed confidence in the basic historicity of the story of Christ. This presumes the credibility of the community that handed on the Gospel. Second, and more fundamentally, "Mother Kirk" commands the pilgrim "John" in *The Pilgrim's Regress* to put aside his desire for self-preservation and dive headfirst into a pool. By what authority can she make this demand?

When the pilgrim first meets Mother Kirk, she is a repulsive figure, an old crone in rags. According to "Vertue", some think she has second sight, and others consider her crazy. John does not trust her, and besides, she looks too old and weak to carry him across the Grand Canyon. Only after many adventures does he meet her again, not as a wizened hag but as a radiant queen. Formerly, she had offered help, and this had been refused. Now she commands: the pilgrim must dive into the pool. John would prefer to jump, but she says that this is not an option—it represents yet another attempt of his to save himself. The personifications of philosophies and attitudes that he encountered on his quest return and try to dissuade him from taking the dive. In spite of their appeals, the pilgrim ". . . rubbed his hands, shut his eyes, despaired, and let himself go. It was not a good dive, but, at least, he reached the water head first."[18] It is significant that it is not the Landlord who commands the pilgrim to dive, nor the Landlord's Son, but the Landlord's daughter-in-law—that is, the Bride of Christ.

Lewis had come to realize that the acceptance of Christianity demanded far more than acquiescence to certain theological statements about Jesus Christ: it was necessary to submit to the Church, whether she appeared as a grimy

[18] C. S. Lewis, *The Pilgrim's Regress: An Allegorical Apology for Christianity Reason and Romanticism* (Grand Rapids: Eerdmans, 1958 [1935]), p. 170.

hag or as an elegant monarch. How to express this submission? Lewis was already attending church, but on Christmas morning 1931, he received the Eucharist at Holy Trinity, Headington Quarry. A letter written to his brother a few weeks later (January 17, 1932) indicates that Lewis was still very unclear about the meaning of the sacraments, but his reception of Holy Communion was the way he showed that he was now a Christian. Many of his academic colleagues treated Lewis' conversion with indifference or disdain. Rumors of some religious epiphany in Lewis' life circulated around Magdalen College, although he had been attending chapel for several weeks before it became generally known. This prompted T. S. Eliot to observe that if someone in an Oxford college wished to escape detection, the best place to hide is the chapel!

The story of C. S. Lewis' conversion is a tale of faith lost and found. Ronald Knox's experience is very different. His decision to enter the Catholic Church came at the end of prolonged and exhausting spiritual struggle, and there is no doubt that his "conversion" completely altered his relationship to those who were nearest and dearest to him. And yet, looking back on the chain of events that led him to take this step, he saw his conversion, not as a break with his past, but as the natural goal of his spiritual journey. Toward the end of an account of his conversion, Knox traces the main stages of that journey. Up to the age of fifteen, his religious life was grounded in the fundamental Christian doctrines: the Trinity; the Incarnation, death, and Resurrection of Christ; belief in Heaven and Hell; and the conviction that sins are forgiven through the atoning merits of Christ's Precious Blood. While at Eton he added to these core beliefs a sense that the Christian tradition can make claims on the obedience of the believer, an awareness of the importance of a continuous ministry in the history of the Church, and a sense of special graces attached to sacraments and sacramentals. At Oxford these beliefs were augmented by an increasing recognition of the miraculous efficacy of the Eucharist, a heightened sense of the place of the saints in our lives, and a conviction that the successor of Saint Peter was the "first bishop" of Christendom. To his mind, none of these subsequent doctrines conflicted with previously held beliefs. Knox espoused these beliefs as an Anglican, as did many others in the Anglo-Catholic movement. Why did he find it necessary to join the Catholic Church?

The only account Knox wrote of this process was his *Spiritual Aeneid*; it was written immediately after his entrance into the Catholic Church, and it is filled with names and incidents that were meaningful to his circle of acquaintances in 1918 but signify little to most readers today. He recounts the struggle of Anglo-Catholics to influence the mainstream of the Church of England, and he notes that they were making headway: practices like reservation of the Blessed Sacrament and the use of Eucharistic vestments, which had formerly cost clergymen their jobs, were now gaining acceptance. Why abandon the field just when his considerable talents were so useful to the Catholic cause in Anglicanism? The *Spiritual Aeneid* describes *how* Ronald Knox came to the Catholic faith, but it must be read carefully, and in the context of other writings, to discover *why* he did.

To set the stage, let us briefly review some strands of Ronald Knox's history and personality; here we find again the same combination of logical thought and romanticism that were so marked in C. S. Lewis. Ronnie was a philosophical little boy. When asked at the age of four what he liked doing, he responded that he thought all day, and at night he thought about the past. His excellent education at Eton and Oxford greatly enhanced his acuity, and he developed a passion for debate. Regarding his experience at Oxford, Knox wrote: "If the object of undergraduate life be to gain experience of men and their ways of looking at things, assuredly I filled my measure; but I am afraid little remains . . . except a complete inability to remain inattentive while a fellow-creature is on his legs, whatever his message, and a painful difficulty in restraining myself from taking the floor the moment he has sat down."[19] Like the post-Kirkpatrick Lewis, Knox approached life's questions from a very logical perspective.

Is faith, then, the conclusion of a syllogism? Knox did not see it this way, and at the outset of the *Spiritual Aeneid*, he states that coming to believe certain doctrines is not a strictly logical process: there are unconscious ways of thought learned from others or gained in prayer; and beyond that, the whole complex of one's personal psychology, while not altering the facts, alters how we interpret them. If Knox sought the philosophical highway of "the True", he did not neglect the winding path of "the Beautiful". His romantic side was nurtured by the Pre-Raphaelites, Gothic architecture, and the metaphysical poets of the seventeenth century. It was from this perspective that he first encountered Catholicism, when at the age of fifteen he read R. H. Benson's *The Light Invisible*. This book had been written while Benson was still an Anglican, but for the first time, Ronnie was exposed to the Catholic vision of life in a positive way. Knox's romanticism also found expression in a fondness for lost causes and sympathy for the underdog, which came into play a year later when he first read about the Oxford Movement.

[19] Ronald Knox, *A Spiritual Aeneid* (London: Longmans, Green and Co., 1918), p. 59.

Ronnie's father was a leading bishop in the Evangelical expression of Anglicanism, and to his great consternation it became apparent that his youngest son was becoming a "Ritualist" who sought to combine fidelity to the Book of Common Prayer with the adoption of Catholic ceremonial practices. It may be hard to imagine that chasubles and birettas could be badges of revolution, but they were in some Anglican circles at the beginning of the twentieth century. Knox enjoyed the audacity such accoutrements involved, but the true value of Catholic ritual was for him spiritual. Pleated surplices he could take or leave, but devotion to the reserved Blessed Sacrament was of a different order.

Even as Ronald was taking on more Catholic doctrines, many of his scholarly friends were striving to lighten the doctrinal load of Anglicanism in an effort to make it more acceptable to contemporary hearers. Initially, Knox was sympathetic to their position; why not make the way easier for those who at present held no belief in supernatural religion? "This is, of course the beginning of all Modernism; you misinterpret the lack of faith in others as a need of intellectual conviction, and try to trim the sails of your theology accordingly."[20]

Upon graduation, Knox applied for a fellowship at Trinity College, with an eye to filling the post of chaplain in two years. The approach of ordination to the Anglican clergy transformed the theoretical difficulties surrounding Anglo-Catholicism into concrete dilemmas, and the prospect of exercising ministry in the milieu of Oxford meant dealing with the challenges that some modern scholarship presented to traditional faith. For Knox, these issues crystallized around the question of authority in religion. It is crucial to explore

[20] Ibid., p. 70.

this matter in depth in order to understand why he became a Catholic.

As a candidate for Holy Orders in the Church of England, Knox examined the traditional doctrines of the faith and the scholarly efforts to "restate" those beliefs in a modern way. Many leading advocates of the modernizing approach were prominent churchmen. Several of them were also Knox's friends, but this did not prevent him from experiencing discomfort that official representatives of the Church seemed to be calling into question basic Christian doctrines. How liberal might a clergyman be in presenting the traditional teachings of the Church? On the other hand, given his own decidedly Catholic leanings, Knox wondered how far a churchman could go in advancing a cause that many bishops (his own father among them) resolutely condemned. Knox and his fellow Anglo-Catholics were not interested in leading Anglicans into the Roman Catholic fold; they wanted to restore authentic elements of the English Church that had been lost in the wake of the Reformation. To what extent could he do this as an official representative of the Church of England?

These were internal ecclesial questions; a third issue concerned the relationship between the Church and the academic world. Scholars of "higher criticism" were applying their historical and literary tools to ancient texts and proposing theories that, when applied to the Bible, seemed to call into question some basic presuppositions of the Christian faith.[21] Knox was at home in the academic world; indeed, he had excelled there. How was he to contend with the

---

[21] Higher Criticism refers to a critical study of the sources and literary forms used by the biblical authors; Lower Criticism deals with the recovery of the earliest authentic texts.

authority of scholarship when it challenged the authority of traditional Christianity? Knox carefully studied the arguments of contemporary theologians but did not share their conclusions. He stated his situation with characteristic wit: "I could not accept the disbeliefs which the theologians propounded for my acceptance. If I was to go to heaven with the Higher Critics, it must be on the plea that invincible ignorance blinded me to the light of doubt."[22] At root was a challenge to his logical mind: "When I found that I could not accept the German doctrines which claimed the homage of an expert theologian like Mr Streeter, what was I to do? Was I to say, I am a heretic because Mr Streeter believes this? Or was I to say, Mr Streeter is a heretic because I, merely because I, think that?"[23]

Every Friday, Knox dined with a group of clerical friends who held varying theological perspectives. Soon after his ordination, this group began discussing a forthcoming book that was to offer a "restatement" of theology in contemporary terms; several of its authors belonged to this group, and other contributors were Knox's friends. The book was called *Foundations*, and even before it was published, Knox lampooned its general positions in a poem entitled "Absolute and Abitofhell".[24] The poem was an immediate success,

[22] Knox, *Spiritual Aeneid*, p. 124.

[23] Ibid., p. 135. Burnett Hillman Streeter (1874–1937) was a theologian and New Testament scholar, one of the contributors to *Foundations* and an active supporter of the Modern Churchmen's Union.

[24] The poem was a pastiche of Dryden's "Absalom and Achitophel" and is included in Knox's *Essays in Satire* and *In Three Tongues*. One line is particularly memorable: "When suave Politeness, temp'ring bigot Zeal, Corrected, 'I believe', to 'One does feel'." Lewis quotes it (without attribution) when describing his loss of faith while studying at Cherbourg House; cf. *Surprised by Joy*, p. 60.

but Knox also felt the need to provide a serious rebuttal. This he presented in *Some Loose Stones*, a book that is essential to understanding the development of Knox's religious views.

In the preface, Knox claims that liberal theologians seek to reduce the deposit of faith to the smallest possible dimensions in order to attract the largest number of converts to the Church. Knox advocates a different position, one that he knows many will consider obscurantist: "that there are limits defined by authority, within which theorizing is unnecessary and speculation forbidden; that there are some religious principles of such a priori certainty, that any evidence which appears to conflict with them does not destroy them, as it would destroy a mere hypothesis, but by conflicting with them proves itself to be erroneously or inadequately interpreted."[25] *Some Loose Stones* presents a comparison of the traditional and modernist approaches.

Knox realizes that many people today find it difficult to accept the assertions of Christianity. He creates a figure called "Jones" who represents the ordinary English person. In confronting Jones, the modern theologian seeks to present the truth not most adequately but most palatably: "We ask of a doctrine, not, 'Is it sound?', but, 'Couldn't we possibly manage to do without it?'; not, 'Is it true?', but, 'Can I induce Jones to see it in that light?' "[26] The goal seems to be, not to identify a fixed body of truth, but to describe the minimum expression of truth that will be acceptable to Jones.

In his second chapter, Knox lays out what he considers to

[25] Ronald Knox, *Some Loose Stones: Being a Consideration of Certain Tendencies in Modern Theology Illustrated by Reference to the Book called "Foundations"* (London: Longmans, Green and Co., 1913), p. x.

[26] Ibid., p. 9.

be the crucial difference between traditional and modernist theology: traditional theology begins with certain a priori assumptions and is deductive; modern theology begins with certain hypotheses and is inductive. Knox defends the traditional approach and begins by asking if there are situations in ordinary life where presuppositions are accepted. Certainly there are presuppositions in mathematics: that things that are equal to the same thing are equal to one another is not a truth gained by observation and experiment; it is self-evidently true. What about the uniformity of nature, such as "every effect has a cause"? If one accepts this merely as a hypothesis, every "extraordinary" event (levitation, faith healing, etc.) upsets the hypothesis; more importantly, science itself becomes a nightmare because all scientific hypotheses are founded on the presupposition that things remain what they are and behave in a uniform manner. There is also a moral presupposition: good, not evil, is ultimately the explanation of the world. This could be treated as a hypothesis, and observation of much of what happens in the world could point to an opposite conclusion: that the creator of the world is evil. We recoil from the notion, but why? Not because the hypothesis is flawed, but because we have an a priori conviction that existence is fundamentally good. Thus, when Jones approaches theology, he does so with certain presuppositions: the uniformity of nature, the validity of logic, and, as an heir to Western thought, the basic goodness of creation. (Of course, unbelievers have presuppositions, too: for example, that miracles cannot happen.)

Traditionally, the theologian has applied reason to the accepted presuppositions of Christian faith as these are articulated in Scripture and Tradition and has worked deductively to a more profound understanding of revealed Truth. The modern theologian begins inductively, applying to the Bible the critical principles he would use for any book and examining doctrines from the standpoint of the modern mind; then, as an afterthought, he seeks to demonstrate that his results are substantially identical with received doctrine. At root again are a priori presuppositions: traditional theology presumes that God sent his Son into the world to give us a definitive revelation of himself and to offer us sure guidance in our lives; the presupposition of the modern approach is that man has no authoritative revelation from God but has to work out his own theology.

Toward the end of *Some Loose Stones*, Knox returns to the question of the a priori presuppositions in the Christian faith. What are they, and how are they determined? There is need for some kind of "corporate witness" to determine what the faith of the community is. The orthodox view, according to Knox, is that the faith is handed down through the traditions of the Church; communities interpret the Gospel on the basis of the tradition they have received. When traditions are in conflict, it is necessary for the leaders of the various communities to come together and, under the guidance of the Holy Spirit, to determine which interpretation is true. The authors of *Foundations* suggest a different meaning of "corporate witness": the testimony of holy people whose spiritual experience validates the traditions of the Church. For Knox the traditional approach holds that the authority of the Church determines what belongs to the a priori deposit of faith; the modern approach views the deposit as a hypothesis that is confirmed by experience.

Ronald Knox proposes a dichotomy: the final arbiter must be either authority or "experience". ("Experience" in quotes, because he examines three different meanings of the word: extraordinary revelations, inner special experiences of conversion, and the daily life of believers.) Knox tests "experience" and finds it wanting: historically, holy people never claimed that their experience was constitutive of the Christian faith, except in extremist sects, and in fact their lives were shaped by the Christian faith they received from the tradition of the Church and believed on the authority of the Church. How does someone today determine what constitutes the a priori presuppositions that Christian faith demands? Knox's answer at this point could be a description of Lewis' "mere" Christianity: "Let him trust orthodox tradition to determine what he is to believe, *and common sense to determine what is orthodox tradition.*"[27]

As Knox pondered the conflicts between received teaching and liberal scholarship, he had to wrestle with apparent contradictions and uncongenial implications: Can "common sense" reveal what orthodox tradition is? Does the Church have the authority to claim which a priori presuppositions are off limits to theological speculation? Does the Church of England possess such authority, and does it even want to have it?

Knox was conducting these meditations at a time when Anglican traditions and authority were the subject of public debate. In the same year that *Some Loose Stones* was published, 1913, two incidents took place that highlighted these issues. First, the Anglican monks of Caldey came into conflict with the leadership of the Church of England, and most of the community chose to enter the Roman Catholic Church. Second, an Anglican bishop in Africa invited members of the Free Churches to receive Holy Communion; since these Christians rejected the necessity for episcopal orders in the Church, a neighboring Anglican bishop demanded that the

---

[27] Ibid., p. 216; italics are the author's.

archbishop of Canterbury convoke a court to condemn the heretical proceedings at Kikiyu. Incidents such as Kikiyu bothered Father Knox, but his conviction that the Church of England was part of the great Latin Church of the West remained unshaken.

Larger events were to dwarf these internecine battles: the guns of August heralded the beginning of the Great War. This tragic conflict struck down the cream of European youth, among them many of Ronald's closest friends; but in addition to the great personal cost, it represented a religious challenge to him and his circle. The British military did not take into account the various theological gradations across the Anglican spectrum: the choices were "C of E" or "RC". Some of Ronald's closest friends made the decision to enter the Catholic Church before shipping out, and he did not try to dissuade them. Knox had to confront the fact that although he could adroitly defend the claims of the Church of England in the lecture hall and the pulpit, he could not commend the faith of the Church of England to friends on the battlefield.

Ronald frankly discussed his situation with his father and sought advice from learned Anglican friends and acquaintances. He began to reexamine the classic responses to Roman claims. Interested readers may consult the *Spiritual Aeneid* for a detailed description of his explorations; here it suffices to observe that whatever avenue he took led him back to the papacy. When speaking of the early Church, his solidly Protestant handbooks confidently distinguished between "Arian" and "Catholic" bishops—but the Arian bishops certainly believed they were Catholic. Who was to say that they were not? Or that the followers of Nestorius were not Catholic? Knox notes that "it had never occurred to me before that *what we mean when we talk of the Catholic party is*

the party in which the Bishop of Rome was, and nothing else."[28]
Some appealed to the authority of ecumenical councils; but
councils were decided by majorities, and the majority of
Christendom believed in the Pope. If one rejected authority and believed only in the "experience of Christendom",
the papacy was *the* certain thing of the Middle Ages. If you
sought the *consensus fidelium*, you either despaired of defining
the *fideles* or else defined them as the people in communion
with the visible center of Church unity, the successor of
Saint Peter.

Knox endured this inner struggle for two years, while
fresh news of battles and the deaths of loved ones came to
him. Added to all of this sorrow, and to the awareness of the
great pain he would inflict on those he most dearly loved
should he convert, Knox also records that during this time
the Catholic Church held out no sensible attraction to him
at all. Her services did not provide the excitement he had felt
when he had conducted Anglo-Catholic services; her doctrines, which he had believed for many years, now seemed
strange to him. Of this point in his journey, Knox wrote:
"No isolated doctrines were real or vivid; I was all one great
aching bruise, cared about nothing except one point—was
I in communion with the Church Christ ordained?"[29]

His spiritual struggle had brought him to a crisis: the
choice was not between Rome and Canterbury but between
Rome and unbelief. He went to Farnborough Abbey to make
a retreat, and while there, he read some chapters from *Creator
and Creature* by the Oratorian Father Faber. Knox phrased
his dilemma this way: " 'That', I told myself, 'is the real
trouble: it is not the Pope, or Indulgences, or Infallibility:

---

[28] Knox, *Spiritual Aeneid*, p. 221; italics are the author's.
[29] Ibid., p. 231.

you do not really believe in God as Catholics do. If you can steadily face all this mountain of assertion about the greatness of God in comparison with man, you may be a Catholic yet—but can you?' "[30] This retreat was to be the crucial test: if, after all he had gone through, his soul still sought to serve God, if the world of religious faith was still one in which he could live, then the Kingdom of Heaven was close at hand.

Although, true to his principles, Knox neither expected nor received any sensible illuminations, he knew before the end of the first week of his retreat that grace had triumphed. In attempting to capture something of his relief, and of his previous blindness, Knox offered the following "crude allegory":

> It was as if I had been a man homeless and needing shelter, who first of all had taken refuge under a shed at the back of an empty house. Then he had found an outhouse unlocked, and felt more cheerfulness and comfort there. Then he had tried a door in the building itself, and, by some art, found a secret spring which let you in at the back door; nightly thenceforward he had visited this back part of the house, more roomy than anything he had yet experienced, and giving, through a little crack, a view into the wide spaces of the house itself beyond. Then, one night, he had tried the spring, and the door had refused to open. The button could still be pushed, but it was followed by no sound of groaning hinges. Baffled, and unable now to content himself with shed or outhouse, he had wandered round and round the house, looking enviously at its frowning fastnesses. And then he tried the front door, and found that it had been open all the time.[31]

[30] Ibid., p. 242.
[31] Ibid., p. 243.

On September 22, 1917—the fifth anniversary of his ordination as an Anglican priest—Ronald Knox walked through that open door and entered the Catholic Church.

C. S. Lewis and Ronald Knox wrote about their conversions because they wanted to explain to others why they took the step they did; but they also wrote to explain their conversions to themselves. They asked themselves: How did God use this book or that conversation to bring about the most important event in my life? How did grace touch my mind and heart in order to bring me to faith? Reflection on the dynamics of their conversions shaped their religious writings; the alchemy of intellect, will, imagination, and divine grace created the foundation for their religious lives.

As regards the intellect, Ronald Knox would heartily concur with Lewis' simple statement: "All possible knowledge, then, depends on the validity of reasoning."[32] Both of our authors valued logical thinking, and they professed that the Christian faith should be embraced, not only because it is good, but because it is *true*. Reason provides the intellectual foundation of belief and, as the common ground of believers and unbelievers, holds a central place in the apologetical works of both our authors.

Confident though they were about the reliability of the intellect, both Lewis and Knox expressed the relationship between reason and faith with great care. The truth of Christian revelation, while consonant with reason, goes beyond it. In a letter describing his conversation with Tolkien and Dyson about Christianity as a "true myth", Lewis writes, "The 'doctrines' we get *out* of the true myth are of course *less* true: they are translations into our *concepts* and *ideas* wh.

[32] C. S. Lewis, *Miracles: A Preliminary Study* (New York: Macmillan, 1948), p. 26.

[which] God has already expressed in a language more adequate, namely the actual incarnation, crucifixion, and resurrection."[33] Doctrinal definitions may be secondary, but they
are necessary, and reason continues to play a role after one
comes to believe. Although some opponents of traditional
Christianity hold that to embrace the faith is to sacrifice the
mind, Knox suggests that in fact it is modern thinkers who
prefer vagueness (what Lewis would call "mish-mash") but
that theological mystery requires the hard lines of definition:

> Thus, if you assert by definition that in that which you see
> before you the accidents remain those of Bread, but the sub-
> stance is that of the Body of Christ, you have mystery; you
> have confessed the inadequacy of your reason to understand
> a reconciliation which is nevertheless a necessary one. But
> if you say, "All I know is that Christ is here", that is not
> mystery but vagueness; your statement may mean anything
> or next to nothing; your mind has nothing to bite on, and
> you are left with a merely emotional attitude.[34]

As we have seen, central to the writings of C. S. Lewis is
the theme of "longing", the desires of the heart that motivate us to seek truth and love. Ronald Knox agrees: people
are searching for something that will "save themselves from
the alternative of committing suicide or collecting postage
stamps".[35] This is why for both these writers Christianity is
much more than a doctrinal system: it is above all a personal
relationship with Christ that entails romance, struggle, and
loyalty. It was important for Knox and Lewis that the mind

[33] Lewis, *Letters* I, p. 977.

[34] Ronald Knox and Arnold Lunn, *Difficulties: Being a Correspondence about
the Catholic Religion* (London: Eyre and Spottiswoode, 1952 [1932]), p. 180.

[35] Philip Caraman, ed., *University Sermons of Ronald A. Knox, Together with
Sermons Preached on Various Occasions* (New York: Sheed and Ward, 1963),
p. 72.

and the heart converge, that truth could be defended by reason and not simply by an appeal to feelings. At the same time, they realized that the heart needs to prod the mind if notional truths are to become real Truth, a truth upon which a person is willing to risk everything.

One important way in which the heart influences the mind is in the matter of credibility. In *The Lion, the Witch and the Wardrobe*, Lucy's sister and brothers do not know what to make of her description of Narnia. The Professor tells them there are only three possible explanations: she is deluded, or she is lying, or she is telling the truth. Ultimately, they have to ask themselves if she is mentally unbalanced or the kind of person who would lie. If the answer is no, then they have to believe she is telling the truth, however remarkable her report. Religiously, this credibility is given ultimately to God and, for a Christian, to Jesus Christ, which necessarily entails the credibility of "Mother Kirk" (Mother Church). This trust supports the believer when confronting evidence that seems to contradict the faith or feelings that weaken it. How the mind and the heart interact is crucial to the question of believing.

John's journey in *The Pilgrim's Regress* takes him into strange lands: in the North dwell the shapers of rigid systems, the cerebral intellectuals; in the South are found those guided by their passions, the emotional mystagogues. Most people are constitutionally oriented toward one or the other (Lewis stated that he was of the Northern type, and the same could be said of Knox), but both mind and heart are at work in all of us. The goal is integration, as Lewis suggests in his preface: "With both the 'North' and the 'South' a man has, I take it, only one concern—to avoid them and hold the Main Road. We must not 'hearken to the over-wise *or* to the over-foolish giant'. We were made to be neither cerebral

men nor visceral men, but Men. Not beasts nor angels but
Men—things at once rational and animal."[36] By sticking to
"the Main Road", Lewis does not counsel avoiding *both* the
North and the South (for this is impossible) but seeking the
balance in which the mind guides the heart and the heart
inspires the mind. Knox suggests that the ideal apologist
would combine the lucidity of Saint Thomas with the ardor
of Blaise Pascal.

Lewis and Knox sought to love God with their whole
mind and their whole heart; the work of integrating the
two did not end, it really only began, with their conversions. How did they seek to deepen the marriage of mind
and heart?

Perhaps one of the most common adjectives applied to
C. S. Lewis and Ronald Knox as writers is "imaginative".
As far back as *Some Loose Stones*, Knox identified a lack of
imagination as a great hurdle to the profession of faith. He
related the story of a man he had overheard in a pub who said
he could imagine living several thousand years, but he could
not imagine living for all eternity. Knox commented that
of course we cannot fully imagine infinite space or time
because we are finite creatures. We need to develop our
imaginative skills in order to approach religious truth. He
thought that the majority of his fellow clergy were intellectually convinced about the doctrines they preached, but he
added, "Your failure is a failure of imagination; you believe
the doctrine, but you do not realize it."[37] Lewis also sees
imagination as a privileged path leading to a deeper apprehension of the truth, and he makes an instructive distinction: the difference between fantasy and imagination is that

[36] Lewis, *Pilgrim's Regress*, p. 13.
[37] Knox, *Some Loose Stones*, p. 218.

fantasy represents an escape from the real world, whereas imagination affords a view of the real world from a different angle. As an example, he states that a fairy tale evokes in a child "the dim sense of something beyond his reach and, far from dulling or emptying the actual world, gives it a new dimension of depth. He does not despise real woods because he has read of enchanted woods: the reading makes all real woods a little enchanted."[38]

So far we have considered how Lewis and Knox understood the dynamics of conversion from the point of view of the human faculties of the mind, the heart, and the imagination. But this is only half the story, because there is another actor in the drama. At the heart of the Judeo-Christian tradition stands the conviction that God enters into human history: the history of our race, and our personal histories, too. This means, Lewis observes, that we are playing poker, not solitaire. One of the fascinating elements in conversion stories, going all the way back to Saint Augustine's *Confessions*, is how God allows free play to the seeker, and yet through the whole saga of poor choices, dead ends, and false starts, God patiently waits to welcome the prodigal home. The interplay of grace and free will is one of the most notoriously difficult issues of Christian theology, but both Lewis and Knox were convinced that in the "blessed defeat" of their conversions grace was triumphant and that they had in fact attained a deeper and truer freedom.

They also recognized that, in the beautiful image of Knox, by means of grace "the water of conviction is changed into the wine of faith".[39] Speaking about religious truths, Lewis urged people to pray for the gift of faith, because without

---

[38] Quoted in Hooper, *Companion*, p. 565.
[39] Ronald Knox, *The Belief of Catholics* (New York: Sheed and Ward, 1953 [1927]), p. 145.

it, "Reason may win truth; without Faith she will retain them just so long as Satan pleases."[40] How does the gift of faith alter our certitude about what we believe? Knox distinguishes three kinds of certitude: logical, psychological, and theological. The act of faith does not alter the believer's logical certitude: it does not do away with the arguments that led a person to a moral certitude that the Christian faith is true. The act of faith may or may not alter psychological certitude, the *feeling* that Christianity is true; but such feelings tend to be transitory. The gift of faith alters theological certitude. Grace does not substitute for the natural operations of our mind and heart; it perfects them, raises them to a supernatural level. For Lewis, it is faith in this theological sense that can support a believer when temptation comes, moods change, or arguments are presented that seem to contradict Christian faith. But for him, too, this faith does not substitute for the reasons of the mind or the reasons of the heart.

Our two authors examined the experience of their conversions in order to share their faith with others. They were convinced that the Christian faith rested on sound reasoning and that it fulfilled their deepest human longings. But their own experience and their dealings as spiritual guides to others taught them that the role of an apologist for the Christian faith was not to score debating points or to smother their adversaries in a torrent of suasions. God is a mystery, and so is the human heart—and in the face of these twin mysteries, C. S. Lewis and Ronald Knox approached their evangelizing efforts in a spirit of humility. Let us now explore how they appealed to the mind, the heart, and the imagination in presenting the Christian faith.

[40] C. S. Lewis, "Religion: Reality or Substitute?" quoted in Hooper, *Companion*, p. 604.

CHAPTER ONE

"Proving" God

When Evelyn Waugh published the fragments of Ronald Knox's new apologetics posthumously, he gave them the title "Proving God". Is such a thing possible? Both Knox and Lewis believed that there are rational arguments for the existence of God. Are such arguments wanted? For some people the existence of God is simply a given: they have never grappled with unbelief and thus feel no need to examine the arguments pro and con. For others the existence of God is a part of revelation, to be accepted on faith without recourse to reason. Then there are nonbelievers, for whom the question never comes up, perhaps because the marvels of human achievements have pushed God into the background: "Because our promised land flows with pasteurized milk and synthetic honey, we forget where the raw materials came from, and so we are in danger of forgetting who it was that gave them, and what he asks of us."[1]

More challenging is the case of those who purposely avoid the question of whether God exists because, if he does exist, it would be inconvenient to know what he asks of us. Lewis compares this type of person to a man who avoids going to the doctor because he may hear bad news; such a person "has lost his intellectual virginity".[2] According to Lewis,

[1] Philip Caraman, ed., *Occasional Sermons of Ronald A. Knox* (London: Burns and Oates, 1960), p. 374.
[2] C. S. Lewis, *God in the Dock, and Other Essays on Theology and Ethics* (Grand Rapids: Eerdmans, 1970), p. 111.

this cowardice or laziness carries its own punishments. Knox wonders if this avoidance is always due to idleness, pride, or moral rebellion: he recognizes that habit, convention, and a hundred other remote influences can keep the unbeliever where he is; and if he dreads a heroic decision, it is not for us to cast a stone at him.

So, many people simply presume God exists, and many others simply presume he does not; neither group feels the attraction of arguments "proving" God's existence. It is only when a person moves beyond these presumptions that philosophical arguments come into play. Such a move may be triggered when someone raised in the sheltering cove of a religious family faces the harsh winds of an unbelieving world or when some traumatic event leads a person to seek a meaning to reality beyond the limits of daily routine. In *Surprised by Joy* Lewis describes his own journey to belief in God as one he undertook very reluctantly; and, while Knox did not go through a period of atheism as Lewis did, his own struggles ultimately challenged him to question the truth of a world view based on belief in God. In both cases, they sought an intellectual foundation for belief. In one of his essays, Lewis draws a distinction between "Faith A", which is a settled intellectual assent to the existence of God, and "Faith B", which is a trust or confidence in the God whose existence is assented to.[3] He suggests that for most people who embrace the faith as adults, the philosophical arguments leading to "Faith A" are a necessary precondition of "Faith B". What arguments did he and Knox offer to those exploring the question of the existence of God?

Before we consider which arguments they judged to be more or less helpful, we should bear in mind that our au-

---

[3] "Is Theism Important?" in *God in the Dock*, pp. 172–76.

thors never viewed these arguments in isolation. This is important to remember, because otherwise it might seem that they were advocating a coldly cerebral approach to faith. In practice, philosophical arguments are not separated from spiritual, moral, or historical ones; the conversion experiences of Lewis and Knox illustrate this fact. While neither man would allow a gap in logic to be filled in with the putty of sentiment, they also recognized that coming to faith is more than the conclusion to a syllogism.

Religious Experience

There are many ways to approach the question of the existence of God, and Lewis and Knox found some avenues more helpful than others. Some arguments appeal to the existence of a religious sense that is part of human experience. A superficial version of this argument might be called "anthropological": since widely diverse cultures throughout history all have had some kind of religious component to them, there must be some "higher power" toward which this religious expression is aimed. Knox contends that this boils down to urging someone to believe in God because everyone else has. He compares this argument to the mythical village in which everyone made a living by taking in someone else's laundry, and he does not consider it persuasive. Students of comparative religion can make interesting explorations into the spiritual expressions of various cultures without believing that these religions point to any objective reality; indeed, for a time the young C. S. Lewis engaged in such studies and determined that *all* religions were false. Another problem Knox notes with the anthropological approach is that the conclusions about the nature and attributes of this "higher power" are contradictory: is "it" personal or impersonal? One or many? Eternal and infinite, or limited by time and space? At most this religious aspect of human culture testifies to a common experience of the numinous. Is this apprehension evidence for the existence of God?

With his interest in the power of myth, Lewis gives greater weight to the testimony of the numinous than Knox does; one of his favorite books was Rudolf Otto's *The Idea of the Holy*. The perception of a beauty and goodness beyond the range of our human resources points to a Reality beyond our world. For example, in *The Silver Chair*, the Witch who rules an underground realm tries to convince the children that their memories of a world of sunlight and green grass are but a dream; they respond that it is amazing that they could invent a world so much more vivid than her dark kingdom. The intuition of a longing for something (or someone) that nothing in this world can satisfy has a real object. Religious experience (with a small *e*, to differentiate it from extraordinary mystical experiences) is a part of human life, and for the postconversion Lewis, it serves as a pointer to God. However, the preconversion Lewis dismissed myths as "lies breathed through silver"; what had changed? In his essay "Is Theism Important?" he suggests that "Faith A" (which is approached through philosophical exploration) converts into religious experience what was formerly only potentially or implicitly religious. Thus even for Lewis the testimony of the numinous calls for an intellectual conviction about the existence of God in order to be admitted as evidence.

Knox is more negative on the probative value of religious experience. This is not to say that such experience was unimportant to him, for he was a deeply religious man; rather, he holds such experiences are not valid as *proof* that God exists. In *Broadcast Minds*, he notes that modern skeptics can reduce such experiences to psychological states and demand, "Why cannot the religious sense be a new window opening on this world, instead of a skylight giving on the next?"[4] He contends that you cannot argue from the ideal to the real order of things, from a state of mind to objective reality. Regarding the Cartesian claim that the two "clear and distinct ideas" are the existence of the thinker and the existence of God, Knox asks why, if that is the case, there are so few people who doubt their own existence, and so many who doubt God's. Some of Knox's contemporaries compared a "religious sense" to a "musical sense" and suggested that a person deficient in this "religious sense" should simply rely on "the expert", such as the mystic. Knox will have none of this:

> If a musical enthusiast, after listening to some rare but gay piece, should tell me that as he listened he could actually see elves and gnomes dancing before his eyes, I should be perfectly prepared to reverence both his own superior sensitiveness to musical impressions, and the subtle power of the art which could evoke such an imaginative experience. I should not suppose that elves or gnomes had been present, unseen to myself. And I confess that if I lacked the sense of religion quite so thoroughly as I lack that of music, the disclosures of the mystic would leave me in very much the same position.[5]

In a sense, Knox is saying that religious experience is nontransferable: it may well be probative to the one who has it, but it does not bear that weight for another. (This is

[4] Ronald Knox, *Broadcast Minds* (London: Sheed and Ward, 1932), pp. 49–50.

[5] Ronald Knox, *The Belief of Catholics* (New York: Sheed and Ward, 1953 [1927]), p. 45.

consonant with traditional Catholic teaching about private revelations: whatever impact they may make on the recipient, other parties are not bound to accept them.) Even apart from extraordinary religious occurrences, it is not uncommon for people to have spiritual experiences that convey a feeling of certitude. When such a person, striking his breast, affirms, "I know God exists, because I feel it *in here*", Knox observes that such an assertion admits of no refutation, but it likewise produces no proof. In later life he came to view the mystical and rational as more complementary than contradictory, but he continued to hold that the mystical approach was exceptional and that the road of the intellect was the way that led most people to God. Similarly, while C. S. Lewis recognized that some people, like the Apostle Paul, came to faith through a profound religious encounter, most adult converts (including himself) come to faith primarily by the path of intellectual exploration. For both men, the place to begin a reflection on the existence of God was our human interaction with the world around us, with "experience" itself.

Matter, Mind, and Metaphysics

For Lewis and Knox, the most fruitful starting place for a discussion of the existence of God is the nexus between mind and matter. They approach this relationship in various ways, but their fundamental arguments are two: first, how is it possible for the material world to generate something that is qualitatively different from anything material, the human mind? Second, how is it possible for there to be an observable order in the material world, which the human mind can perceive, but of which the human mind is not the source?

Regarding the first question, both Knox and Lewis hold that there is no *natural* explanation for the origin of the human mind, because it is unlike anything else in the material world; Knox calls the human intellect "the cuckoo's egg in the nest of a bewildered creation".[6] Neither he nor Lewis were troubled by the assertions of Darwinian evolution about the biological development of human beings; both pointed to a chasm between that organic development and the existence in human beings of something unique, as Knox explains:

> Run "instinct" for all it is worth; show how Man's delicate sensibility in a thousand directions is but the hypertrophy of such instinct; collect whatever instances you will of inherited tendencies, of herd-psychology, and the rest of it—you still come up against a specific difference between man and brute which eludes all materialist explanation: I mean the reflective reason. When your attention, instead of being directed towards some object outside yourself is directed towards yourself as thinking or towards your own thinking process, that is the work of the intellect, that is Man's special prerogative. When Adam awoke in the garden, we dare not guess what monstrous forms of animal life, what wealth of vegetation our world has forgotten, his eye may have lighted upon. But we do know what was his strangest adventure, because it was an adventure he shared with none of his fellow-tenants in Paradise. His strangest adventure was when he met himself.[7]

[6] Ronald Knox, *The Beginning and the End of Man* (London: Catholic Truth Society, 1921), p. 6.

[7] Knox, *Beginning and End of Man*, p. 4.

Lewis concurs: in *Miracles* he contrasts naturalist and supernaturalist views of reality, and he states that the former, which sees existence simply as a self-contained series of events with irrational causes, cannot account for the existence of human intellectual consciousness. In a paper read to the Oxford Socratic Club, Lewis noted that even the ability to argue that the material world is irrational was an exercise of reason, and he offered a *reductio ad absurdum* of the agnostic position of Professor H. H. Price: "He appeared to himself to be studying the nature of things, to be in some way aware of realities, even supersensuous realities, outside his own head. But if strict naturalism is right, he was deluded: he was merely enjoying the conscious reflection of irrationally determined events in his own head."[8]

Reflective reason is something distinct from the material world and yet, in our human experience, relies upon it. The material world seems to have an independent existence—that is, it is there whether we attend to it or not; and furthermore, it impinges on the mind: a blow to the head or inebriation affects our ability to reason. On the other hand, it is hard to conceive of mind existing for the sake of matter, because the mind introduces the relationship of subject to object; as Knox observes, we can picture Mary Jane looking up at Venus, but we cannot picture Venus looking down on Mary Jane. Or, as Lewis notes, "The silence of the eternal spaces terrified Pascal, but it was the greatness of Pascal that enabled them to do so."[9] The existence of the human mind

[8] C. S. Lewis, "Religion without Dogma", in *God in the Dock*, p. 136. In *Miracles* Lewis developed this idea that it is self-contradictory to make a rational argument that everything is irrational, which prompted G. E. M. Anscombe's celebrated critique of Lewis' position. Her observations led him to rewrite a chapter of his book, but his basic insight remains that human knowing cannot be attributed to nonrational causation.

[9] Lewis, *God in the Dock*, p. 41.

creates an audience for the great theater of experience, and for Lewis and Knox there is no "natural" explanation for this phenomenon.

In *Broadcast Minds* Knox crosses swords with Bertrand Russell on this question. Can the philosophy of materialism explain the existence of intelligence? Russell believes it can: given the vastness and complexity of the universe, it is probable that among the various combinations you will have one or two that produce intelligent organisms. This, for Knox, obfuscates the question: "If the police were to discover a human body in Mr Russell's Saratoga trunk, he would not be able to satisfy them with the explanation that, among all the innumerable articles of luggage in the world, it is only natural that there should be some few which are large enough to contain a body. They would want to know how it got there."[10] By airily talking of hypothetical possibilities in a vast universe, Russell is avoiding the question of how in fact our material world has produced the spiritual reality of intellect. The existence of something different from the material world requires a cause that is other than material, and points to a Mind which is the source of our human ability to reason. And, when the human mind studies the world around it, it discovers that the material world too points to a Cause beyond itself.

The Five Ways

Ronald Knox referred to what he called the "the crossword of creation" as the oldest detective story in the world, and C. S. Lewis observed that nature, although not apparently

---

[10] Knox, *Broadcast Minds*, p. 47.

intelligent, is intelligible. The tradition of inferring the existence of God from the observation of the world around us is a venerable one in the West and finds its classic expression in the "Five Ways" (sometimes called "Five Proofs") articulated by Saint Thomas Aquinas. Given the Neoscholastic revival in Catholic thought throughout the first half of the twentieth century, it is not surprising that Knox devoted a good deal of attention to these arguments. He recognized that some of his contemporaries might find other proofs more cogent: the Cartesian approach, based on the necessity for an infinite Intelligence; the Kantian argument from conscience; the Hegelian appeal to an Absolute. But, while many find these approaches more direct, more intimate, and perhaps more profound, they are for Knox the afterthoughts of an introvert. For most people what is most familiar is not what is nearest to us but what we can hold at arm's length: "I remember, long ago, the late Archbishop of Canterbury [William Temple] describing to me his attempts to argue a working-man out of his materialism on Hegelian principles; all he got was, 'Ow, don't talk like that; you make me feel quite funny.' "[11] Knox realizes that the five classical proofs may seem arid in an age unaccustomed to metaphysical language, but they represent a reasoned statement of the idea that what we see around us is the work of an invisible Creator.

What about C. S. Lewis? Superficially, it seems that this approach did not carry much weight with him. He wrote to Dom Bede Griffiths in 1952 that "the Cosmological argument is, for some people at some times, ineffective. It always has been for me."[12] Decades earlier Lewis had expressed hostility to Neoscholasticism, claiming that philosophies come

---

[11] Ronald Knox, *God and the Atom* (New York: Sheed and Ward, 1945), p. 100.

[12] Walter Hooper, ed., *The Collected Letters of C. S. Lewis*, vol. III (San Francisco: HarperCollins, 2007), p. 195.

and go, but only the Word remains. An examination of his correspondence reveals that the sources of this antagonism were twofold. First, Lewis identified the Neoscholasticism of the thirties with a "highbrow fad" pursued by some people who struck him as very harsh and who seemed to be motivated more by hatred of their fathers' religion than by anything else. He mentions T. S. Eliot in this regard, so it seems that his objection is less to a philosophical system than to what he perceived to be an elitist "catholicizing" tendency in some High Church circles. Second, he commented on his statement about "only the Word remaining" in a later letter, in which he explains that he did not mean to imply that one philosophy is as good as another or that pure reason is mutable. Rather, his point was simply that different schools of philosophical thought draw their practical effectiveness from the broader intellectual context, which changes.[13] Against these hesitations it should be noted that Lewis possessed the works of Saint Thomas and consulted them regularly and, more importantly, that several of Lewis' arguments are in truth variations of the classic "Five Ways".

The first two approaches of Saint Thomas are derived from the observation of cause and effect in the world around us. Things change, potentialities are actualized, and such processes are set in motion by other agents. Could this state of affairs regress infinitely? Saint Thomas says no, because each agent has itself been acted on by another agent; something (or someone) has to be the first, a Mover that is itself "unmoved", for the process of change to start. Also, in our

---

[13] This correspondence may be found in the second volume of Lewis' collected letters. His first letter on the subject was written to Bede Griffiths on April 4, 1934, with the explanation appearing in a letter to Griffiths on April 24, 1936. In a letter written to Sister Madaleva on June 7, 1934, Lewis expresses his dislike of such Neoscholastics as Eliot and Jacques Maritain, although he praises Étienne Gilson. His description of harsh, high-brow faddists is in a letter to Sister Penelope written on November 8, 1939.

experience, nothing exists that has brought itself into being; again, something or someone has to be the ultimate Cause, without having been caused itself, in order for anything to exist. The reality of change in the world points to a source outside the process, as Lewis observes: "An egg which came from no bird is no more 'natural' than a bird which existed for all eternity. And since the egg-bird-egg sequence leads us to no plausible beginning, is it not reasonable to look for the real origin somewhere outside the sequence altogether?"[14] He also notes that the laws of nature do not *cause* events to happen but simply determine *how* they happen; thus, even the smallest events lead us back to a mystery that lies outside the realm of natural science.

In his presentation of these first two approaches, Knox suggests that they require nothing more than the mind of a four-year-old, like the one with whom he shared a compartment on a train. The child asked his mother questions and responded to every answer by asking, "Why?"; the string of "whys?" must come to an end somewhere. Knox also tells his Oxford students that the first two proofs are the ones that make most sense to a schoolboy, because schoolboys are familiar with pushing in line and passing the blame— juvenile manifestations of the first two "proofs". However, he also admits that there are difficulties. For one thing, science today does not speak so much of cause and effect, of one thing acting upon another, as of the mutual interaction of things; and he wonders if the Scholastics were guilty of reading into their interpretation of "agents" in the natural world notions that belong to the self-conscious experience of human agents. Another objection can be raised: it is one thing to say every effect has a cause; it is a very different

---

[14] Lewis, *God in the Dock*, p. 211.

thing to assert that a *natural* effect has a *supernatural* cause and so shift from physics to metaphysics. Knox says he does not want to suggest that there is not a response to this objection, but he continues, "I only want to say that it bothers me when the whole argument resolves itself into a discussion about whether metaphysics exist at all, and people start talking about the blind man in the dark room looking for the black cat that isn't there. That is the point in the discussions at which I slide out of the room and say I've got to put out the vestments for tomorrow." [15]

Knox tells his Oxford listeners that they probably skipped the third proof as schoolboys because it seemed to be too much work but that he considers it the most persuasive of the five. This approach begins with the fact that in nature things are born and die, they come into existence and go out of existence. Because of this, their being can be described as "contingent"; but again, this chain must lead to some Being who is not contingent and as such is the Necessary Being who imparts existence to other beings. In *Miracles* Lewis describes this as the one independent being upon whom all other beings depend. Knox asks, what is the mysterious "plus factor" that imparts real existence to mere possibility? The chimera is an exotic creature that does not exist, and the duck-billed platypus is an exotic creature that *does* exist. Why is that? Neither is more or less likely than the other—and yet one "is" and the other "is not". Actuality is a gift imparted from a reservoir outside the closed circle of our thought. And Knox feels it is helpful to "humanize" this third proof and to remind his listeners, "This means you!": "I should be surprised if Mr. Pickwick came into the room;

[15] Philip Caraman, ed., *University Sermons of Ronald A. Knox, Together with Sermons Preached on Various Occasions* (New York: Sheed and Ward, 1963), p. 169.

why am I not surprised to find myself in the room? The problem, if you come to think of it, is the same. Pickwick was projected into the world by Dickens, but as an idea only—man could do no more. By what means, then, am I projected into the world, an actuality?"[16] We know that we exist, and we know that we are not the source of our own existence. An added advantage of the third proof is that it not only points to the existence of God but highlights our dependence on him.

The fourth approach is based on the observation of "degrees of perfection" in the world around us: some things are more or less good, noble, and so on; but such judgments imply an Absolute against which lesser things are judged. When we recall that, for Saint Thomas, being itself is good, we can appreciate how this argument is related to the preceding one: just as the existence of everything is contingent upon God's being, so it is good or true to the extent that it participates in the goodness of God. Being Itself is also Goodness Itself, and so the Absolute is not simply an ideal by which we measure but the source of the varying degrees of goodness that we observe.

Neither Lewis nor Knox has much to say about this "proof", but they both used an argument for the existence of God that is related to it: the testimony of conscience and moral judgment. This was the starting point for Lewis' first series of radio broadcasts, entitled "Right or Wrong: A Clue to the Meaning of the Universe".[17] In this series, he begins with a discussion of the moral law, seeking to determine the source of the "ought" that makes demands on every human being. He contends that its source is not to be found

---

[16] Ronald Knox, *Proving God: A New Apologetic* (London: *The Month*, 1959), p. 39.

[17] This was originally published as part of a collection called *Broadcast Talks*, and later as the first part of *Mere Christianity*.

in either instinct or human convention—rather, it lies in a controlling power outside the universe. In fact, for Lewis the existence of right and wrong yields more insight into the nature of God than creation itself: "You find out more about God from the Moral Law than from the universe in general just as you find out more about a man by listening to his conversation than by looking at a house he has built."[18]

Knox also uses the argument from conscience. In the same conference in which he reflected on the relationship between mind and matter, he observed that the words can function as verbs as well as nouns: things "matter" and people "mind". In everyday speech, these terms simply refer to preference or convenience, but something can "matter" in an absolute, not a relative, way. "If we say that it matters a great deal when Hitler starts persecuting the Jews, we don't simply mean that the Jews mind; of course they do. . . . We mean that there is some order of justice external to himself which Hitler is violating. The thing matters IN ITSELF."[19] But, he goes on to ask, can anything really matter "in itself"? It is a personal Law-giver who is the source of right and wrong: can anything matter, unless there is Somebody who minds?

The final "way" to God is from the existence of order in the world; this is often called the argument from design. Natural bodies lacking intelligence nevertheless act for a purpose, and act always, or nearly always, in the same way. This is the basis of science: the predictability of the elements of nature acting in a consistent and ordered way is a precondition for any valid statement about natural processes. The argument from design appealed to the eighteenth century,

[18] C. S. Lewis, *Mere Christianity* (New York: Macmillan Publishing Co., 1943), p. 37.

[19] Knox, *University Sermons*, p. 13. It is interesting to note Knox makes this reference to the plight of the Jews under the Nazis in a conference delivered sometime in the 1930s.

since advances in the discovery of the laws of nature pointed to an intelligent Designer of the world. By the middle of the twentieth century, a cloud overshadowed this conception of a world governed by consistent and predictable laws: and it was a mushroom cloud. Scientists discerned an essentially random force at work on the atomic level, because the explosions of radium atoms followed no predictable pattern. Knox observes that this exception to "the laws of nature" would have been more shocking to an eighteenth-century Deist than to a thirteenth-century Scholastic: Saint Thomas had included the caveat "nearly" in his assertion that natural bodies always act in the same way. The fact that atomic interactions are unpredictable does not take away from the fact that most elements in nature *do* function in a consistent and predictable way; in fact, for Knox this simply increases the sense of awe with which we should regard the creative power of God: "We had admired the pattern as a mosaic; admire it more, now we find its medium to be a powdery gesso which, nevertheless, does not slip between the Craftsman's fingers."[20] Lewis, too, considers the issue of unpredictability on the atomic level. He is reluctant to believe it, holding that our science may not have advanced far enough to discern the laws that are at work on that level. But if this unpredictability is true, and if there are events that act on their own and do not "interlock" with events around them, then we have discovered something outside nature, which he calls the "subnatural". And if nature can have a back door opening onto the subnatural, why can she not have a front door opening onto the supernatural?

From this brief survey, we see that both our authors were familiar with the traditional cosmological arguments for the

[20] Ronald Knox, *God and the Atom* (New York: Sheed and Ward, 1945), p. 110.

existence of God. Given the prominence of Neoscholasticism in Catholic circles at this time, it is not surprising that Knox referred to the traditional arguments more often and more explicitly than Lewis did. At the same time, Knox was aware of their limitations. In one conference, he contrasted Protestant and Catholic approaches to apologetics and conceded, "Our metaphysics are as incredible to the modern Protestant as the doctrine of Indulgences."[21] If an agnostic asks his Christian neighbors for an account of the faith that is in them, the Protestant will move him by the sincerity of his convictions, while the Catholic will impress him with an ingenious network of argumentation. The result, Knox suggests, is that the Protestant approach gives an impression of reality without truth, while the Catholic approach gives an impression of truth without reality. This observation provides an interesting background for something Knox wrote late in life. In *Proving God*, he contrasts the zeal of youth to champion a particular idea with the mellowness of old age, which allows greater sympathy for another's point of view: "Experience has softened the hard edges of his affirmations. If I may use words in a grossly unphilosophical sense, what he demands now is not so much truth as reality."[22] In his earlier works, like *The Belief of Catholics*, Knox gives pride of place to the "Five Ways" and asserts that they provide the most lucid and cogent evidence to the inquirer. Later, as for example in his conferences to students at Oxford, he makes more modest claims about the arguments and recognizes that there are many factors that influence our intellectual reflections. He suggests that the arguments may not

[21] Ronald Knox, "Humanizing the Third Proof", unpublished conference, 1943, Knox Papers, Mells, Somerset; in Milton Walsh, *Ronald Knox as Apologist* (S.T.D. disser. Gregorian University, Rome, 1985), p. 311.

[22] Knox, *Proving God*, p. 10.

be strictly cogent in and of themselves but that they confirm that our God-dependent construction of reality is true. Throughout his life, but especially in his later years, Knox would not treat these "proofs" in isolation. But he refuses to set them aside, because they remind us that differences in religion are not matters of taste but matters of truth.

But if Knox wanted to unite the "reality" of the heart and the "truth" of the mind, it is true that Lewis desired this, too. The "Five Ways" are not as prominent in Lewis' writings, but elements of them are present. He preferred to approach the question of God via the path of conscience, and as we have seen, he felt that we learn more about God from the moral law than we do from the world in general. But Lewis certainly believed we learn *something* about God by studying the world he made and that the cosmological argument has its place in the intellectual armory of the faith. Having been cured of his "chronological snobbery" by Owen Barfield, Lewis would not allow his adversaries to dismiss medieval arguments for the existence of God simply because they were medieval. In an essay entitled "Dogma and the Universe", Lewis contends with those who reject traditional doctrines because they claim that modern science has made them obsolete. He asserts that even where there is real progress in knowledge, there is some knowledge that is not superseded: "There is a great difference between counting apples and arriving at the mathematical formulae of modern physics. But the multiplication table is used in both and does not grow out of date."[23] The traditional Christian arguments for inferring the existence of God from the world around us are not negated by scientific advances and indeed can be enhanced by them, as, for example, when modern

---

[23] Lewis, *God in the Dock*, p. 45.

physics theorizes that the universe had a beginning. Lewis argues that ultimately we have two choices when we look at the world around us: the naturalist view, which holds that the whole vast process of space and time goes on of its own accord, a self-contained system that embraces everything that is; and the supernaturalist view, which holds that there is One Self-Existent Thing that is outside nature and is the thing upon which everything else depends. This "God-dependent" interpretation of the world is what the cosmological argument of the "Five Ways" articulates, and Lewis argues that this interpretation is at least as reasonable as the naturalist one, and he believes it is more so.

What God Is Like

If the supernaturalist view is correct, and God exists apart from time and space and has chosen to create the universe, then we can know something about the nature of God. (It should be noted, however, that for us even to use a word like "exist" apart from time and space takes us beyond the reach of human understanding, which is why often these statements really tell us what God must *not* be.) Thus, for example, we say God is eternal; that is what "being outside time" means. Both Knox and Lewis reflected on the challenge of this seemingly simple assertion. Because the only existence we know is time-bound, we cannot imagine what it means to be outside time altogether. In *Difficulties*, Arnold Lunn wrote that he found the term "outside time" meaningless. Knox responded that we cannot "comprehend" timelessness because we are conditioned by time and space. But time and space are not necessities of rational thought, like the law of contradiction; I can "think" God outside time, even though I cannot imagine what that is.

Knox and Lewis both try to illustrate a timeless perspective, although they concede that their images are very imperfect. Knox invited Lunn to picture a cemetery in which the members of a family are buried next to one another, with the most recently deceased closest to where Lunn is standing. The series of tombstones reflects the chronological series of deaths in the family: 1927, 1895, 1870, and so on. Now, he says, imagine flying over the cemetery in an airplane: there is now no nearer or farther to the graves, no before and after—the whole sequence is present at the same time. Lewis draws his example from the craft of writing: an author describes a character who hears a knock at the door and goes to answer it. There is a time sequence in the story, but the author is not within that sequence; he could write the first half of the sentence and finish it hours later. Both of these images are very limited, because unlike Lunn in the airplane, God is not in a space relative to the cemetery, and unlike the human author, God is not in a time-series apart from the novel. But what both Lewis and Knox try to convey is that God is not only aware of the whole sequence of events in time as "present" to him, but God is outside the bounds of time altogether. They will draw on this understanding of divine eternity when treating both the issue of predestination and the question of how God answers our prayers.

The existence of order in creation and the existence of human minds capable of discerning that order and able to think self-reflectively suggest that the source of this world and ourselves is a knowing Mind. Because this Being is limitless, he must be all-knowing and all-powerful. If this Being were to be limited, we would have to ask, "By whom

or by what?" and *that* Being would be God. We might be
tempted to say that by definition what we mean by "God"
is an omniscient and omnipotent Being. There is a major
(many would claim insurmountable) objection to this assertion: how could such a God create a world in which suffering and evil abound? What our authors have to say about
the problem of evil will be presented in a later chapter. For
now we should simply note that for Lewis this objection
is ultimately self-defeating: to say that there is evil in the
world implies that good and evil exist. But if they do, this
points to the existence of a Being outside the world who is
the source of a standard of good.

Is this Being personal? Both Lewis and Knox affirm that
God is indeed profoundly personal, although this was a truth
that Lewis resisted for a long time. He took refuge in terms
like "the Absolute", because he sensed that if this Being
were personal, he could make personal claims on Lewis.
The philosophical terms employed in the cosmological arguments can contribute to an "abstract" understanding of
God, as Knox demonstrates when he suggests substituting
them for the name of God in phrases taken from everyday
life: "For the sake of the First Cause, do turn that gramophone off . . . I'm not a narrow-minded man, the Supreme
Intelligence knows."[24] Similarly, Lewis warns that abstrac-
tions are every bit as much a concession to our human limitations as anthropomorphic pictures of God are.

On what basis can Lewis and Knox claim that God must
be personal and not simply some "force"? For both of them,
the fundamental answer is the same: in this material world,
we have direct experience of only one kind of spiritual being, and that being is personal. They mean ourselves, and

[24] Knox, *University Sermons*, p. 172.

by extension, other human beings. In fact, it is the spiritual aspect that differentiates these various organisms; materially speaking, one human being is like another. In the words of Knox: "The idea of personality, of self-conscious individuality, is so vital to my whole conception of the spirit nature that I cannot even think it away. A purely impersonal spirit is as unthinkable to me as a moral agent who has no will."[25] For Lewis, an examination of the spiritual aspect of human nature brings us face to face with the moral law, which again points to a personal Being. He suggests that a concept like "Life-Force"[26] is attractive to many precisely because it is a "tame God" which offers us the thrills of religion without any moral demands.[27]

Lewis rejected this "tame God" and recognized that God is a personal Being, infinitely beyond creation, who freely brought everything into being and who commands some things and prohibits others. It was the awareness of this truth that led Lewis, the reluctant convert, to accept God as God. Coincidentally, not a mile away from the room where Lewis knelt down on that night in 1929, Ronald Knox was serving as chaplain to the Catholic students. In one of his conferences, entitled "If God Exists—", he pointed out to his listeners that many people want God to exist as a sort of background to their lives but that once you prove he exists, you will find he fills the whole stage. God, not man, is the center of the universe. God, not man, is the measure of all

[25] Ronald Knox, *Caliban in Grub Street* (London: Sheed and Ward, 1930), p. 74.

[26] Of this term, and words like "Energy" and "Activity", Knox comments: "Let me implore the reader not to be taken in by the use of capital letters; they are the modern Englishman's refuge from thought." *Caliban in Grub Street*, p. 78.

[27] Lewis, *Mere Christianity*, p. 35.

things. All our actions are no longer regulated by our own measure but by his. For both of these men, the realization that God exists should bring you to your knees.

Conclusion

At the outset of this chapter, we noted that both Knox and Lewis believed that there were rational arguments for the existence of God. This does not mean that they considered people who did not believe in God to be stupid. Lewis' own experience with atheism and Knox's personal and pastoral sympathies for the doubts and objections of other people (some of them very close to him) prevented them from dismissing nonbelievers as fools. They did experience frustration when their adversaries refused to even take the question of the existence of God seriously. One example is Knox's contemporary from his Eton days, Julian Huxley, who maintained that there is next to no evidence for the existence of God. Knox asks what kind of evidence would carry weight with him: Huxley rules out miracles as intrinsically impossible; he dismisses religious experience as the workings of the unconscious. When presented with cosmological arguments, he responds that he is bored with metaphysics and considers it "idle speculation". Knox asks, "I wonder if it has ever occurred to him that the refusal to speculate may be a mark of idleness? Truth . . . is something that deserves by its own right to be found and to be held. It has crowns which are refused to the incurious."[28] In their sermons, conferences, broadcasts, and books, Lewis and Knox sought to

---

[28] Knox, *Broadcast Minds*, p. 57.

disturb the idleness of their opponents and to pique others' curiosity.

Their fundamental starting point was the experience of their listeners, who found themselves to be self-reflective beings in a material world. How could a material, physical world bring about the existence of an intellectual, spiritual being? When that thinking biped reflected upon itself, it discovered a sense of moral purpose, an "ought" that was something distinct from self-preservation and convention. When that mind looked out on the world around it, it discovered an amazingly complex reality that functioned according to reliable laws. Everything in this world seemed dependent on something else for its existence: did this state of affairs simply stretch back through all eternity? And why did anything exist at all? An inner moral law and an outer natural law: can these be explained on the basis of materialism alone? Lewis and Knox argued that they could not, but what troubled them was that many of their contemporaries refused to even entertain such questions; they simply presumed that eventually science would solve all our problems.

Our authors believed that the "God-dependent" view of the world made sense and that when you accept that a personal, omnipotent Being has brought everything into existence, it is reasonable to desire a conscious relationship with that personal Being. According to Lewis, once a person has attained a settled intellectual conviction that God exists (Faith A), he will be moved to pray for confidence and trust in God (that is, for Faith B). You will want to know more about that Being and of his will for you. The beautiful things of this world will tell you about their Maker, even as you recognize that God must be infinitely more beautiful than anything else. Knox suggests that we cannot face up to the thought of God directly, and we need to think of something else and look at God out of the corner of our eye: "If you go out into the garden on a bright, sunny day, you don't look up at the sun and exclaim, 'How beautiful the sun is!' You look round you at the flowers, at the dew on the grass, at the trees just in bud over there on the hill-side, and exclaim, 'How beautiful everything looks, in the sun!' "[29]

So, to be convinced *that* God exists may come at the end of an arduous intellectual climb, but the human mind cannot rest for long on that plateau; the mysterious summit beckons. Our minds want to know what God is like, and our hearts want to know what God wants us to do. But what if God is more anxious to find us than we are to find him? What if he, whom we have understood to be the one Being who is outside time and space, should choose to step onto the stage of human history?

[29] Ronald Knox, *The Layman and His Conscience* (New York: Sheed and Ward, 1961), p. 49.

CHAPTER TWO

Jesus Christ

Some contemporary popular religious books promise to show us the real Jesus of Nazareth: to strip away the mythological adornments with which his pious followers have clothed him for centuries and get to his real doctrine; to discover the prophetic moral teacher beneath accretions like the Virgin Birth, miraculous healings, and Resurrection appearances. C. S. Lewis resolutely opposed such an approach to the Gospels. One reason he was so effective an adversary was that these were views he once held himself.[1] For many years Lewis viewed Christianity as one mythological system among many, and not the best of them. Even after he recovered his faith in God, it took him some time to reach the conviction that Christ was God. Although Ronald Knox did not experience such a denial, some of his friends and family did. The young Catholic students at Oxford in the twenties and thirties were exposed to the same views as those espoused by Lewis ten years before, and it was incumbent on their chaplain to provide these young men with rational arguments for their belief in the divinity of Christ.

While publishers trumpet the findings of "the Jesus Seminar" and other such projects as unprecedented, bold discoveries that shake the foundations of traditional belief, the

---

[1] See his letters of the 12th, 18th, and 27th of October, 1916 in Walter Hooper, ed., *The Collected Letters of C. S. Lewis*, vol. I (San Francisco: Harper, 2004).

writings of Lewis and Knox suggest that people might ask for their money back—the same claims were made a hundred years ago. How did these two Christian authors respond to them?

The Divinity of Christ

Many people who do not believe that Jesus of Nazareth was divine (in any unique meaning of that word) still consider him to be a great teacher and a heroic man. As common as this view is, for both Knox and Lewis it is completely untenable. *If* the New Testament provides a reliable picture of Jesus, then he claimed to be much more than a teacher; *if* the Gospels are taken seriously, this itinerant preacher was an impostor, a lunatic . . . or God himself. (The "ifs" raise the issues of the reliability of the Scriptures and the historicity of Jesus' miracles. Both Lewis and Knox have much to say about these topics; their arguments will be presented in subsequent chapters.) There is no doubt that the Gospels present us with a moral teacher of profound insight and originality; but they also present us with much more.

Our authors argue that the Gospels describe a man who claims to teach with unique authority. From the beginning of his ministry, when Jesus reads out a Messianic text from the prophet Isaiah and claims, "Today this scripture has been fulfilled in your hearing" (Lk 4:21), his teaching reflects remarkable self-assurance. In the Sermon on the Mount, he quotes the highest authority acknowledged by the Jews, the Law of Moses, and in each case says, "But I say to you . . ." He claims that in him his listeners meet someone who is greater than Jonah, greater than Solomon, greater even than the Temple (Mt 12:6, 41, 42). He states that he is the Lord

of the Sabbath (Mk 2:28). While the Pharisees and the disciples of John fast, Jesus tells his followers that there is no
need for them to do so, because the Bridegroom (a biblical
image of God) is with them (Mk 2:19). Jesus says that *he*
sends prophets (Mt 23:34). He forgives sins: forgives them
himself, as if he were the injured party. (Lewis notes that we
have become so comfortable with the Gospel Christ that we
are not shocked by Jesus' claim to forgive sins but that his
contemporaries certainly were.) And Jesus not only forgives
sins now but claims that he will return at the end of time
to judge the world.

What is the basis for such audacity? Jesus presumes a
unique relationship to God, such that the only word that can
express it is "Son". Son with a capital *S*, because while we
are all children of God inasmuch as God has brought us into
being, Jesus claimed to be *the* Son in a unique way. He pays
the Temple tax but notes that he is actually exempt because
he is the Son. In the parable of the wicked tenants, Jesus describes the owner of the vineyard (another Jewish image for
God) sending his servants, the prophets; then, "Afterward
he sent his son to them, saying, 'They will respect my son'"
(Mt 21:37). In the midst of his preaching rounds, Jesus cried
out one day, "All things have been delivered to me by my
Father; and no one knows the Son except the Father, and no
one knows the Father except the Son and any one to whom
the Son chooses to reveal him" (Mt 11:27).

That Jesus' contemporaries understood him to claim to be
more than a teacher and something greater than a prophet
is reflected in the question put to him by the high priest
at his trial: "Are you the Christ, the Son of the Blessed?"
When Jesus responds affirmatively, the high priest tears his
garments and denounces the answer as blasphemy. When
Pilate asked Jesus if he was a king, Jesus had also responded

affirmatively but offered a qualification; with the high priest, no qualification is offered, no clarification given. In a sermon preached on this trial, Knox imagines a liberal higher critic rushing into the courtroom to defend Jesus by means of all kinds of qualifications and scholarly explanations of terms like "Christ", "Messiah", and "Son of God". These pleas are met with noble scorn, and while Knox is saddened by the blind hatred of Jesus' judges, they at least pay him the compliment that he means what he says. It is no good, Knox observes, "to seek to flatter him with half divine titles, too high praise for a madman, too cold homage for a God."[2]

This is the figure we encounter in the Gospels, and Knox and Lewis agree that Jesus is unlike any other great religious teacher. Mohammed described himself merely as a prophet, and Buddha described himself simply as a guide to the path of Enlightenment; such figures never had the audacity to claim, "I am the way, and the truth, and the life; no one comes to the Father, but by me" (Jn 14:6). But Jesus did. A great teacher? Lewis suggests a more apt description would be an arrogant megalomaniac. During his years of unbelief, friends encouraged him to read the Gospels, assuring him he would find there a figure he could not help loving. He frankly confessed later, "Yes, I could!" and said that if Jesus is not truly God, a great deal about him is not lovable or even tolerable.[3]

Was Jesus an impostor, deliberately giving the impression that he was something more than human? It is hard to square that hypothesis with everything about his character that emerges from his teachings. And what would be

---

[2] Philip Caraman, ed., *Pastoral Sermons of Ronald A. Knox* (New York: Sheed and Ward, 1960), p. 381.

[3] Walter Hooper, ed., *The Collected Letters of C. S. Lewis*, vol. II, (San Francisco: Harper, 2004) pp. 374–75.

the motivation for such a pretense? Jesus showed a decided disinterest in political power, wealth, and the adulation of the crowds, the usual goals of such trickery. Finally, would he endure a horrendous death to prolong what he knew to be an imposture? A negative response to the high priest's question would have concluded the trial in his favor.

Was he mentally disturbed, a lunatic? History has known figures who suffered from delusions of grandeur, who sincerely believed that they were more than mere mortals. Sincerely, but mistakenly. Again, Lewis and Knox appeal to the teachings of Jesus: these are marked by originality, common sense, and a simple shrewdness that are the antithesis of lunacy. As Knox notes, "As well expect a motor-car to find its way through crowded traffic without a driver, as a mind that is unbalanced commit itself to literary expression without being guilty of extravagances that betray it."[4]

The third alternative is that Jesus really was both a human being and God incarnate. Is such a thing probable? Lewis says that this is the wrong question to ask: for that matter, he asks, is the existence of the universe itself "probable"? Rather, we should ask on what historical grounds it can be asserted that this remarkable event did in fact happen. Lewis uses the analogy of a symphony or novel, or rather, the parts of such a work. Someone produces a newly discovered manuscript and suggests that this is the missing piece, the key to the whole work. The test would be: does this missing piece illuminate all the other parts of the work and pull them together? He argues that the doctrine of the Incarnation provides a much better explanation for the data of the Gospels than either of the other alternatives.

This is not to say that this explanation does not also raise

[4] Knox, *The Belief of Catholics* (New York: Sheed and Ward, 1953 [1927]), p. 96.

questions; indeed, most of the theological controversies of the first six centuries of the Christian era dealt with the doctrine of the Incarnation. And, if the "incarnational" explanation were self-evident, there would be no need to defend it; and both our authors felt the need to defend it. Lewis devoted a chapter of his book *Miracles* to the difficulties surrounding this doctrine; we will review what he had to say about them and also invite Ronald Knox into the conversation.

The first, and central, difficulty is this: what does it mean to say "God became man"? How is it conceivable that the eternal, self-existent Spirit could be combined with a human, limited organism? Lewis counsels caution in trying to describe what it would be like for Jesus to be both God and man: "I do not think anything we can do will enable us to imagine the mode of consciousness of the incarnate God."[5] For two thousand years, people have asked about Jesus' identity, "What did he know, and when did he know it?" Church teaching has steered a course between the extremes of a Christ so divine that his human behavior was mere play-acting, and a Christ so human that he was not aware of his divinity. Since the nineteenth century, the latter temptation has been the stronger, and Knox devoted a chapter of *Some Loose Stones* to those who argued that the "kenosis" or self-emptying of the Son in the Incarnation meant the abandonment of the divine attributes such as omniscience and omnipotence. These theologians were striving to defend the true humanity of Christ, but the farthest Knox would travel down the path they took was to hold that Christ always possessed the divine attributes but that

[5] C. S. Lewis, *Miracles: A Preliminary Study* (New York: Macmillan, 1948), p. 133.

he intentionally chose not to draw on them. While this may strike many as naïve, it is important to see the truth Knox was defending: that while Jesus Christ possessed a human nature and a divine nature, he was (from all eternity) a divine Person. *Who* he is, is the Son of God; this is the Personality we encounter in the Gospels. The man who made the audacious claims Jesus did could not be the Son of God suffering from amnesia.

While we cannot imagine the consciousness of God-made-man, Lewis says that we do have some experience of beings that combine natural and supernatural elements: ourselves. In human beings we encounter creatures that possess the biochemistry, instinctive reactions, and sensuous perceptions of the animal world, and the rational thought and moral will that cannot be explained by any material process, and so are termed "spiritual". If the Christian doctrine of the Incarnation is true, we can understand that "our own composite existence is not the sheer anomaly it might seem to be, but a faint image of the Divine Incarnation itself—the same theme in a very minor key."[6] This truth opens up for Lewis a new and beautiful principle, the ability of the higher to come down and include the lower. This is the "kenosis" that the Fathers loved to contemplate: not a self-emptying that robs the Son of his divinity but the loving condescension by which he wills to express his divine life in human terms. When we talk to babies we use baby talk because we want to communicate with them on their level. This is what the Son of God did in becoming man: he revealed the things of eternity on the screen of time. About this condescension Knox writes: "If Einstein were to teach

[6] Ibid., p. 134.

schoolboys geometry, he would need a blackboard; but that is the schoolboys' fault, not Einstein's."[7]

If the first objection is that the idea of God becoming man is so extraordinary, the second is that it is so common: many religions have stories of gods and goddesses who assume a mortal form and whose deaths and risings become the pattern for the cycle of the seasons. Lewis has great sympathy for this objection, since it was his own position for some years. The turning point in his conversion to Christ came when Tolkien and Dyson challenged him to see the Christian story as a "true myth": a story that shares the imagery and drama of the great myths of every culture—what Joseph Campbell called "the hero with a thousand faces" —but that was also a historical event. Unlike the heroes of legend who lived "once upon a time", Jesus Christ lived at a particular moment in history and in a particular culture. (It is interesting, Lewis notes, that the religion of Jesus' Jewish culture differed significantly from the dying-and-rising cycle of pagan nature religions. In fact, he says that in his comparative religion days, he was chilled and puzzled by the virtual absence of pagan "dying god" ideas in early Christian literature.) Once Lewis accepted Tolkien's argument that Christianity was a myth that is also historically true, his understanding both of myth and of Jesus changed radically: in Christ, myth becomes fact. But Lewis did not conclude that because the myth of Christ was true, all other myths were false: "It is not the difference between falsehood and truth. It is the difference between a real event on the one hand and dim dreams or premonitions of that event on the

[7] Ronald Knox and Arnold Lunn, *Difficulties* (London: Eyre and Spottiswoode, 1952 [1932]), p. 156.

other."[8] Knox would agree; he said that pagan myths shaped the human mind to receive the truth of revelation just as a bird shapes a nest for the eggs it will lay.

The fact that in Jesus myth becomes fact raises another difficulty: the idea of a "chosen people", or what is sometimes called "the scandal of particularity". Lewis knows that in the modern egalitarian world there is a desire for a level playing field in our search for God: no individual, group, or culture should be able to claim preferential treatment or a corner on the truth. He states that Christianity offers no concessions to this point of view. The fundamental reason for this is that we are not dealing with our search for God but God's search for us. God sustains all creation and touches the human spirit in every civilization, but for him truly to enter into creation on human terms requires that he do so in a particular culture. The drama of the Old Testament is the account of how God works through the history of one people, narrowing and sharpening the process until it comes to a single bright point: a Jewish girl saying her prayers, the representative of her people and of all humanity. But the Jewish people, and this woman, are chosen not for their own honor but for the sake of the unchosen: through Abraham's seed, all nations will be blessed. And this choice brings suffering: "On the finally selected Woman falls the utmost depth of maternal anguish. Her Son, the incarnate God, is 'a man of sorrows'; the one Man into whom Deity descended, the one Man who can be lawfully adored, is pre-eminent for suffering."[9] Here we touch the mystery of Vicariousness, which we will explore in the next section of this chapter.

---

[8] "Is Theology Poetry?" in C. S. Lewis, *The Weight of Glory* (San Francisco: Harper, 1980), p. 129.

[9] Lewis, *Miracles*, p. 142.

Why?

Why did the Incarnation take place? In the ministry of Jesus, we see an ardent champion of compassion who gave the world a powerful example by word and deed. Recalling Knox's image of Einstein teaching children, we could say that Christ came to teach the geometry of divine love on the blackboard of human experience. His teachings have enlightened and inspired millions of people over the centuries. Lewis and Knox draw particular attention to two incidents in the life of Christ: his temptation in the wilderness and the Agony in the garden. These events manifest the mortality of Jesus, who tasted the basic human experiences of hunger and the fear of death as well as the wounds of rejection and betrayal. It is consoling to us in our weakness that Christ did not face these trials with Stoic impassivity, and it is instructive that he opposed them, not with the miraculous powers of his divinity, but with the human resources of self-denial, prudence, and humility—the same weapons he commends to us. But as important as the teaching and example of Jesus are, they do not address the crucial issue; as Knox observes in *Some Loose Stones*, the whole language of Christianity professes, not, "Jesus lived for me", but "Jesus died for me".[10] Christ himself described his mission in these words: "The Son of man also came not to be served but to serve, and to give his life as a ransom for many" (Mk 10:45).

What does he mean? This is something that frankly puzzled Lewis in the months leading up to his Christian conversion. He could not see how the life and death of "Someone Else" two thousand years ago could help us here and

[10] Ronald Knox, *Some Loose Stones* (London: Longmans, Green and Co., 1913), p. 173.

now, except as an example: "And the example business, tho' true and important, is not Christianity: right in the centre of Christianity, in the Gospels and Saint Paul, you keep on getting something quite different and very mysterious expressed in those phrases I have so often ridiculed ('propitiation'—'sacrifice'—'the blood of the Lamb')—expressions wh. I cd. only interpret in senses that seemed to me either silly or shocking."[11] Lewis recognized that the central belief of Christianity is that Christ's death has somehow put us right with God and given us a fresh start. While he and Knox were aware of theological speculations over the centuries that have proposed that the Incarnation would have taken place even apart from the catastrophic event of the Fall, for them this was a theoretical issue: in fact, we had fallen and we needed to be saved.

Regarding the effects of the Fall itself, the evidence surrounds us. Lewis suggested that nature itself has the air of a good thing spoiled. It can be viewed as something imperfect, on the way to some greater good; but there is also what he calls a "positive depravity" that is the result of human sin. In the realm of our human experience, the spiritual element seems to be under siege, and our network of relationships is skewed. They are abnormal or pathological, and Lewis suggests that nothing but custom could make this state of affairs seem natural, and nothing but Christian doctrine can make it intelligible. There is the final crisis of death itself, which is the sign of the triumph of Satan. It might be urged that the misfortunes of Lewis' childhood combined with a Protestant emphasis on the seriousness of the Fall gave him a rather pessimistic vision of life. But in fairness to Lewis,

---

[11] Lewis, *Letters* I, p. 976.

it should be noted that he is addressing people who have closed their eyes to the need for salvation; and more importantly, this rather bleak vision is presented primarily as a setting in which the saving power of God's love can be seen at work. Knox, too, speaks of the Fall, suggesting that we human beings are misfits, made for a destiny that we have missed.

The root cause of the Fall is the misuse of free will; God created us for love, and love requires freedom. In a primeval revolt, our first parents refused God's love and sought to usurp the place of God. We are in a state of rebellion, which has been reinforced by thousands of years of self-will and conceit. This has poisoned our relationship with God, with one another, and with the rest of creation. That sin leaves its mark on the sinner and on injured parties is a matter of experience; but to understand the significance of the Fall and the way Christ becomes our Savior, it is important to see that both Knox and Lewis believe that sin also creates an objective disturbance in the moral order and that this calls for some kind of restitution. According to Knox, what the sinner needs is not only an impetus to change for the future but a reprieve from the past.

Lewis offers a vivid illustration of this truth in *The Lion, the Witch and the Wardrobe*. Edmund has chosen to betray his family and Aslan; he later realizes what he has done, and he repents. But the "deep magic" of Narnia demands that he must pay the price; Edmund's guilt cannot simply be ignored. The White Witch demands his life, and in justice she can claim it. Aslan offers to die in Edmund's place, and it appears that the triumph of evil is complete: the Witch taunts the dying Lion by saying that with him out of the way, she can kill Edmund, too. But she is unaware of the "deeper magic" of Narnia, which the resurrected Aslan explains to the girls: "When a willing victim who had committed no treachery was killed in the traitor's stead, the Table would crack and Death itself would start working backward."[12]

How can the suffering of one person atone for the sins of another? Knox admits that many people consider such an arrangement immoral, and Lewis comments that there have been many theological explanations for this core conviction of Christianity, some more valuable than others. The wages of sin is death, not as an arbitrary punishment but as the necessary consequence of our severing our connection with God, the source of life. Mankind is caught in a double bind: first, the party rejected is God himself; how can a mere creature make restitution? Second, because we are sinners, even our good actions possess an element of selfishness. In response to the first difficulty, God becomes man in order to offer his life in sacrifice, providing "the ransom that only divine Justice could have demanded and only divine Mercy would have afforded."[13] God could not die in his own nature, but he could in ours. As regards the second difficulty, Lewis observes that in order to convert death to life, death must be *freely accepted*; only one who did not need to die unless he had chosen to could die perfectly. Christ is the innocent Man "who has committed no treachery" who gives his life in the traitors' stead.

This invasion of enemy-occupied territory entails humiliation for God. Lewis likens him to a strong man stooping lower and lower to pick up a huge burden. He also employs the poetic image of a diver (recall that in *The Pilgrim's Regress*, this is what the pilgrim had to do to be saved):

[12] C. S. Lewis, *The Lion, the Witch and the Wardrobe* (New York: Harper Trophy, 1950), p. 179.

[13] Philip Caraman, ed., *The University Sermons of Ronald A. Knox* (New York: Sheed and Ward, 1963), p. 367.

Or one might think of a diver, first reducing himself to naked-
ness, then glancing in mid-air, then gone with a splash, van-
ished, rushing down through green and warm water into black
and cold water, down through increasing pressure into the
death-like region of oose and slime and old decay; then up
again, back to colour and light, his lungs almost bursting, till
suddenly he breaks the surface again, holding in his hand the
dripping, precious thing that he went down to recover. He
and it are both coloured now that they have come up into
the light: down below, where it lay colourless in the dark, he
lost his colour too.[14]

This pattern of descent and reascent runs all through creation: it is the story of all vegetable and animal life, reduced
to a tiny seed cast into the cold ground or the dark womb;
it is the pattern of our moral and emotional lives, which also
endure many deaths in order to be reborn. "Through this
bottleneck, this belittlement," Lewis claims, "the highroad
nearly always lies."[15] These are but minor manifestations of
the great divine patterns of the death and Resurrection of
Christ and of the momentous act of creation itself.

Together with this pattern of descent and ascent, Lewis
perceives something else at work in nature: what he calls
"Vicariousness". While many people today, with their emphasis on individualism, might be scandalized by the notion
that one person's suffering can make satisfaction for another
person's sins, Lewis maintains that the principle is constantly
at work in nature: "Self-sufficiency, living on one's own resources, is a thing impossible in her realm. Everything is indebted to everything else, dependent on everything else."[16]

[14] Lewis, *Miracles*, p. 135.

[15] Ibid., p. 136.

[16] Ibid., p. 143. Lewis' friend Charles Williams believed in "substitution"
or "the way of exchange", which enabled one person to take on the pain of

What is true of nature is true as well of human society: no man is an island. According to Knox, this dependency was the hallmark of Jesus' life: from his infancy when he received milk from his Mother until his death agony when he received wine from the soldier, Christ was indebted to his creatures. Saint Paul, the first writer to explore the meaning of Christ's atoning death, saw the solidarity of the human race as crucial to understanding the mission of Christ: as in Adam all die, so in Christ all are restored to life. Lewis calls this principle of Vicariousness the rule of the universe— "one can paddle every canoe *except* one's own"—and emphasizes its salvific significance: "That is why Christ's suffering *for us* is not a mere theological dodge but the supreme case of the law that governs the whole world: and when they mocked him by saying 'He saved others, himself he cannot save' they were really uttering, little as they knew it, the ultimate law of the spiritual world."[17] The "deeper magic" of Christ embraces death and transforms it from the sign of the final triumph of evil into the gateway to eternal life. As Lewis observes, the good strategist makes his opponent's strong point the pivot of his own plan.

The Impact of Jesus' Death and Resurrection

The proof that Christ has destroyed the power of death is his Resurrection. It is also the vindication of his divine claims and is at the heart of the Good News of Christian-

---

another. Lewis actually experienced this during his wife Joy's illness: for a period of time, the spread of cancer in her bones was arrested, and he endured a debilitating bone disease.

[17] Lewis, *Letters*, II, p. 953.

ity: "The message which electrified the world of the first century was not 'Love your enemies', but 'He is risen'."[18] Through his glorious Resurrection, Christ brings life out of death, not just for himself, but for us, too. He tasted death that we might have life. Knox offers a refinement to the traditional idea of "substitution": "He didn't suffer instead of a guilty race; he identified himself, not by a legal fiction, but by a real (though mystical) union, with a guilty race, and suffered as its representative. . . . For St Paul, Christ did not die in order that we might live; he died in order that we might die."[19] He goes on to explain what he means by this paradoxical statement. In Christ's death, we died to our sins; death cancels all obligations. "For you have died, and your life is hid with Christ in God" (Col 3:3). But it is also true that we share in Christ's victory: "When Christ who is our life appears, then you also will appear with him in glory" (Col 3:4). Deliverance from sin and death is an essential part of Christ's mission, but it does not exhaust it —the risen Christ gives us much more than forgiveness.

In the risen Christ, Lewis sees a qualitative advance in human nature; while the secular world speculates about what level of existence humanity might evolve to, the glorified humanity of Christ offers a glimpse of what human perfection will be. It is not the result of some innate organic development, but it is the gratuitous gift of God. From the risen Christ, the "good infection" of life and glory spreads through the human race and touches all of creation. Since everything in our universe is interconnected, the salvation given by Christ has a glorifying effect, just as the selfishness of sin taints everything. With his vivid imagination, Lewis

[18] Ronald Knox, *Caliban in Grub Street* (London: Sheed and Ward), 1930, p. 113.
[19] Knox, *Pastoral Sermons*, pp. 508–9.

probes the impact of Christ's death and Resurrection on the whole cosmos. Are we the only rational beings in the visible universe? Are we the only fallen creatures in that universe? These are questions that have not been answered (yet!), although they tantalized Lewis when he wrote his science fiction trilogy. But if it is true that the Creator himself shared our human nature, tasted death, and rose from the dead in such a way that our mortal nature was transformed, then the whole universe has been changed by those events. And that startling and glorious transformation will not be the "mere" byproduct of our redemption: "Where a God who is totally purposive and totally foreseeing acts upon a Nature which is totally interlocked, there can be no accidents or loose ends, nothing whatever of which we can safely use the word *merely*."[20] Reflecting on the beautiful imagery at the beginning of Saint Paul's Letter to the Colossians, Knox also sees Christ in relation to both the human race and the whole creation. As the Word through whom all things were made, he is the "elder Brother" of every created thing; as Redeemer he is the head of the Body, the Church:

> The eternal generation of the divine Word is the first echo, as it were, which breaks the mysterious silence of heaven. And the Resurrection of Jesus Christ is the first echo which breaks the silence after the long sleep of death which has gone on undisturbed since Adam fell. Christ as God stood in a vague relation to all his creatures as in some sense their elder Brother; Christ as Man stands in a definite relation to them as the Head, the clan Chief in whom and with whom the whole clan is mystically united; all creation is summed up in him. Nothing henceforward is complete without him; everything lives, with a new life now, in him; he, the centre of their being, is now also the magnet which draws them

[20] Lewis, *Miracles*, p. 149.

back towards him. To him, whether as God or as Man, both priority and primacy belong.[21]

Mention of the Letter to the Colossians highlights the fact that the first generation of Christians already had some intuition of the Son's preexistence before the Incarnation. While it is not unusual to hear people say (as Lewis himself believed for many years) that Jesus was simply a human being who was "eventually" deified long after his death, in fact his divine preexistence is a theme that appears in the New Testament. It took centuries for the Church to clarify some basic truths of this mysterious preexistence, and in describing these, Lewis reflects on the difference between "making" and "begetting": "To beget is to become the father of: to create is to make."[22] The difference, Lewis says, is that when you beget, you make something like yourself; but when you make, you make something unlike yourself. Since the Son is "begotten" of the Father, he possesses the divine attributes of the Father—omnipotence, existence from all eternity, and so on. On the other hand, while everything that God has created bears some resemblance to its Maker, created realities do not share God's own nature. This distinction is so important to Lewis that he proposes that we use two different words for "life"—*Bios* for the life found in nature, a life that is limited in duration; and *Zoe* for the spiritual life that exists in God from all eternity. *Bios* has a resemblance to *Zoe*, but it is like the resemblance between a photo and an actual place or between a statue and a real person. Christ, as the only begotten Son of the Father, possesses *Zoe*, while we as creatures have the life of *Bios*.

Every Sunday millions of Christians throughout the world

[21] Knox, *Pastoral Sermons*, pp. 502–3.

[22] C. S. Lewis, *Mere Christianity* (New York: Macmillan Publishing Company, 1943), p. 138.

affirm this truth about Christ when they profess in the Nicene Creed that Christ is "God from God, Light from Light, true God from true God, begotten, not made"; but what keeps this from being abstract speculation is a subsequent line: "For us men and for our salvation he came down from heaven." From his meditations on the relationship between the Father and the Son, Lewis speaks about what this doctrine means *for us*. In the mystery of the Incarnation, the *Zoe* of the eternally-begotten Son is united to the *Bios* of the created human nature of Jesus. This has happened, not for God's sake, but for ours: we become sons and daughters of God by sharing in the life of the Son of God. The Son is completely dependent upon his Father, but his eternal self-surrender does not mean the loss of his identity—on the contrary, it *is* his identity as the Son. To be the Son is to receive everything from the Father and to give everything back to the Father. This is why the obedience of Christ is so liberating: whereas Adam and Eve sought to establish their identity apart from God, Christ celebrates his identity in communion with the Father. Our first parents tried to snatch at equality with God, and in so doing brought about the reign of death; Christ Jesus "did not count equality with God a thing to be grasped, but emptied himself" (Phil 2:6–7) and through his death restored life.

For Knox, too, the Trinity is not simply a mystery we contemplate, but it is a communion in which we have been invited to participate:

> I am accepted in the beloved; God loves me in Christ, loves Christ in me—it does not matter which way I look at it; the point is that by virtue of the Incarnation I have become identified with, included in, the Divine Word—that same expression of the Father's being which he contemplates eternally, and is well pleased. And the Holy Spirit, who in virtue

of his eternal mission is the response evoked from the Son
by the Father's love, in virtue of his temporal mission is my
response to God's love of me in Christ. My prayer is made in
union with, and indeed in some sort is continuous with, that
breath of love which unites the Father and the Son; and so it
is in rhythm with the very life of the Godhead. No stirring
of grace within me but is, remotely, a pulsation of the Divine
activity.[23]

"But Only Christ"

Throughout this chapter, we have examined what C. S.
Lewis and Ronald Knox had to say about three fundamental Christian truths: the Incarnation, the saving death, and
the glorious Resurrection of Jesus Christ. They wrote to
defend these truths from the attacks of nonbelievers and the
corrosion of half-believers. They sought to offer clear, reasonable, and attractive presentations of these central beliefs.
We have not explored what implications they drew from
these doctrines for themselves. In the case of Lewis, this is
because he was reticent about such matters, and apart from
these apologetical issues, he wrote relatively little about the
Person of Christ. The one place he felt free to set aside
such reticence was in the kingdom of Narnia. There Aslan
not only creates Narnia; he sings it into being. The risen
Aslan not only appears to his dejected followers, but he
romps with them in the joy of a new dawn. At the end of
Narnia time, Aslan the Judge appears, but the inhabitants
of that kingdom judge themselves when they look into his
eyes and feel in themselves either profound love or intense
hate. The magical quality of Aslan is that he combines great
majesty and humble companionship. In the face of a world

[23] Ronald Knox, "The Blessed Trinity", unpublished conference, n.d.,
Knox Papers, Mells, Somerset; in Milton Walsh, *Ronald Knox as Apologist*
(S.T.D. diss., Gregorian University, Rome, 1985), pp. 394-95.

that denied or minimized the claims of Christ, Lewis wrote to defend Christ's majesty; but in the kingdom of his heart, he rejoiced in Christ's companionship.

With Knox we face the opposite problem—an embarrassment of riches. His sermons and conferences fill thousands of pages, and the great majority of these writings speak of Christ. For example, every year, Knox preached in the same church for the feast of Corpus Christi: he preached over thirty sermons on the Eucharist, each of them focusing on a different facet of the mystery of Christ. In a retreat conference entitled "But Only Christ", Knox takes as his starting point the end of the story of the Transfiguration, where it relates that the three Apostles saw no one else any more but only Jesus. This, he says, is the goal of the Christian life: to see only Jesus in everything and everyone. Such an idea could easily become simply an instance of pulpit rhetoric, but Knox teases out both the challenging and consoling aspects of this desire:

> Is there someone who has done you an injury, who provokes you to anger? Is there someone whose conversation bores you, whose importunity wearies you, whose outward manners offend you? Here too you will see Jesus only—the Crucified appealing to you out of these human souls, that need your care, your forbearance, your compassion. Jesus with you, not an abstract idea, not a historical memory, not enthroned in the terrors of Judgement, but a Friend, human and divine, constantly at your side, sharing your burdens, understanding your difficulties, sympathizing with your work.[24]

These are the words of a man who has looked into Aslan's eyes and has seen both his own shortcomings and his Savior's compassion.

---

[24] Ronald Knox, *The Layman and His Conscience: A Retreat* (New York: Sheed and Ward, 1961), p. 218.

CHAPTER THREE

Gospel Truth

As we saw in the last chapter, both C. S. Lewis and Ronald Knox believed that the image of Jesus as a mere human being deified by later ages could be sustained only by doing great violence to the biblical text. Lewis complained that liberal scholars created their picture of Jesus the teacher by dismissing as "unhistorical" any elements in the Gospels that implied that he claimed to be more than that. (Ironically, in his atheist days, Lewis believed that his friend Arthur Greeves could maintain that Christ was divine only by a selective reading of the New Testament: "I am still inclined to think that you can only get what *you* call 'Christ' out of the Gospels by picking & choosing, & slurring over a good deal."[1]) For the Christian Lewis, a theology that simply dismisses *tout court* the miraculous and denies the historicity of nearly everything in the Gospels leaves the uneducated person with only two options: atheism or Roman Catholicism. In *Caliban in Grub Street* Knox described this line of attack as "scissors and paste" and argued that such efforts reduce Christ to the "gentle Jesus" of Victorian piety.[2] The corrosive effect of this approach continues in our own day, as a perusal of the religion section of many bookstores shows.

---

[1] Walter Hooper, ed., *The Collected Letters of C. S. Lewis*, vol. I (San Francisco: Harper, 2004), p. 862.

[2] Ronald Knox, *Caliban in Grub Street* (London: Sheed and Ward, 1930), pp. 107–23.

Both of our authors lived in the academic world that produced much of this scholarship, and throughout their lives
they opposed the higher critics. We have already seen how
Knox held that it was dangerous to interpret the Bible solely
on the basis of literary forms, divorced from dogmatic foundations. Lewis shares this antipathy and bases his opposition
on personal experience: he has read how reviewers have re-
constructed the history of his own books, and those of his
friends, and found that in 100 percent of the cases, the reviewers were wrong about the events and personalities that
influenced them. Given this rate of failure, how can critics
be so assured about the formation of writings two thousand
years ago? It should be noted that neither Lewis nor Knox
claimed to a be a biblical expert: they were literary scholars,
and it was on these grounds that they challenged the methods of higher criticism.[3] In fact, Knox states in *A Spiritual
Aeneid* that he was initially outraged more by the application
of these principles to the poetry of Homer than to the books
of the Bible. As a student at Oxford, he studied the handbooks that maintained that the *Iliad* was a work of composite
authorship. But as he checked the references, he discovered
a curious thing: while the experts all held this view, they
contradicted one another as to which parts of the epic poem
were composed earlier. If the first critic claims part A is late
and part B is early, while the second critic claims the reverse,
which are you to believe? To further complicate the matter,

[3] One biblical scholar who took exception to Knox's approach suggested
that in Knox's 1946 commentary on the Epistles and Gospels he showed a
tendency to "apotheosize the insignificant", and the scholar likened Knox to
the hero of one his detective stories, finding clues left by the sacred writers
that were missed by the professional "Scotland Yard" exegetes. Cf. John F.
McConnell, "Monsignor Ronald Knox, *Malleus Exegetarum*", *Catholic Biblical
Quarterly*, April 1947, pp. 155–69.

he found that the handbooks assumed one writer's views in one place and the other's in another, without any sense of the inconsistency. When he came to study books about the Old Testament, he found the same pattern: "all the *petitiones principii*, the splitting up of books into various strata of authorship on the ground of criteria arbitrarily assumed, and then suspecting interpolations everywhere merely in order to make the facts square with the theories."[4] What were some of the theories that the higher critics propounded? Knox and Lewis discuss four principal ideas.

First, there is the presumption that since the Enlightenment, scholarship has taken a quantum leap forward: we are much better informed than past ages, and the new "scientific" approach to the Bible has made earlier interpretations obsolete. Both Lewis and Knox suggest that it is arrogant simply to dismiss the biblical interpretations of nearly nineteen centuries and claim that they shed no light on the meaning of the Scriptures. One form of this theory is the suggestion that very early on, the real meaning of Jesus' life and teaching had been seriously misunderstood and misrepresented by his followers and has only now been recovered by modern scholars. But, Lewis objects, the very modernity that these scholars boast of creates an obstacle: how can they, who live in a world vastly different from the first-century Mediterranean, claim to understand Jesus better than the people of his time? "The idea that any man or writer should be opaque to those who lived in the same culture, spoke the same language, shared the same habitual imagery and unconscious assumptions, and yet be transparent to those who have none of these advantages, is in my opinion preposter-

[4] Ronald Knox, *A Spiritual Aeneid* (London: Longmans, Green and Co., 1918) pp. 123-24.

ous."[5] Such ideas exemplify "chronological snobbery" and are generated in an academic environment that values originality, creativity, and innovation. For Knox, such an attitude is symptomatic of modernism, which he describes as a tendency, not an intellectual system: it is "the tendency to be up to date. It is an affection of the soul."[6] Of course, this weapon can turn in the critics' hands: a subsequent generation could react to its forbears and "discover" that the *Iliad* was indeed all the work of one poet.

A corollary of the first theory is the assumption that, unlike us, people in the ancient world were credulous, and their ignorance of science led them to impute divine or diabolical causes to events that have a natural explanation. Rebecca West suggested that the stories in the Bible were pretty fables that served their purpose in the nursery years of the human race but that we have outgrown them; Knox observes, "Christianity is a pedagogue, to bring us to Miss West."[7] In fact, while it is true that people in the ancient world did not possess our scientific knowledge, they did possess *some* scientific knowledge, some understanding of the laws of nature. Lewis uses the virginal conception of Jesus as an example. Saint Joseph knew as well as any modern doctor that in the ordinary course of things, pregnancy can be the result only of sexual intercourse: "In any sense in which it is true to say now, 'The thing is scientifically impossible', he would have said the same: the thing always was, and was always known to be, impossible *unless* the regular processes

[5] Lewis, *Christian Reflections* (Grand Rapids: Wm. B Eerdmans, 1967), p. 158.

[6] Knox, *Some Loose Stones* (London: Longmans, Green and Co., 1918), p. 214.

[7] Knox, *Caliban in Grub Street* (London: Sheed and Ward, 1930), p. 119.

of nature were, in this particular case, being over-ruled or supplemented by something from beyond nature."[8]

In fact, belief in the miraculous requires some knowledge of the laws of nature; the extraordinary can be recognized only when one knows what the ordinary is. The presumption of credulity is refuted by the Gospels themselves: some people denied that Jesus performed miracles, while others attributed such powers to sorcery; even those closest to Jesus expressed doubts during his ministry and even after his Resurrection.

The third theory is a particular instance of the second: belief in miracles is considered to be a prime example of credulity in the ancient world. Both Lewis and Knox addressed this question extensively, and we will explore what they had to say in the next chapter. Here it is sufficient to note Lewis' objection that the question of the miraculous does not pertain to biblical scholarship as such; it is a philosophical question: "The canon 'If miraculous, unhistorical' is one they bring to their study of the texts, not one they have learned from it. If one is speaking of authority, the united authority of all the Biblical critics in the world counts here for nothing."[9] Biblical scholars can, of course, delve into specific instances, as for example to ask if there was one miraculous feeding in the wilderness or two, but Lewis' point is that the question of the possibility of miracles lies outside the bounds of biblical scholarship.

The fourth theory is that the dogmatic assertions about the identity and mission of Jesus grew up long after his death. What motivates the "scissors and paste" approach of

[8] Lewis, *Miracles* (New York: Macmillan, 1948), p. 57.
[9] Lewis, *Christian Reflections*, p. 158.

critics in the various quests for the historical Jesus is the conviction that the true figure has been obscured by subsequent theological interpretations. But these dogmatic assertions are found already in the Epistles, many of which predate the Gospels. Knox urges us to remember that Christianity is older than the Gospels; Lewis agrees, although he admits that it is hard not to think of the Gospel story as the original and the rest of the New Testament as an elaboration. The Gospels certainly reflect an interest in the teachings of Jesus, but this interest is prompted by the experience of his Resurrection, as Lewis explains: "Nothing could be more unhistorical than to pick out selected sayings of Christ from the gospels and to regard those as the datum and the rest of the New Testament as a construction upon it. The first fact in the history of Christendom is a number of people who say they have seen the Resurrection."[10]

In opposing these ideas, both Knox and Lewis deliberately assumed a conservative position. They did so because they believed that the data of Christian tradition demanded this and because they believed that the methods employed by the critics were flawed. (It should be noted that Lewis and Knox showed a similar hostility to the application of these methods to secular literature.) Lewis realized that some viewed his position to be "Fundamentalist", but he considered this an unfair accusation. Neither he nor Knox believed the Bible to be the product of divine dictation, and they recognized the human elements in the production of the Bible. While recognizing the human efforts that shaped the compilation and editing of the sacred books, as well as their inclusion in the canon of Scripture, Lewis stated, "On all of these I suppose a Divine pressure; of which not by any means all need

[10] Lewis, *Miracles*, p. 172.

have been conscious."[11] He drew again on a favorite image in describing the relationship between these divine and human elements: the human being, who is a combination of an animal organism and a rational soul. We can study the human being as a mammal, and we can examine the Bible as a human text; but just as human beings possess a spiritual quality that makes us more than mere animals, so there is a spiritual component given by God to the Bible such that it is uniquely God's word.

Lewis realized that the whole Bible, but especially the Old Testament, employs a rich variety of literary forms, some of them fictional; it did not trouble him to think that the Creation accounts in Genesis were drawn from earlier legends. The saga of Israel over those long centuries reveals great truths gradually coming into clearer focus. Reading these texts prayerfully allows us to enter into that experience, and for this reason Lewis held that even if it were possible to sort out history from legend, we would lose something essential in the process. Knox shared this understanding of the gradual unfolding of God's plan, which culminates in the coming of Christ; he says that according to Saint Paul, the whole providential history of the Chosen People was a great overture, introducing in advance all the motifs in the New Testament.

We find a variety of literary forms in the New Testament as well, but unlike the Old Testament, these writings were composed within a short space of time: they describe a series

---

[11] Lewis, *Reflections on the Psalms* (New York: Harcourt, Brace and World, 1958), p. 111. Knox rejects Arnold Lunn's contention that papal pronouncements demand that Catholics take a literalist position about Scripture, and that while he asserts that the Holy Spirit is the author of Scripture, this is not to be understood as "dictation" in the sense that the human authors received their words in some kind of trance; cf. *Difficulties*, pp. 92–96.

of events, and reactions to these events, which took place within a hundred years. Here, too, we find the human element: Paul writes letters to address specific problems, and Luke organizes materials to compose his Gospel; the other evangelists arrange similar material in different ways. Knox tells his Oxford students that they should not picture the Apostles as a group of reporters at a press conference, each eager to get the story published: "Think, rather, of some meal you have taken with some religious community, and how they sat round afterwards and told stories of old Father So-and-so, now dead; how some of the stories, to the community, were chestnuts, and there were others the young ones hadn't heard before. That is the sort of atmosphere in which the stories of the Founder are cradled."[12] As students of literature and as writers themselves, Lewis and Knox knew the characteristics of the creative process, and they could perceive the contours of the Bible as literature. From having spent a lifetime on their knees, they could read there the inspired word of God.

Their greatest concern from an apologetic point of view was to defend the historical reliability of the New Testament, especially in what it tells us about Jesus Christ. In this regard the Letters of Saint Paul are remarkable. They betray practically no interest in the life and ministry of Jesus, yet they are full of theological statements about him. Knox states that what makes all of this theology even more notable is that most of the time, Paul is not writing to present new doctrines to his readers, but he is writing in response to specific situations. The Apostle assumes that the general content of this theology is something with which his audience is familiar. Knox suggests that for Paul, "the life of Christ"

---

[12] Philip Caraman, ed., *University Sermons of Ronald A. Knox* (New York: Sheed and Ward, 1963), p. 209.

did not mean a biography on the shelf; it was experienced in the lives of believers now:

> His nature was Divine, but the incommunicable privileges of Godhead were not allowed to detain him; somehow, he took upon himself the nature of Man, accepted all its inadequacies, shouldered all its responsibilities. He, our Elder Brother, our Representative, became our Victim, the Representative of our sin; hung upon the Cross, and, as if by the shock of that unparalleled encounter, shattered all the barriers that had existed till then—the barrier between God and Man, the barrier between life and death, the barrier between Jew and Gentile. He died, and in his death mankind, as mystically associated with him, died too, so that the old debt incurred by Adam's sin was cancelled. He rose again, and thereby acquired a second title to the headship of the human race; he was now the Elder Brother of all risen men. The life into which he rose was not a force that quickened his natural body merely; it quickened to birth a new, mystical Body of his, the Church. In the power of that life the individual Christian becomes supernaturally alive; dead to sin, dead to the fetters of the old legal observance, he lives now in Christ, lives now in God. Baptism, his initiation into his Master's death and resurrection, leaves him, as it were, gasping for breath and tongue-tied, while the Holy Spirit within him cries out "Father, Father", to claim the promise of adoption. . . . Our whole life now is Christ-conditioned, he is the medium in which we exist, the air we breathe; all our nature is summed up, all our activities are given supernatural play, in him.[13]

This citation sketches what Knox calls Saint Paul's "program", and as we read it we see how quickly Christian dogmas clustered around Jesus. These theological assertions about Christ appear in writings that were either earlier than or contemporary with the Gospels themselves. Lewis

---

[13] Knox, *University Sermons*, pp. 214–15.

echoes Knox's understanding that in Paul we see "the life of Christ" lived out, and in doing so he highlights the human touches in the Epistles that underscore their authenticity: "The crabbedness, the appearance of inconsequence and even of sophistry, the turbulent mixture of petty detail, personal complaint, practical advice, and lyrical rapture, finally let through what matters more than ideas—a whole Christian life in operation—better say, Christ himself operating in a man's life."[14]

What about the Gospels? Those who attack the historicity of these texts point out many difficulties, and our authors are aware of them. In the introduction to his commentary on the Gospels, Knox lists some: apparent contradictions, sayings challenged on historical grounds, obscure or cryptic sayings, stories that are similar but not identical, and manuscript variations. Often critics make much of such issues by treating passages in isolation. For example, early in the twentieth century Albert Schweitzer put forward the thesis that Jesus was an apocalyptic preacher who mistakenly believed that the world was about to end, and he based this thesis on certain of his statements in the Gospels. In response to this hypothesis, Knox pointed out that in many other teachings, Jesus spoke in a way that suggests he expected the growth of the Kingdom to be a lengthy process.

While Lewis and Knox occasionally addressed objections raised about specific incidents in the Gospels, their usual approach was to invite the reader to consider the Gospels as a whole. Whatever the discrepancies among the four Gospels, they present the broad outlines of Jesus' life and teaching in the same way, and what we read in them "rings true". This may seem a rather vague defense, but Knox says that

---

[14] Lewis, *Reflections on the Psalms*, p. 114.

if we compare them with the apocryphal Gospels, we sense the difference immediately: they belong to real life, not to legend or an elaborate literary fraud. Lewis concurs with Knox's point about the canonical and apocryphal Gospels and offers a more specific version of this justification from the "feel" of the Gospels. When critics dismiss the Gospels as legends or romances, Lewis asks how many legends or romances they have read: "I have been reading poems, romances, vision-literature, legends, myths all my life. I know what they are like. I know that not one of them is like this."[15]

Unlike in the apocryphal Gospels, and unlike in the great legends and myths, one senses in the Jesus of the Gospels a real human being. Here Lewis crosses swords with Rudolf Bultmann, who claimed that the earliest Church did not preserve any picture of the personality of Jesus: "It is Bultmann *contra mundum*. If anything whatever is common to all believers, and even to many unbelievers, it is the sense that in the Gospels they have met a personality."[16] He goes on to argue that there are many historical figures about whom we have no personal knowledge, such as Alexander the Great; and there are fictional characters whom we feel we know as real people, like Falstaff; but there are very few who fit into both categories. Lewis proposes only three candidates: Plato's Socrates, Boswell's Johnson, and the Gospels' Jesus. For Knox, the story of Jesus in the Gospels complements the doctrinal assertions about him in the Epistles:

> St Paul tells me that God became Man; the Evangelists tell me that he became *a* Man. Not merely in the sense that he belongs to his background; that the sort of proverbs he quoted, the sort of references he made to the Scriptures, the sort of illustrations he used in his teaching, were all in character; not

---

[15] Lewis, *Christian Reflections*, p. 155.
[16] Ibid., p. 156.

beyond the compass, ideally anyhow, of a Galilean peasant. They tell me more than that; how God made Man was God made a Boy, who grew in wisdom with the years; how he underwent baptism, the baptism which was ordained for the remission of sins; how he was tempted by the devil; how he was surprised, and asked questions; how he chose a scoundrel to be one of his most intimate friends; how he wept with disappointment over the infidelity of Jerusalem; how he shrank from the near approach of death; how he complained aloud, on his Cross, that God had forsaken him. And as paradox after paradox comes out, the theologians sit there making it all right, and saying, "Here we distinguish; in one sense yes, and in another sense no", but the Evangelists just go on with their story; "we don't know about that" they explain; "all we know is that this is what happened."[17]

The critics seem to want it both ways: either Jesus is merely a great moral teacher but not divine; or he is a mythical, legendary character who is not human. Knox and Lewis believe that if you read the Gospels in their entirety, and put away the scissors and paste, you encounter a figure who is both deeply human, and more than human—in fact, the Son of God. About the liberal critics, Lewis concludes: "These men ask me to believe they can read between the lines of the old texts; the evidence is their obvious inability to read (in any sense worth discussing) the lines themselves. They claim to see fern-seed and can't see an elephant ten yards away in broad daylight."[18]

---

[17] Ronald Knox, "The New Testament Record", unpublished conference, 1952, Knox Papers, Mells, Somerset; in Milton Walsh, *Ronald Knox as Apologist: Wit, Laughter and the Popish Creed* (San Francisco: Ignatius Press, 2007), pp. 209–10.

[18] Lewis, *Christian Reflections*, p. 157.

CHAPTER FOUR

Miracles

For many sophisticated people, the major stumbling block to the credibility of the New Testament is the presence of the miraculous woven throughout its narratives. The "signs and wonders" that gave credence to the claims of Christ in the first century can be obstacles to credibility in a post-Enlightenment world. The conflict between a materialistic and a theistic world view is most patent in the debate about whether or not miracles happen. Both Lewis and Knox wrote extensively on this question; they shared a conviction that miracles are not only evidence for the existence of God but are central to our understanding of the life and mission of Jesus Christ.

Knox first addressed the question in *Some Loose Stones*, where his adversaries were Christian scholars who attempted to explain away miraculous events as "special providences", which Knox distinguishes from authentic miracles as "a marvelous conjunction of circumstances, not any circumstance marvelous in itself."[1] The doctor passing by just when the child was ill, the storm splintering the ships of the Armada, and other such events can be viewed as marvelous, but they are not strictly speaking miraculous. For Knox, a miracle is something that traverses the law of uniformity in nature and does so in such a way that it gives evidence of divine power

[1] Ronald Knox, *Some Loose Stones* (London: Longmans, Green and Co., 1913), p. 53.

directly at work. This evidentiary quality of the miraculous is crucial for him. Someone reading the Gospels now may be unconvinced by the miracle stories (Knox suggests that many people today believe in Christianity not because of these stories but in spite of them); but what is clear is that they certainly were accepted as evidence in the first century. After his conversion Knox discussed miracles in *The Belief of Catholics*, and in the same year (1927), he wrote a pamphlet on this topic for the Catholic Truth Society. He also addressed the subject in his conferences at the Oxford chaplaincy. In these writings, Knox defended the possibility of the miraculous against Deists and pantheists: for the Deist, miracles are impossible because God would not interfere with the workings of creation that he has set in motion; for the pantheist, miracles are impossible because God is caught up in the cogs of the universe. Knox did not address the objections of the atheist, for whom there can be no miracles because there is no God. Presumably, Knox felt that the atheist position should be met on philosophical grounds, not on the basis of miracles. Most of his writings on miracles, however, concerned the miracles' evidentiary quality regarding the mission of Jesus Christ.

Lewis first engaged the question of the miraculous in a sermon he preached in 1942. The talk was well received, and Dorothy Sayers urged him to write more extensively on the topic. By 1945 Lewis had completed *Miracles: A Preliminary Study*, although it was not published until 1947. The title is significant, because Lewis aimed at offering a philosophical defense of miracles, not a historical examination of the miracles of Christ; only the final three chapters deal directly with Christian beliefs. However, those three chapters offer insights into the significance of Christ's miracles, both for an understanding of who he is and for what he does for us. Thus Lewis, like Knox, presents both a philosophical argument in defense of the miraculous and a theological reflection on the miracles performed by Jesus Christ.

Are Miracles Possible?

Whether or not it is true that simple people in the past were overly credulous regarding the miraculous (and that in itself is a question our authors considered open to discussion), there can be no doubt that in our post-Enlightenment world, there is an opposite prejudice: the supposition that miracles simply cannot happen. With customary humor Lewis sketches this world view at the beginning of his 1942 sermon:

> If the end of the world appeared in all the literal trappings of the Apocalypse, if the modern materialist saw with his own eyes the heavens rolled up and the great white throne appearing, if he had the sensation of being himself hurled into the Lake of Fire, he would continue forever, in that lake itself, to regard his experience as an illusion and to find the explanation of it in psycho-analysis, or cerebral pathology.[2]

In a world without God, there can be no miracles; everything must have a "natural" explanation. Most of Lewis' book *Miracles* addresses two fundamental ways of looking at our universe: the natural and the supernatural. We have seen his arguments for the latter approach already—how both our reason and our moral judgments point to something or someone beyond the natural universe. Knox summarized Lewis' description of the naturalist approach in one

[2] Lewis, "Miracles", in *God in the Dock* (Grand Rapids: Eerdmans, 1970), p. 25.

of his Oxford conferences: "Mr Lewis is so good, isn't he, at the beginning of his book on miracles, about the rationalist wanting to inhabit a self-contained world of *nature*, ascertainable fact, what he calls 'the whole show', outside which there is nothing. A sealed-off, God-proof little universe, an egg which never hatches, that's what he wants. Any divine interference he resents exactly as a man with a bad cold resents a draught."[3] For such people, extraordinary events are perplexing but not troubling: it is the idea of divine intrusion that they resent. Knox goes on to say that if a dog made a public speech in the middle of Carfax, it would worry the rationalist, but he wouldn't really *mind* (so long as the dog kept off theological topics): "It may be preternatural, but it's not supernatural, there is no hen's beak *from the outside* cracking his eggshell."[4]

Treating the supernaturalist alternative as a hypothesis, how does the miraculous interact with "the laws of nature", which are so central to our modern view of the world? One position is that miracles simply cannot happen because the laws of nature exclude them. This is often presented as a "scientific" objection to the miraculous, but both Lewis and Knox observe that it is nothing of the kind: miracles are by definition exceptions to the laws of nature; science *ex hypothesi* is strictly limited to nonmiraculous occurrences. The objection to miracles is philosophical, not scientific. Still, Lewis recognizes that for the scientist, miracles might be seen as a form of doctoring or cheating the laws of nature; and Knox suggests that some think the idea of God constantly rearranging his scheme to fit human needs is "like a child continually altering the direction of its clockwork toy to prevent its edging off the

[3] Philip Caraman, ed., *University Sermons of Ronald A. Knox* (New York: Sheed and Ward, 1963), p. 188.

[4] Knox, *University Sermons*, p. 189.

table."[5] But far from denying the laws of nature, the miraculous presumes them. As Knox notes, you cannot be astonished at a miracle of levitation unless you believe in the law of gravity.

For both Lewis and Knox, there is a synergy between the laws of nature and the miraculous, between the natural and the supernatural. Knox draws on a biblical image to illustrate their relationship. In the Book of Judges, Gideon is given two signs that he has been chosen by God: during the first night, dew settles only on his fleece, and the ground around it stays dry; on the second night, the dew settles everywhere but on the fleece (Judg 6:36–40). The dew on the fleece alone symbolizes unusual, miraculous occurrences, while the dew on the ground surrounding the fleece represents the ongoing reality of creation with which we are so familiar. The ordinary operations of nature are as sensational as the exceptional miracle, and both come from the same hand:

> Ordinarily, in all the million details of our daily experience, He works thus, expressing His will through the laws which Science tabulates for us, laws which operate uniformly, no effect without its cause, back to the first amoeba in which life was found, back to the first nebula from which matter took birth—and yet, all the time it is His power, directly exercised, which lends these causes their efficacy. You are puzzled by miracles? I tell you, if you would only recognize the necessity of God's action in the world, the fall of a sparrow to the ground would be ten thousand times more staggering to your poor, finite imagination. It is a thing to make you dream at night, and wake gasping with the wonder of it.[6]

As we shall see later, both he and Lewis find that the ordinary actions of God in sustaining creation and the miracles

[5] Knox, *Some Loose Stones*, p. 61.

[6] Ronald Knox, "Miracles" (London: Catholic Truth Society, 1927), p. 7.

of Our Lord dovetail: God does locally and exceptionally what he is doing universally in the ordinary processes of nature.

Lewis expresses this synergy by describing a miracle as an event that has its source in God apart from the laws of nature but that subsequently conforms to those laws: "Miraculous wine will intoxicate, miraculous conception will lead to pregnancy, . . . miraculous bread will be digested."[7] Once the miraculous enters the realm of nature, it obeys all her laws. The reason for this is that nature is a system, but a partial system. Both it and the miraculous have a common origin in God, and the source of their interlocking must be sought outside the limited system of nature: "Everything *is* connected with everything else: but not all things are connected by the short and straight roads we expect."[8] By definition, miracles interrupt the usual course of nature, but in doing so, they assert the unity of reality at a deeper level. Lewis draws on his expertise as a literary critic to suggest a parallel: poets will break the superficial uniformity of rhyme or meter occasionally, but they do so in the service of a higher unity in their work. The novice student might consider this an error, but the connoisseur recognizes the hand of genius. Like Knox, Lewis suggests that the miraculous draws our attention to the ongoing miracle of our universe and its operations. In fact, he suggests that only the supernaturalist truly sees nature, because distance lends perspective. Just as the "Englishness" of our language can be appreciated best by someone who knows a second language, so the "natureness" of the world can be appreciated best by someone whose horizon is not limited by this world. While working

[7] Lewis, *Miracles* (New York: Macmillan, 1948), p. 72.
[8] Lewis, *Miracles*, p. 74.

on this subject, he described to Bede Griffiths some of the thoughts he was "drunk with": "You don't *see* Nature till you believe in the Supernatural: don't get the full, hot, salty tang of her except by contrast with the pure water from beyond the world."[9]

Lewis appeals to this combination of affirming *both* the uniformity of nature *and* the possibility of the miraculous in his response to the antimiraculous position of David Hume. Hume had argued that the uniformity of natural laws suggests that the miraculous is so improbable that accounts of miracles may never be accepted as true; there *must* be some other explanation, no matter how improbable it is. Again, for Lewis this is to assume that nature is a complete, self-contained system, and on the basis of that assumption to define the dogma that miracles cannot happen. From Lewis' perspective, the question "Do miracles occur?" and the question "Is the course of nature absolutely uniform?" ask the same thing from two different perspectives; for Hume, an affirmative response to the latter demands a negative response to the former. The only kind of probability Hume allows is one which respects the absolute uniformity of nature. But here Lewis discerns a finger pointing to the supernatural: Hume's presumption of this uniformity argues against a closed, all-inclusive understanding of nature. The laws of nature point to a legislator, and our rational assumptions indicate a Rational Spirit behind the universe. The supernatural perspective accounts for both the uniformity in nature and the possibility of miraculous occurrences. The "probability" of specific miracles can be examined on historical grounds, and no doubt in some cases alternative explanations will emerge. But to assume that all such stories

[9] Walter Hooper, ed., *Collected Letters of C. S. Lewis*, vol. II (San Francisco: Harper, 2004), p. 648.

must be untrue because we know that miracles have never occurred is to beg the question. (Lewis devotes an entire chapter to the question of probability; Knox's approach is more succinct: a "Miracle cannot be probable or improbable; it is either possible or impossible."[10])

Having considered the post-Enlightenment prejudice that miracles cannot happen, our authors address another objection: the presumption that people in the past were credulous and had a prejudice in favor of miracles. There are two related questions here: Were they credulous? And does a belief in miracles necessarily demand an acceptance of the primitive cosmology (from a scientific perspective) of the ancient world? We have seen that Lewis recognizes that the ancients did not possess our scientific understanding of the laws of nature, but they certainly had an experiential knowledge of those laws. Saint Joseph was unaware of the biological complexities of conception, but he certainly knew that in the course of nature there was only one way a woman could be with child; Mary's pregnancy could have only one natural explanation. Both Lewis and Knox point out that the reaction of the witnesses to miracles in the New Testament is one of wonder and awe: Jewish witnesses claimed that they had never seen anything like this, and pagan witnesses thought that Paul and Barnabas were gods come down to earth. Such reactions suggest that people did not expect miracles and knew enough about the workings of nature to realize that something remarkable had happened.

But is it not true that primitive peoples often ascribed a miraculous cause to an event that might have another explanation? Both Knox and Lewis acknowledge that unusual events may be inexplicable without being miraculous; some,

[10] Knox, *Some Loose Stones*, p. 84.

or even many, faith healings could have a psychosomatic origin. But that does not cover every case; it would take an exaggerated trust in merely human restorative powers to account for the raising of Lazarus from the grave four days after he died. Our authors ask for an examination of miracles that begins with an open mind: what we are looking at may have a natural explanation, but it also may not. As to the suggestion that belief in the miraculous demands the acceptance of a primitive cosmology, Lewis makes two points. First, whenever we speak of supernatural realities, we necessarily employ images; but Christian doctrine is not inextricably linked to any images, past or present. For two thousand years the Church has preached doctrines about Christ in situations with various philosophical and cosmological presuppositions, and Christians have been able to distinguish core doctrines from the language and imagery with which they are expressed. The growth of scientific understanding does not threaten the dogmatic assertions of the Christian faith. Second, while spiritual realities are expressed in metaphorical or analogical terms, historical events can be described literally. Miracles are occurrences that people claim to have witnessed in the material world, and miracles' historicity should be examined with the same criteria we use for other alleged events. (Lewis showed impatience with attempts by modern Christian scholars to dismiss the miracles of Jesus as unhistorical. After reading through Alec Vidler's sermon "The Sign of Cana", he said he found it incredible that we should have to wait two thousand years to be told that what the Church has always regarded as miracle was only a parable.)

Before proceeding with such an investigation, there is another difficulty to face: granted that God *can* do miracles, *would* he? Many modern people, Lewis observes, seem to

have an aesthetic objection to the miraculous: "to violate
the laws he himself has imposed on his creation seems to
them arbitrary, clumsy, a theatrical device only fit to impress
savages—a solecism against the grammar of the universe."[11]
Is God "showing off" in performing miracles or, to recall
Knox's image, constantly redirecting his windup toy to keep
it from running off the desk? It is dangerous to presume to
know the mind of God, and both Lewis and Knox always
expressed a great reserve in this regard. But if God does perform miracles, he does so for a very good reason: we need
them. We forget God so easily; he needs to catch our wandering attention. Even apart from miracles, the whole story
of the Judeo-Christian tradition is of a God who enters into
creation and history to seek us out, to reveal himself to us.
We could come to the understanding that God exists from
a study of the world around us, but often people do not;
in our fallen condition, a revelation is needed: "The spiritual blindness of man is not a functional disorder which will
yield to treatment; it is an organic disease which calls for
an operation."[12] If Christ's coming into the world is what
Christians believe it to be, it represents nothing less than
an invasion of the supernatural into the natural world; and
the reaction of the natural world can express itself only in
miracle.

In answer to those who consider it "unseemly" for God
to perform miracles, Lewis draws on the teaching of Saint
Athanasius: God incarnate did in a localized, limited way
what God is always doing in a universal way. Miracles do
not conflict with our understanding of the natural world but
illuminate it: "The miracles in fact are a retelling in small

[11] Lewis, *God in the Dock*, p. 28.
[12] Knox, *University Sermons*, p. 189.

letters of the very same story which is written across the whole world in letters too large for some of us to see."[13] Miracles tell us something about Christ, but that is only half the story: they also tell us about the wonders of the world in which we live. Knox shares this view: "Miracles are God's signature, appended to His masterpiece of creation; not because they ought to be needed, but because they are needed."[14]

By way of summary, our authors maintain that before we begin to examine the miracle stories in the New Testament, we must set aside certain prejudices: that the only reality is the spatiotemporal world in which we live; that the laws of nature exclude the possibility of the miraculous; that God would not "stoop" to do miracles. It is not easy to put these presuppositions aside, because many intellectuals since the Enlightenment have claimed insistently the contrary: there is no world beyond what we can experience with our senses; miracles are impossible; God does not enter into the workings of our world. It is also challenging to put these presuppositions aside because a living, personal God makes demands on us that that the Enlightenment "Watchmaker" or pantheist "Absolute" do not:

> Here lies the deepest tap-root of Pantheism and of the objection to traditional [biblical] imagery. It was hated, at bottom, not because it pictured Him as man but because it pictured Him as king, or even as warrior. The Pantheists' God does nothing, demands nothing. He is there if you wish for Him, like a book on a shelf. He will not pursue you. There is no danger that at any time heaven and earth should flee away at His glance.[15]

[13] Lewis, *God in the Dock*, p. 29.
[14] Knox, "Miracles", p. 10.
[15] Lewis, *Miracles*, p. 113.

To entertain the possibility of a personal God, especially of a God who cares for us and comes in search of us, means that one may be in for *anything*—and that includes the very real possibility that "just in the millionth instance He multiplies bread instead of multiplying wheat."[16]

The Miracles of Jesus

While sophisticated readers today may find the Gospel miracles an embarrassment, for both Lewis and Knox they are an essential part of the story. Knox observes that the miraculous haunts the story of Jesus at every turn and that while it is difficult to dismiss Jesus as a deluded fanatic, such a theory would not be untenable if the miracles are cut out of the Gospels. Lewis claims that to exclude them deals a mortal blow to our religion: "A naturalistic Christianity leaves out all that is specifically Christian."[17] In their writings, they argue that the miracles of Jesus really happened, and they explore what those miracles mean.

Were not miraculous stories part and parcel of the primitive culture of the first century? Lewis and Knox challenge this assumption. Because we tend to squeeze "the ancient world" into a flat, coterminous picture, we may not advert to the fact that Jesus was born into a world where the miraculous was largely a memory. There are hardly any miracles recorded in the Jewish Scriptures after the Babylonian captivity; the miraculous exploits of the pagan gods belonged to a fairy-tale world of "once upon a time"; the ancient oracles were mute. Then, suddenly, in the first century, "a blaze

---

[16] Knox, "Miracles", p. 7.
[17] Lewis, *Miracles*, p. 83.

of credulity flares up through the world".[18] A remarkable series of miraculous events are experienced in the space of a very short time in the life of Jesus and his immediate followers. And these miracles are not like the exploits of the gods in pagan antiquity, whose miracles consisted largely of peculiar punishments; reading Ovid's *Metamorphoses*, Lewis suggests that the least suspicion that they were actually true would have ruined the fun. It may be, Knox says, that people were ignorant or stupid in ascribing the wonders of Jesus to supernatural causes; but this sudden outburst of credulity suggests that *something* must have triggered it.

Knox emphasizes the evidentiary importance of Jesus' miracles. They are the only adequate proof that he was who he claimed to be: "Put Raphael down at a street-corner as a pavement-artist, what proof can he give of his identity but to paint like Raphael? Bring God down to earth, what proof can He give of His Godhead but to command the elements like God?"[19] The first followers of Jesus saw his miracles in this way. In the Acts of the Apostles, Saint Peter says that Jesus went about doing good and healing all who were oppressed by the devil, and then adds: "We are witnesses to all that he did both in the country of the Jews and in Jerusalem" (Acts 10:39). What they witnessed was not simply the Sermon on the Mount, but also the healings; not simply the Crucifixion, but also the Resurrection. For the disciples and the evangelists, the miracles of Jesus gave evidence that their Master was more than human.

Not only did the disciples understand the miracles to be evidence, but Jesus himself claimed they were. When the imprisoned John the Baptist sent some of his disciples to ask

[18] Ronald Knox, *The Belief of Catholics* (New York: Sheed and Ward, 1953 [1927]), p. 101.
[19] Knox, "Miracles", p. 17.

Jesus if he was the one who is to come, Christ's answer was: "Go and tell John what you hear and see: the blind receive their sight and the lame walk, lepers are cleansed and the deaf hear, and the dead are raised up" (Mt 11:4-5). Some of Jesus' adversaries conceded that he performed marvelous deeds, but they attributed his power to demonic possession. This obstinacy in the face of the evidence is understood by Jesus to be the reason for their condemnation: "If I had not done among them the works which no one else did, they would not have sin; but now they have seen and hated both me and my Father" (Jn 15:24). The Gospels testify that both followers and foes of Jesus credited him with miraculous deeds; Knox says that we either have to believe that Christ performed these signs in order to convince people that he was the Son of God or that he deliberately allowed them to believe he was performing miracles when he was not. The latter explanation is hard to square with the moral teaching of Jesus, and this brings us to the second important point to be made about his miracles: how they connect with his message.

Our Lord's miracles were not isolated displays of thaumaturgic power; they were inextricably linked to one another and to the whole pattern of Jesus' life and teaching. Knox describes them as the sign language between Heaven and earth, pictures of eternity projected onto the screen of time. Their significance is illuminated by Jesus' teaching, and they in turn illustrate the doctrine he taught. For example, the Gospel of John devotes twenty-one verses to the miracle of the multiplication of the loaves and fishes, and fifty verses to Christ's discourse about himself as the Bread of Life. Knox reflects on this fact and the relationship between what Jesus did and what he taught:

You know how people telling a story, after dinner, will illustrate what happened by moving knives and salt-cellars and
so on about, to illustrate how the land lay? Well, just so,
our Lord in this miracle uses the common need of hunger,
the common substance of bread, to give his hearers a sort of
diagram of the supernatural life, and how it has needs, and
how those needs are to be satisfied. So with the blind man
who was sent to wash in the pool of Siloe; it was all a lesson
in the meaning of baptism—the enlightenment from above
which is necessary to all of us if we are going to open our
eyes to a spiritual world. . . . The water turned to wine—
our poor human effort transformed and energized by grace.
The fig-tree that withered—God's judgement on the life that
runs to leaf and bears no fruit. The swine at Gadara—how the
madness of one man can drive a whole nation to its ruin. The
palsied man, carried in by his friends and let down through
the roof—how faith can triumph over obstacles, how prayer
can avail for others besides ourselves. The miraculous draught
of fishes—the blind obedience, the untiring patience which
faith demands of us. The stilling of the tempest on the lake
—what confidence we ought to derive from the presence of
our Master in and with his Church. All working up to that
astonishing miracle, the raising of Lazarus—the human soul,
dead in sin, the prey of corruption, reawakened and disin-
terred.[20]

For Knox, the miraculous element not only haunts the
Gospel story at every turn, but it suits that story: the miracles harmonize with the identity, the mission, and the doctrine of Jesus.

Lewis concurs: the miracles should not be studied indi-
vidually but in relationship to one another and to the message of Jesus' preaching: "Not one of them is isolated or

[20] Knox, *University Sermons*, pp. 221–22.

anomalous; each carries the signature of the God whom we know through conscience and from Nature. Their authenticity is attested by their *style*."[21] He devotes two chapters of *Miracles* to the way the miracles of Christ bear witness to his divinity. In some cases, we see in Jesus' miracles God incarnate doing in sudden and particular ways what he is always doing universally, what Lewis calls "Miracles of the Old Creation". In other cases, the miracles are previews of what God will do in the future, "Miracles of the New Creation". Some of the former are miracles of fertility: events like the multiplications of the loaves and fishes and the water turned to wine at Cana are localized manifestations of the same creative power by which each year God produces wheat and grapes from the earth. "The Miracle consists in the short cut; but the event to which it leads is the usual one."[22] Regarding miracles of healing, Lewis readily admits that in some cases marvelous cures can be attributed to hysteria and the power of suggestion; but not all the miracles of Jesus can be dismissed in this way. Lewis proposes a spectrum of healings: natural processes, natural processes influenced by the mind, and direct interventions by God. His point is that these are all related, and in all of them God's power is at work. In Christ, "the Power that always was behind all healings puts on a face and hands."[23]

What Lewis calls "Miracles of the New Creation" are foreshadowings of what God has in store for us. The greatest of these is the Resurrection of Christ, to which we will turn in a moment. But that new creation occasionally shines through in the earthly life of Jesus. For example, when Jesus

[21] Lewis, *Miracles*, p. 166.
[22] Ibid., p. 163.
[23] Ibid., p. 168.

stilled the storm, he did what God always does, bringing about storm and calm; but when he walked on the water and allowed Peter to do the same, he was prefiguring a new kind of relationship between the human body and the rest of the visible creation. Similarly, in the Transfiguration, we get a glimpse of a future glory, a glory Christ wants to share with us. Jesus can perform miracles because he is truly God, but he performs them through his human nature.

The Two Great Miracles

If it is true that in Christ we see God doing in a localized manner what he does throughout creation, this is because it is God himself who is acting. The Incarnation is "the Grand Miracle" which forms the basis of the miracles of the old and new creation for Lewis. The Resurrection is the greatest miracle of the new creation and a confirmation of the unique claims of Jesus. For Knox, it is at the terminal points of Christ's entry into this world and his departure from it that the invasion of supernature shakes the natural world to its depths:

> Matter and Life, the two main conditions of our mortality, are challenged by this contact with a higher order of things. Matter must see its own laws defiled, when a Man comes into the world leaving his Mother still a Virgin, when he goes out of the world leaving the stone and the seal of his virgin tomb unviolated. Life must see its own laws defied, when he comes into the world unbegotten, when he goes out of the world alive.[24]

[24] Knox, *University Sermons*, p. 222.

In these spectacular miracles Knox finds lessons for us too: in the Virgin Birth, we see the promise of our own regeneration by the Holy Spirit in the womb of the Church, and in the Resurrection the sowing of the seed of immortality that is to take root in us.

We have already examined the thought of Knox and Lewis on the Incarnation; now we will review what they had to say about the Resurrection. This was Jesus' greatest sign, which he predicted several times during his ministry. These predictions are associated in some way with a statement about the destruction and the rebuilding of the Temple, a charge that was brought against him at his trial. In Matthew's Gospel, a guard is mounted at the tomb of Jesus in answer to his claim that he would rise from the dead. But the Resurrection was not just one more miracle—Knox and Lewis believe that the essential proclamation of the first Christians was that Jesus had risen from the dead: "to preach Christianity meant primarily to preach the Resurrection."[25] We should recall that the liberal scholarly bishop consigned to Hell in Lewis' *The Great Divorce* started down the road that brought him there by denying the Resurrection of Christ. What proof do we have for the Resurrection, and what does it mean for us?

Knox devotes a great deal of attention to evidence for the Resurrection. His starting place is the empty tomb, because this is a matter of fact. If the first disciples had proclaimed that Jesus was risen and his body was still in the tomb, their preaching would have had no effect. Knox surveys the most common alternative explanations. Some of the earliest liberal critics had suggested that Jesus did not really die on the Cross; he faked his death intentionally in order

---

[25] Lewis, *Miracles*, p. 131.

to delude posterity that he had risen from the dead. This solution was so patently contrary to everything the Gospels tell us about the personality and values of Jesus that it was quickly abandoned (only to be "resurrected" in the second half of the twentieth century in books like *The Passover Plot* and *Holy Blood, Holy Grail*, the inspiration for *The Da Vinci Code*). Some scholars suggested that the women had gone to the wrong tomb; or that in an earthquake the body had slipped underground; or that the body had been eaten by wild animals—explanations that testify to the hardiness of Hume's contention that any rationalization, no matter how wildly improbable, is preferable to miracle. Setting to one side such farfetched solutions, the only reasonable natural explanation is that someone removed the body from the tomb. But who? Some suggested the enemies of Jesus— the Roman authorities or Jewish leaders—who wanted to prevent disturbances. But if they had done so, they certainly would have produced the corpse once the disciples began speaking of the Resurrection. The more likely suspects are the followers of Jesus themselves, an explanation circulating in the Jewish community when the Gospel of Saint Matthew was written (Mt 28:12–15). The disciples stole the body, invented stories about seeing Jesus alive, and spread this fiction all over the Mediterranean world—that is the best *natural* explanation; but Knox asks, does this square with the behavior of the disciples during the Passion? Is it credible that these men (less courageous than the women!) would have denied their Master, abandoned him to a horrible death, and then concocted a story they all knew to be a lie and endured imprisonment and execution for the sake of this deception?

Knox then turns to the risen Christ's appearances to his disciples. The evidence for these is remarkably ancient: Saint

Paul writes to the Corinthians within twenty-five years of the events, and he quotes a list of appearances that is already traditional. The accounts of specific appearances related in the Gospels overlap this list somewhat, but Paul lists appearances we do not read about in the Gospels, and the Gospels describe appearances that do not appear on Paul's list. A comparison of the Gospels themselves reveals inconsistencies, more than we find in the Passion narratives. Knox suggests that these discrepancies in fact argue for their authenticity: if the disciples had really invented the story of the Resurrection, their accounts would have agreed more closely: "The evidence on these points of detail is not exactly clear. True evidence very seldom is. Bribe a handful of soldiers, and they will spread the same lie all over Jerusalem. Take three women to the tomb, none of them expecting to find anything unusual, and you will have to piece the story together for yourself."[26] What adds to the confusion is that Jesus is changed after his Resurrection. As Lewis points out, his humanity is something radically new yet corporeal. The disciples do not describe "visions" of Christ: he can be touched, and he eats. (Later they have visions, but this is after the privileged time of these unique appearances.) Were these hallucinations? Both Lewis and Knox dismiss this explanation, since on several occasions the disciples did not at first recognize Jesus. A hallucination makes us mistake a stranger for a friend; they mistook their friend for a stranger. It was not just that Jesus had come back to life, like Lazarus or the daughter of Jairus; the disciples were encountering a transformed human nature, the great miracle of the new creation.

[26] Philip Caraman, ed., *Pastoral Sermons of Ronald A. Knox* (New York: Sheed and Ward, 1960), p. 387.

With his vivid imagination, Lewis probes some of the implications of the humanity of the risen Christ. After the Resurrection, Jesus relates differently to space and time but is not cut off from them. He has not retreated from the world of nature back into some kind of unconditional and utterly transcendent existence: "The old field of space, time, matter and the senses is to be weeded, dug, and sown for a new crop. We may be tired of that old field: God is not."[27] One of our limitations is that we presume that if there is anything beyond our three-dimensional world, it is purely spiritual in a negative, abstract way (Knox describes this as an impression of something which is pale, imaginary, and unsubstantial); in fact it is *more* real and possesses dimensions of which we are unaware. Lewis says that our initial choices seemed to be between a one-story house (nature) or a two-story house (nature with some kind of unconditional "Something"). But Christianity, especially in light of the Resurrection, suggests something richer: a multistoried universe whose various levels are increasingly spiritual, multidimensional, and personal. What we see in our own world hints at this: there are chemical and material objects; plants, which possess in addition to material existence a vital principle; animals, which are more intelligent and sensate than plants; and human beings, who are endowed with reason. Each plateau is natural in its own right but is "supernatural" to the level below; it possesses a quality that is more than natural to the lower form; and they are all interconnected. What the disciples experienced in their encounters with the risen Christ was a humanity that defies description, not because it is less real than our humanity, but because it is *more* real.

[27] Lewis, *Miracles*, p. 179.

The first remarkable truth is that this new human nature is made out of the old one; the second remarkable truth is that, above the topmost floor of creation, there still is God, the ultimate Fact, and that it is God the Son himself whom we meet in the humanity of Jesus; the third remarkable truth is that God wants to share this Sonship and this glorified humanity with us.

The Resurrection is "Good News" for us because it does not concern Jesus alone. His disciples not only proclaimed that Christ was risen; they believed and hoped that they would share in the glorified humanity they had seen and handled in his flesh: "He did not simply convince men that he had risen; he convinced them that they would rise. That change of the body from a passible to a glorious state, which they admired as a portent in him, they looked forward to as a common experience for themselves."[28] The disciples enjoyed these experiences only for a limited period of time; with the unique exception of Saint Paul's encounter with the risen Lord on the road to Damascus, the appearances came to an end at the Ascension. We might envy the first disciples—although even they experienced doubts—and draw the conclusion that meetings with the risen Christ belong to the distant past or to some vague future time when Christ will return in glory. Both Lewis and Knox resolutely oppose such thoughts: we encounter the risen Christ in the visible world around us, in other human beings, in his Body the Church, and in her sacraments. If we do not see him, we do well to recall that his own friends often did not recognize him at first, and as Knox suggests, this was because his comings were so simple:

[28] Knox, *Pastoral Sermons*, p. 400.

It is not only then that the Resurrection promises us a future existence in glory. It does do that. It guarantees heaven here and now, all about us and in our midst. That is the exciting sense which everyone must feel who reads about the encounters the disciples had with our Blessed Lord after his Resurrection. For they were sudden, unlooked-for encounters in the course of ordinary workaday pursuits. You went to the garden to mourn a friend lost, and you found him whom your soul loved. You hid in the upper room, and locked the doors on yourselves; you looked round and he was there. . . . You went fishing on the lake; somebody hailed you, and told you how to cast your nets better: and even as you struggled with your sudden catch, it occurred to you, "Where have I heard that authoritative ring in the voice before?" And all in a moment the truth flashed on you. Doesn't that mean, possibly, that heaven is a good deal nearer to us than we know?[29]

The risen Christ meets us in the ordinary circumstances of life. Does he still perform miracles?

Lewis and Knox give somewhat different answers to this question, and it is an area where their diverse ecclesiastical loyalties appear. In general, Protestantism tended to limit the miraculous to exceptional moments in history, above all to the period of the New Testament. At the end of *Miracles* Lewis tells his readers that they are probably right in assuming that they will never witness a miracle: "God does not shake miracles into Nature at random as if from a pepper-caster. They come on great occasions: they are found at the great ganglions of history."[30] In fact, he warns them against wanting to see one, because the great moments of history are usually marked by both miracles and martyrdom. He cer-

[29] Knox, *University Sermons*, p. 340.
[30] Lewis, *Miracles*, p. 201.

tainly was open to the miraculous and considered his wife's recovery from cancer as a miracle with a small *m*; but for the most part, his defense of miracles was limited to the miracles of Jesus in the Gospels.

Ronald Knox was writing from a Catholic perspective, and the Catholic Church has always believed miracles to be part of Christian experience since the New Testament. He sees this as a belief that distinguishes Catholicism from the other forms of English Christianity and suggests that the rejection of the miraculous after the sixteenth century offers an example of discontinuity in the post-Reformation Church of England. Knox notes that Anglican and Protestant theologians distinguished "biblical miracles" from "ecclesiastical miracles", meaning by the latter those reported in later centuries. The latter are often dismissed as manifestations of superstition or ignorance: it is fine to believe that Saint Peter the Apostle walked on water but not to believe that Saint Peter of Alcantara did. Knox considers this view illogical and suggests that a more appropriate division would be between "Gospel miracles" and "ecclesiastical miracles". If miracles were limited to the direct actions of Jesus, they would have ended with his Ascension. But they did not; the followers of Jesus continued to perform miracles, or, more accurately, the risen Lord continued to perform miracles through the members of his Body, the Church. If that was true in the first century, why would it not be true in the second? Or the thirteenth? Or the twentieth?

This is not to say that Knox expected God to "shake miracles at random as if from a pepper-caster": they are very uncommon, intermittent, and unpredictable. Usually they are associated with the lives and deaths of exceptionally holy men and women and manifest the power of Christ at work in his disciples. If we are tempted to associate them with some distant "Age of Faith" and presume that they no longer happen with the frequency they once did, Knox suggests we read the *Dialogues* of Saint Gregory the Great, in which a monk in the sixth century voices the same complaint. If miracles take place at the "great ganglions of history", the present moment is the great ganglion for us who are living through it; and the risen Christ is as active now as he ever was.

Non-Christian Miracles

But are miracles unique to Christianity? Here the Christian apologist deals with an objection on a different front: having responded to the materialist claim that miracles never happen, Lewis and Knox now have to answer the contention that they happen everywhere and thus prove nothing unique about the identity and mission of Christ. They found such claims made on three fronts: from other world religions, from the paranormal experiences of Spiritualism, and in the healings of Christian Science.

In regard to other world religions, they observed that miracles do not hold the importance for them that they do for Christianity. The Old Testament describes many miraculous events, but such wonders are rarely recounted after the return from the Babylonian captivity, five centuries before the birth of Christ. In one letter, Lewis wondered whether a Jewish inquirer could find a rabbi who believes in miracles; they do not play a central role in the Jewish religion. Knox suggests that miracle stories in some other religions may have been inspired by Christianity. There are accounts of miracles performed by the philosopher Apollonius of Tyana, a near-contemporary of Jesus; but these appear to be patterned on Christ's miracles, and Apollonius' life was written by Philostratus two hundred years after his death. The earliest lives of Buddha do not describe miracles, and the contention that he was born of a virgin surfaced only after the Christian Gospel had made its way to India. There are no miracles related in the Koran, and miracles are attributed to Mohammed only after his death. Where miracles do appear in other religions, they are far more peripheral than in Christianity. We have seen how both Lewis and Knox held that the miracles and the message of Jesus were intimately connected, both by his own claims and by the testimony of his disciples. Unlike in Hinduism or Islam, miracles are central to the story of Jesus Christ. Regarding Buddhism, Lewis thinks it is absurd that a teacher who claimed nature to be an illusion would occupy himself in producing effects on the natural level: "The more we respect his teaching the less we could accept his miracles."[31] We saw above that Lewis held that a naturalistic Christianity, which denies the miraculous, leaves out all that is specifically Christian; could this be said of other world religions?

Two phenomena in the early part of the twentieth century involved miraculous claims: Spiritualism and Christian Science. In considering the former, Knox expresses some exasperation at having to switch from defending the miraculous at all to having to limit the claims of the miraculous: "We, to whom superstition was once imputed, must now defend ourselves against antagonists who take photographs of fairies, and reproduce the voices of the dead on a gramophone record."[32] The Spiritualists' critique is that Catho-

---

[31] Ibid., p. 160.
[32] Knox, "Miracles", p. 28.

lics deny Spiritualists' stories of the dead holding converse with the living but claim that saints appear in visions; and Spiritualists ask if there is really any difference between the medium in a trance and the saint in ecstasy. From the perspective of Christian Science, our reliance on human treatments and material medicines indicates a lack of faith; we should put all our trust in the healing power of Christ.

Although Spiritualism and Christian Science are very different entities, Knox raises the same objection to both: they fall into the error of tempting God by *demanding* a miracle. The Catholic Church, he says, believes in miracles, hopes for miracles, and encourages us if we wish to pray for miracles; but they are always the exception, not the rule: "God grants supernatural favours in His own way, not in ours."[33] They are not made to order. While there may be similarities between the psychosomatic reactions of a medium and a saint, there is a world of difference between them: the medium seeks paranormal experiences, while the saint simply seeks union with the will of God; extraordinary phenomena are neither sought after nor valued by Christian mystics. In the case of Christian Science, it is a matter of a good thing (faith) exaggerated beyond what God intends: "For us, to refuse to summon the doctor when a child is lying at death's door is murder, nothing else."[34]

To hope for a miracle is an expression of faith; to expect a miracle is to tempt God. The difference between magic and a miracle, according to Lewis, is that magic is held to work more or less automatically, whereas miracle is an answer to prayer. Knox says that the Christian religion has met with magic since the days of the Apostles and has always scorned

---

[33] Ibid., p. 32.
[34] Ibid., pp. 29–30.

it. The Church refuses to put her trust in magical appliances and occult formulas: "Where supernatural occurrences have marked its progress, they have come unsolicited, unpremeditated, unlaboriously."[35] And he contrasts the magician and the priest: the magician tries to see how much he can get out of God for man; the priest tries to see how much he can get out of man for God.

Conclusion

In defending the historicity and significance of Jesus' miracles, Lewis and Knox steered a course between two opposite extremes: materialists who claim that miracles are impossible and magicians who claim they are everywhere, provided you know how to conjure them. Lewis described these two extremes as "Everythingism": "Thus the Everythingist, if he starts from God, becomes a Pantheist; there must be nothing that is not God. If he starts from Nature, he becomes a Naturalist; there must be nothing that is not Nature."[36] Both of these alternatives are avoided by belief in a personal God who is the Creator of the universe, infinitely above it but passionately concerned about it. It is this Creator who is the source of the laws of nature and who has the sovereign authority to intervene directly in the processes of this world. The Christian contention is that in Jesus Christ, this God came into our world as man and, in doing so, performed in a miraculous way the same deeds he performs continually. The miracles and mission of Christ are inseparable, and the miracles bear witness that Christ is truly God.

[35] Ibid., p. 32.
[36] Lewis, *Miracles*, p. 198.

The "Everythingist" does not see this evidence, either because nature is everything and miracles are impossible or because miracles are everywhere and tell us nothing special about Christ. But this blindness is not limited to miracles. Lewis warns: "Everythingism is congenial to our minds because it is the natural philosophy of a totalitarian, mass-producing, conscripted age. That is why we must be perpetually on our guard against it."[37] Both he and Knox sensed in the modern age something far more sinister than a disbelief in miracles, and we will explore what that is in the next chapter.

[37] Ibid., p. 199.

CHAPTER FIVE

Two Loves, Two Cities

Early in the 1940s, C. S. Lewis was invited to join an American organization, and he accepted with delight: "Dear Sir, While feeling that I was *born* a member of your Society, I am nevertheless honoured to receive the outward seal of membership."[1] The invitation had been extended by the Society for the Prevention of Progress. No doubt Ronald Knox would have welcomed nomination as well. Our two authors were conservative by temperament and profession. Although as young men they were rather stylish in dress, in later years they adopted a rather plain appearance and an old-fashioned approach to life. Knox once confessed to feeling more medieval than middle-aged and suggested that the last really good invention was the toast rack.

They were most at home in Oxford, an idyllic and rather timeless setting in which they could pursue their love for things past: classical authors, English literature, medieval and renaissance texts. Not just personal passion but professional duties kept them attentive to bygone ages—Knox pouring his energies into a translation of the Latin Vulgate Bible, Lewis laboring over *English Literature in the Sixteenth Century*. When Lewis gave his inaugural lecture as the new professor of medieval and renaissance English at Cambridge, he entitled the talk "*De Descriptione Temporum*", a title taken

---

[1] Walter Hooper, ed., *The Collected Letters of C. S. Lewis*, vol. II (San Francisco: Harper, 2004), pp. 613–14.

from the writings of a seventh-century bishop, Saint Isidore
of Seville. (In this case Lewis may have been avant-garde:
Saint Isidore has been proposed as patron saint of the In-
ternet!)

The occasion of this lecture was the establishment of the
chair of medieval and renaissance literature at Cambridge.
In this talk, he explained why his interest in the past was
something far deeper than nostalgia. While students of history or literature often contrasted the classical world with
the Middle Ages, or the Middle Ages with the renaissance,
Lewis argued that the greatest cultural chasm of Western history came between the mid-nineteenth century and all that
had gone before. For example, if one wanted to find a time
when someone was unable to read Virgil although his father
could, it was more likely to be the twentieth century than
the fifth. While it was not uncommon to hear people (even
in the 1950s) decry the waning of Christian faith as a return
to paganism, Lewis did not agree. In fact, he suggested, it
might be rather fun if it were: "It would be pleasant to see
some future Prime Minister trying to kill a large and lively
milk-white bull in Westminster Hall."[2] The abyss of modernity cut off our "post-Christian" culture from Christianity,
and doubly so from the pagan past that preceded it.

Much of his lecture presents evidence for this rift in politics, the arts, and religion and for the influential role of
mechanical inventions in this sea change. How, then, does
he see his role as professor of medieval and renaissance literature? Lewis enlists a very contemporary ally: psychology.
"In the individual life, as the psychologists have taught us,
it is not the remembered but the forgotten past that enslaves

---

[2] C. S. Lewis, *Selected Literary Essays* (Cambridge: Cambridge University
Press, 1969), p. 10.

us. I think the same is true of society."³ The study of the past liberates us from the idols of the present and, indeed, liberates us from misinterpreting the past itself. But Lewis offers his services not only as a guide to "Old Western Culture" but as a specimen of it. He suggests that he would give a great deal to hear any ancient Athenian, even a stupid one, talk about Greek tragedy; Lewis' students can hear Lewis discuss medieval and renaissance literature as a native, not a foreigner. And he concludes: "Speaking not only for myself but for all other Old Western men whom you may meet, I would say, use your specimens while you can. There are not going to be many more dinosaurs."⁴

Ten years earlier, Lewis had addressed a similar theme in his introduction to an English translation of Saint Athanasius' *De Incarnatione*. There he asked people to read old books, not simply the commentaries about them by modern authors (including himself). Along with the inherent value of the works themselves, he saw two advantages. First, old books introduce us into the thread of the conversation: if we join a discussion at eleven o'clock that began at eight, we will miss the import of much that is said—allusions that amuse or annoy the conversationalists will go over our heads. Not only do modern authors help us understand old books, but old books help us understand modern authors and help us weigh their opinions more judiciously. Second, the great works of the past give us perspective on our own age: "Not, of course, that there is any magic about the past. People were no cleverer then than they are now; they made as many mistakes as we. But not the *same* mistakes."⁵ Lewis explains that his own approach to Christianity began with

³ Ibid., p. 12.
⁴ Ibid., p. 14.
⁵ C. S. Lewis, *God in the Dock* (Grand Rapids: Eerdmans, 1970), p. 202.

his reading of classical religious texts as literature, and how rich and profound he discovered "mere Christianity" to be. The author of *De Incarnatione* is praised by Lewis as a great model of the fruitful "conservatism" for which he pleads:

> His epitaph is *Athanasius contra mundum*, "Athanasius against the world". . . . He stood for the Trinitarian doctrine, "whole and undefiled", when it looked as if all the civilized world was slipping back from Christianity into the religion of Arius —into one of those "sensible" synthetic religions which are so strongly recommended today and which, then as now, included among their devotees many highly cultivated clergymen. It is his glory that he did not move with the times; it is his reward that he now remains when those times, as all times do, have moved away.[6]

The courage to stand firm requires a deep awareness of the tradition, and it was this that Lewis considered more necessary than ever in a world where mechanical advances suggest to us, perhaps unconsciously, that newer is always better. One of Knox's characters in *Sanctions* echoes this view: "And believing in the iron law of progress, you turn the process around (most illogically) and argue that simply because things are modern, simply because a certain phase of thought has developed out of an earlier phase of thought, we are all bound to sit by and applaud such developments."[7] Both he and Lewis loved the past because they found it beautiful and fascinating; but they commended it to others because they found it instructive.

Their passion for the past was fed by something deeper and more urgent: distress at the shape the Western world was taking after its "liberation" from the past. The most

[6] Ibid., p. 206.

[7] Ronald Knox, *Sanctions: A Frivolity* (London: Sheed and Ward, 1932), p. 119.

explicit expression of this alarm is found in a series of lectures delivered by Lewis in 1943. In the midst of the tragic and horrifying events of the Second World War, his chosen subject seems almost a parody of the misplaced priorities of an ivory tower professor: "Reflections on Education with Special Reference to the Teaching of English in the Upper Forms of Schools". Its alternative title demonstrates just how attuned he was to the war and his grave concern about what could follow it: "The Abolition of Man".

Lewis begins with something that seems remote to a world of blackouts, sirens, and Stukas: two recent English textbooks, which he cloaks with anonymity as "The Green Book" and "Orbilius".[8] What disturbs him about these books is their assumption that only the world of facts is objective and that values are purely subjective: "The schoolboy who reads . . . *The Green Book* will believe two propositions: firstly, that all sentences containing a predicate of value are statements about the emotional state of the speaker, and, secondly, that all such statements are unimportant."[9] The divorce between fact and meaning reduces religion to psychology, politics to economics, and thought to biochemistry. In a sermon delivered soon after the completion of *The Abolition of Man*, Lewis describes the effect of this attitude: "He sees all the facts but not the meaning. Quite truly, therefore, he claims to have seen all the facts. There *is* nothing else there; except the meaning. . . . You will have noticed that most dogs cannot understand *pointing*. You point to a bit of food on the floor: the dog, instead of looking at the floor,

---

[8] In reality, *The Control of Language* (1940) by Alex King and Martin Ketley; *The Reading and Writing of English* (1936) by E. G. Biaggini.

[9] C. S. Lewis, *The Abolition of Man, or Reflections on Education with Special Reference to the Teaching of English in the Upper Forms Schools* (New York: Colliers, 1962 [1947]), p. 15.

sniffs at your finger. A finger is a finger to him, and that is all. His world is all fact and no meaning."[10] What these textbooks exemplify is the modern denial of what Lewis calls "the Tao", which holds that "the good" is something objective and that reason is the faculty by which it is known. This reality goes by various names, such as natural law, traditional morality, or first principles of practical reason; but it consists of universal values that are found in every culture, albeit with local differences of emphasis. This is what must be rescued from the past if we are to avoid "the abolition of man".

In the West this denial of the Tao is linked to a rejection of the supernatural and the assertion that only the natural is real. The claim that the material world is all that is real leads to what Lewis calls "the sweet poison of the false infinite":[11] science becomes "scientism", biological evolution becomes "evolutionism", and history becomes "historicism". The vocabulary is Lewis', but Knox addresses the same issues, as we shall see. The gulf that separates us from everything before "the modern age" has precipitated this crisis. But we are experiencing in a new way the same dynamic Saint Augustine explored sixteen centuries ago in *The City of God*: two loves have built two cities—a love of God to the contempt of self, and a love of self to the contempt of God. In their writings, Knox and Lewis analyze the fruits of "the city of man without God" under construction around them.[12]

Our authors survey in broad terms the dynamics of the

[10] Lewis, "Transposition", in *The Weight of Glory* (San Francisco: Harper, 1980), pp. 113–14.

[11] C. S. Lewis, *Perelandra* (New York: Macmillan Paperbacks, 1944), p. 81.

[12] Gilbert Meilaender and others have underscored how Lewis employed Saint Augustine's imagery of the Two Cities: cf. Meilaender, *The Taste for the Other: The Social and Ethical Thought of C. S. Lewis* (Grand Rapids: Eerdmans, 1978), pp. 102–5.

three centuries preceding their own. Science and philosophy began to go their separate ways in the seventeenth century. There is a gap between the metaphysical (represented by Donne, Milton, and the Cambridge Platonists) and the physical (represented by Bacon and the Royal Society). This division deepened in the following century, with Butler and Berkeley advancing the metaphysical cause, and Hume, Bentham, and the French philosophes championing the physical. Scientists marveled at the laws of nature, which might owe their origin to God but that function as a self-contained system. The nineteenth century saw the rise of an evolutionary world view that obviates the need for even a "watchmaker" God: the laws of nature are not a marvel but are simply a series of events that owe their origin to chance and their development to an innate instinct for the preservation of the species.

From Science to Scientism

Neither Lewis nor Knox had a quarrel with the hypothesis of biological evolution. Their objection was to what Lewis called "popular evolutionism": a tendency to see progress as some kind of universal cosmic law that applied to every category of experience, from civilization to religion. Lewis delineated several differences between scientific evolution and popular evolutionism: evolution was presented as a hypothesis limited to the area of biology but evolutionism as a fact applicable to everything; the former described how organisms changed (and in many cases degenerated), while the latter always assumed improvement. He suggested that this equation of evolution and progress was produced by the observation that in nature it appears that small, chaotic, or feeble things turn into large, strong, and complex things, combined with the phenomenon of real advances in machines. In this atmosphere people assumed that, as the self-improving mantra of Couéism put it, "Every day in every way I am getting better and better."[13] Lewis maintained that science in fact gives no support to popular evolutionism at all. Evolutionism predates Darwinian theories (Lewis found it in the works of Keats and Wagner); in biological evolution, progress is the exception, degeneration the rule; and while it is true that complex trees grow from simple seeds, it is also true that simple seeds come from complex trees. Knox claimed that the continued progress of the human race is for many people a dogma of faith, a principle by which they live: "It is a moral they deduce, with some hesitations of method, from the developments of history. It is a corollary they infer, with no very good title, from the scientific hypothesis of Evolution."[14]

The horrendous events of the twentieth century were to bankrupt the Victorian confidence in human progress with which our authors had to contend. But apart from its naïve optimism, they also were troubled by other aspects of evolutionism. For one thing, if biological evolution is concerned with the preservation of species, this brings it into conflict with the Tao: "The charity which provides for the sick in hospitals, for the lunatics in asylums, is cumbering the earth with useless weeds, with unproductive consumers. . . . Evolution clamours that these inferior specimens of the race should be eliminated; morality revolts from the doctrine."[15] Knox wrote these words in 1927; the next decade was to

[13] Émile Coué (1857–1926) was a French psychologist who taught a system of autosuggestion.

[14] Ronald Knox, *The Belief of Catholics* (New York: Sheed and Ward, 1953 [1927]), p. 207.

[15] Ibid., p. 210.

see the birth of a regime in Germany that embraced the principle of "the survival of the fittest" with catastrophic results. Their other major objection to evolutionism is that it identifies success solely in terms of this world; human advances will create a Heaven on earth. In *The Screwtape Letters* Wormwood explains that the Enemy (God) wants people to attend to the present and to eternity, because the present, with its freedom and actuality, is the moment when time touches eternity. The great business of the tempters is to get people to live in the future, because it kindles hope and fear: "Hence nearly all vices are rooted in the Future. Gratitude looks to the Past and love to the Present; fear, avarice, lust and ambition look ahead. . . . We want a whole race perpetually in pursuit of the rainbow's end, never honest, nor kind, nor happy *now*, but always using as mere fuel wherewith to heap the altar of the Future every real gift which is offered them in the Present."[16] Or, as Knox wryly put it: "The world's future occupied their thought, instead of a future world, and, by a kind of inverted Confucianism, they fell to worshipping their grandchildren."[17]

Evolutionism applied to history produces "historicism", the contention that we can discover the inner meaning of history. Lewis suggests that historians do not usually make such a claim; they are content to confine themselves to their proper field, the relationship between historical events. Historicism is more a temptation for philosophers, theologians, and politicians: "When Carlyle spoke of history as a 'book of revelations' he was a Historicist. When Novalis called history 'an evangel' he was a Historicist. When Hegel saw in history the progressive manifestation of absolute spirit he

---

[16] C. S. Lewis, *The Screwtape Letters* (New York: Macmillan, 1973 [1942]), pp. 69–70.

[17] Ronald Knox, *God and the Atom* (London: Sheed and Ward, 1945), p. 59.

was a Historicist."[18] And it is a temptation for ordinary folk, too—the village woman who describes her wicked father-in-law's stroke as a divine judgment is a historicist. Lewis claims that it is impossible to know the "inner meaning" of history until the end of the story; a person who listens to a joke but misses the punch line is in the same position as someone who has not heard the story at all. Regarding human history, we have not gotten to the end of the story, we know very little of the story itself, and we do not know whether we are in act 1 or act 5. Knox was masterful at evoking different eras of history, as in *Let Dons Delight* and *Barchester Pilgrimage*—but as to what place we occupy in the chronicle of history, he professes the same ignorance as Lewis: on the one hand, he notes that Gregory the Great thought that the world was about to end, but on the other hand, Knox says we may still be living in the age of the early Church.

Both of our authors emphasize that generally speaking, evolutionism is not advanced by scientists, nor is historicism espoused by historians; it is the pundits, not the experts, who seek to extend the claims of science and history beyond their proper limits. In his "Reply to J. B. S. Haldane", Lewis denied that he was hostile to science or to scientists; his foe was scientism, which he described as an outlook casually connected with the popularization of science, much less common among scientists than among their readers. Knox suggests, "In this century it is the camp-followers of science, not its votaries, that came forward as the critics of religion".[19] He believes that scientists are motivated primarily by curiosity; they have an honorable mis-

---

[18] C. S. Lewis, *Christian Reflections* (Grand Rapids: Eerdmans, 1967), p. 101.
[19] Knox, *God and the Atom*, p. 14.

sion, but it is not that of molding the whole character of a civilization: "This, as a rule, scientists recognize, nor do they feel that a slight has been put on their profession when it is mentioned. But of these modern priests of science I am more doubtful; they mean business, and they talk the language of fanaticism."[20] These "priests of science" are the advocates of scientism, and Knox creates a term to describe them: "Omniscientists". And it was against these pundits that Knox wielded his pen in *Broadcast Minds*.

The catalyst for this book was an incident in which Knox's sense of humor had landed him in hot water. On January 16, 1926, he broadcast a parody of a BBC radio news report. Knox's program purportedly described a riot in London sparked by "the National Movement for Abolishing Theatre Queues", and it caused near panic in some places where it was thought to be an actual news bulletin (this was twelve years before Orson Welles' celebrated broadcast of *The War of the Worlds*). The caricature was so broad that Knox was unrepentant about its unintended effects, although he was publicly admonished and the incident almost cost him his appointment as chaplain at Oxford. The serious lesson he drew from this episode was that the novelty of radio and the fact that in England it was under the control of the government invested this medium with a great deal of authority. He feared that people would be tempted to simply take over a philosophy of life from self-constituted mentors rather than construct a philosophy of life for themselves. And these mentors would be the "omniscientists" who popularize points of view for which they can claim no personal expertise, disarming all opposition by an appeal to science.

[20] Ronald Knox, *Broadcast Minds* (London: Sheed and Ward, 1932), p. 275.

Early on in *Broadcast Minds*, Knox describes some of the tactics of the omniscientists. While they profess that the clarity of science dispels the fog of religious illusion, in fact their goal is not clarity but obscurity: "They adopt the tactics of the cuttle-fish, which emits its ink not to enlighten but to confuse its pursuers."[21] They seek to confuse with the riddles of science, not to enlighten with its clarity, so that ordinary people feel they can no longer trust their own judgment or hold any beliefs as certain at all. Another technique is to refer to experts whose work is far beyond the limited understanding of the public and whom the omniscientists generously offer to explain. But Knox cautions that one should attend carefully to who the experts are. For example, both Bertrand Russell and H. L. Mencken cite in opposition to a traditional understanding of the Bible a scholar named Arthur Weigall; Knox did some research and discovered that this author was not a biblical scholar at all but an Egyptologist, journalist, and stage designer. A third device is a preference for prehistory, since the facts cannot be checked: "People will be grateful to you for making the dry bones of paleontology live by the exercise of a little imagination."[22] We really know nothing about the cave dwellers who left paintings on the walls; we do not even know if they were adults or children. (Knox notes that they could draw people as well as he could, and animals better, which suggests they might have been children!) "But I do not know whether the human figures were portraits of their friends or caricatures of their enemies or images of gods."[23] The omniscientists claim to know a great deal. One of them, Gerald Heard, in *The Emergence of Man* addressed the issue of religion and science (a topic that had nothing to do with the subject of his

[21] Ibid., p. 32.
[22] Ibid., p. 34.
[23] Knox, *Belief of Catholics*, p. 209.

book) and claimed that with the Enlightenment the West had moved from the age of faith to the age of hypothesis. Knox responded that we have moved even further, "into the age of pure assertion, without proof, in which we sit down and listen to the expert and wish we could talk like that."[24]

And what do these self-appointed experts tell us? That the inexorable march of science over the past century has engulfed the quaint certitudes of religion like a tide swallowing up a sand castle. The omniscientists are exasperated that the corpse is still twitching: "More than a century since Darwin, and still there are Prayer-book debates, and a Vatican City!"[25] Knox for his part is exasperated that, with the exception of the new field of psychology, the "scientific" arguments against Christianity are the same as they were a century ago, but the presumption is that they have won the day. The omniscientists assume an antagonism between religion and science that religious thinkers do not share. For example, in his *Treatise on the Gods*, H. L. Mencken states that there was a time when a person suffering from ague sent for a priest and made a votive offering; now he sends for a physician and takes quinine. Knox replies, "What an antithesis! We might be pardoned for pointing out that it was the Jesuits who introduced quinine into Europe."[26] Or, in response to Heard's contrast between the age of faith and the age of hypothesis: "But nobody ever suggested that our knowledge of the natural world did, or ought to, depend on faith, and the difficulty of basing our knowledge of another world on hypothesis is that the hypothesis unfortunately cannot be verified until we get there."[27]

Taking a page from the psychologists, Knox wonders if

---

[24] Knox, *Broadcast Minds*, p. 185.
[25] Ibid., p. 29.
[26] Ibid., p. 152.
[27] Ibid., p. 179.

these writers suffer from a "Galileo complex". Their writings presume an inveterate opposition between religion and science: a difference in method, in that science is inductive and religion deductive; a difference in aim, in that science strives to educate people, while religion seeks to keep them ignorant; a difference in effects, in that science makes people free and happy, while religion makes them oppressed and miserable. They suppose, and want their readers to suppose, that the antipathy is mutual and unavoidable, whereas Knox notes that many great scientists were and are believers: "We still measure electricity by volts and amps; Volta and Ampère were convinced Catholics. Mendel, the pioneer of all the study of heredity, was a monk. Pasteur died clasping the Crucifix. With such children as these we Catholics share our nursery and our fairy stories."[28] Knox says that there were only two occasions when it seemed that scientific theories impugned the authority of the Bible: the Copernican theory of a heliocentric universe in the sixteenth century, and the Darwinian theory of evolution in the nineteenth. Copernicus was a priest, and his work—dedicated to the Pope—did not initially meet with opposition. Galileo's furtherance of this theory did lead to his condemnation, which still conjures an implacably obscurantist religious view of the world. But as Knox points out, "The trouble about selecting Galileo as your trump card is that you have nothing to lead up to him with. He is an isolated case, not the symptom of a tendency."[29] The principal theological challenges from Darwinism concerned the age of the earth and the evolution of human beings from other mammals. The first was an issue only for those who held an extremely literalist view of the Bible; the second offered no problem for believers, provided

---

[28] Ronald Knox, "Miracles" (London: Catholic Truth Society, 1927), p. 25.
[29] Knox, *Broadcast Minds*, p. 271.

it concerned the development of the biological organism of the human being and not the production of the soul. Thus, Darwinism as such posed no insurmountable problem for most Christians, but the omniscientists presume that it does.

At the conclusion of *Broadcast Minds*, Knox sets out his reasons for saying that there is no conflict between religion and science in several areas: anthropology and comparative religion, archeology, astronomy, biology, chemistry and physiology, history, physics and chemistry, and psychology. He concludes by suggesting that the conflict between religion and science is due to a backwash from the nineteenth century, not from advances in the twentieth:

> The idea that "science" is to be regarded as a single body in the State with its own interests to maintain, and that there is a specifically "scientific" outlook which must needs have a single philosophy to express it, has arisen, I think from the old Victorian debates, whose influence has now slowly filtered through, by way of the schools, by way of popular literature, by way of newspaper culture, to the apprehension of the man in the street.[30]

It is this atmosphere which has created the impression that the advancing tide of science has swept away the sand castle of religion.

The Triumph of Scientism

The omniscientists' hostility to religion understandably provoked a response from Christian apologists like Knox and Lewis. But their abhorrence for scientism was prompted by something deeper: they feared, not just the abolition of religion, but the abolition of man. Knox's analysis of the techniques of the omniscientists concluded by cautioning that

[30] Ibid., p. 274.

"the priests of science" mean business and talk the language of fanaticism; Lewis' *The Abolition of Man* spells out what this could mean. Ever since Francis Bacon sounded the call to extend human power over all things possible, Western society has pursued "the conquest of nature". This has shaped a culture that sees the world in terms of facts, not values. Again, it is not science as such but the atmosphere of scientism that is corrosive: "It is not the greatest of modern scientists who feel most sure that the object, stripped of its qualitative properties and reduced to mere quantity, is wholly real. Little scientists, and the little unscientific followers of science, may think so. The great minds know very well that the object, so treated, is an artificial abstraction, that something of its reality has been lost."[31] Nature is reduced to an object so that it can be plundered. Our belated sensitivity to the environment is born of the recognition that this objectification of nature has had disastrous consequences.

Lewis points out a more serious result of this approach: ultimately, human power over nature means the power of some people over others: "What we call Man's power is, in reality, a power possessed by some men which they may, or may not, allow other men to profit by."[32] The leaders in a given society can bestow or withhold the benefits of technology, and the same holds true for stronger nations. Power over nature also becomes power over human nature, and the scientific breakthroughs that permit us to make human nature what we want it to be will allow some people to make others what *they* want them to be. Some of Lewis' contemporaries shared this anxiety about a dystopian future (witness George Orwell's *1984* and Huxley's *Brave New World*[33]); what is of

[31] Lewis, *Abolition of Man*, p. 82.

[32] Ibid., p. 68.

[33] Aldous Huxley was the brother of one of Knox's omniscientists, Julian Huxley, and he died on the same day as C. S. Lewis.

interest to us is our authors' analysis of the problem and the alternative they offer.

In a world where fact trumps value, there is a temptation to reduce moral judgments to questions of fact. This, to Lewis, is a usurpation: "Let the doctor tell me I shall die unless I do so-and-so; but whether life is worth having on those terms is no more a question for him than for any other man."[34] Questions of justice and goodness cannot be reduced to facts, and to the extent that our society banishes values, it creates what Lewis calls "men without chests": people who lack the crucial quality of emotions trained into stable sentiments that traditionally mediated between the mind and the appetites. Defenders of fact at the expense of virtue may describe their position as intellectual, but Lewis rejects this: "It is not excess of thought but defect of fertile and generous emotion that marks them out. Their heads are no bigger than ordinary: it is the atrophy of the chest beneath that makes them seem so."[35] This state of affairs has a very negative impact on society, because society needs the very qualities that have been denigrated—virtue, enterprise, and self-sacrifice. Of this contradiction, Lewis observes: "We castrate and bid the geldings be fruitful."[36]

We should remember that Lewis delivered these lectures during the Second World War. A nation at war needs people who are willing to lay down their lives. The Tao instills self-sacrificing virtue: an ancient Roman father who told his son that it was a sweet and seemly thing to die for his country believed what he said. But if questions of value have been dismissed as unimportant, if only facts matter, how do we motivate people to go into battle? Lewis suggests several solutions available to the "innovators", but he considers them

[34] Lewis, *God in the Dock*, p. 315.
[35] Lewis, *Abolition of Man*, p. 35.
[36] Ibid., p. 35.

blind alleys. One approach would be to propose a new ide-
ology in place of the Tao; but all modern attempts to invent a new ethics are really the rebellion of a branch against
the tree, simply a selection of *some* elements of the natural
law and the exclusion of others. It is no more possible to
come up with a completely new set of ethics than it is to
place a new sun in the sky. The innovators could appeal
to reason and argue that it is a fact that some people must
die in order that the country not perish. That may be true,
but someone could object, "Why me?" A culture that den-
igrates values cannot appeal to honor, shame, or patriotism.
An appeal could be made to the instinct for preservation.
But, Lewis objects, "telling us to obey instinct is like telling
us to obey 'people' "[37]—people say different things, and so
do our instincts. There is an instinct for the preservation of
the species, but the individual instinct of self-preservation
is also very strong. We cannot evade the issue of values;
the Tao provides these. But there is one final avenue open
to the innovators: they could manufacture an artificial Tao.
Whereas the ancient Roman handed on to his son a set of
values in which he himself believed, the innovators can condition others under their charge to embrace values that they
do not believe in for themselves. Tao becomes the product,
not the motive, of education.

Tao in the traditional sense offers a wisdom that teaches
us how to conform to reality through knowledge, self-
discipline, and virtue. Divorced from that tradition, the artificial Tao of the innovators strives to subdue reality to our
wishes. Simply put, the goal becomes power. And the search
for power leads to the marriage of government and science,
a union Lewis was not alone in dreading. Knox notes that

[37] Ibid., p. 48.

"it is not a reign of scientists that Lord [Bertrand] Russell anticipates and fears; it is rather a reign of men with organizing ability, who will bend the scientists to their own purposes."[38] Our authors' hostility was not directed against scientists but against officials who would suborn science— a morally neutral means in itself—into a tool to control and dominate others. As Knox observes, it is one thing for science and government to work hand in hand but quite another for them to work hand in glove. The beginnings of such a course are innocent enough: there are the basic needs created by hunger, sickness, and security; these needs can be addressed through scientific advances; and an omnicompetent global technocracy is seen as the solution. But power over the forces of nature is also power over other people: benefits can be bestowed or withheld, and billions could find themselves under the control of a handful of people.

In addition, science provides intellectual credibility to those in power: "If we are to be mothered, mother must know best."[39] Horrible deeds are described in pseudo-scientific words to "disinfect the thing of blood and tears, or pity or shame".[40] Crimes are classified as diseases, and it is the experts who define diseases. This makes Lewis very uneasy: "One school of psychology regards my religion as a neurosis. If this neurosis ever becomes inconvenient to Government, what is to prevent my being subjected to a compulsory 'cure'?"[41] Ironically, the triumph of scientism transforms a secular government into the system Lewis most fears, a theocracy. He views this as the most dangerous form

[38] Knox, *Broadcast Minds*, p. 245.

[39] Lewis, *God in the Dock*, p. 313.

[40] C.S. Lewis, *Of Other Worlds: Essays and Stories* (New York: Harcourt, Brace and World, 1967), p. 84.

[41] Lewis, *God in the Dock*, p. 313.

of government because it has the highest pretensions: its agents are absolutely convinced that their view is the only acceptable one. As an example, Lewis refers to a disagreement with J. B. S. Haldane on the subject of usury; what bothered him was Haldane's instantaneous assumption that the question was so simple that there could be no hesitation about accepting his position.

Then there is the fact that modern life is shaped increasingly by huge, impersonal organizations that possess a dynamism of their own. Knox contends that in his lifetime, people have abdicated many of the rights that had been viewed as personal liberty: "To be free, in these days, means at best to be bullied by your own fellow countrymen rather than by foreigners."[42] In reference to the use of the atomic bomb, Knox says that it was nations, not individuals, that consigned Hiroshima to destruction: "And a nation at war has difficulty in keeping its hands clean, because it cannot keep its hands free. A whole bundle of human interests is concerned, whenever a decision is made, and these cannot be neglected. Generosity, the gesture of claiming something less than your right, is to be found in the individual, not in the group."[43]

As has been noted, Knox and Lewis were not alone in viewing the alliance of science and government with trepidation. What concerns us is their understanding of the source of the problem: the abandonment of objective moral values, binding on rulers and subjects alike. Lewis explored this theme in his space trilogy, with its figure of Weston, the physicist whose goal is to use the advances of science to conquer other planets; the National Institute for Co-ordinated Experiments (N.I.C.E.), an entity that com-

---

[42] Knox, *God and the Atom*, p. 145.
[43] Ibid., p. 147.

bines the state with the laboratory; and Mark, a pseudo-intellectual whose training has been neither classical nor scientific, merely "modern". Lewis' combination of science fiction and Arthurian legend highlights the relationship he sees between science and magic: if unchecked by genuine Tao, science becomes simply a tool in the quest for power. A classic example is Doctor Faustus; although many think he sold his soul to obtain knowledge, in fact he lusted after the power and riches knowledge would give him. Lewis' view is that once the supernatural is banished and reality is reduced to nature, there is no curb on the lust for power. (Lewis' point was underscored in the reception his science fiction received. He wrote to Dorothy Sayers that *That Hideous Strength* got unanimously unfavorable reviews, and added: "Apparently reviewers *will not* tolerate a mixture of the realistic and the supernatural. Which is a pity, because (a) It's just the mixture I like, and (b) We have to put up with it in real life."[44])

Ronald Knox also tried his hand at a fictional treatment of these issues in his short story "The Reprieve".[45] The principal characters are a nuclear physicist named Muldoon and an Oxford don named Masbury. Following a conversation with several others, in which Masbury states that he is absolutely opposed to the use of force in any circumstances, the two men are left alone, and Muldoon presents Masbury with a potentially frightening scenario. When he has obtained a promise that Masbury will hold what he says in strictest confidence, he reveals that he is working on a project that has provided him with a device of hitherto unknown destructive power: "In the modern world, the scientist . . . wields power; he makes decisions. And it's not merely up to me to

[44] Lewis, *Letters* II, p. 682.

[45] Ronald Knox, "The Reprieve", *The Month* (December 1956), pp. 327–39.

see that the world goes on. It's up to me to decide whether the world shall go on or not."[46] Where a man contemplating suicide has to decide whether life is worth living for *him*, Muldoon must decide if it is worth living for *anybody*. Perhaps the ideal final act for the modern world would be a mass-produced, labor-saving death. Would such an event be a tragedy? No: "Tragedy only exists in the minds of those who survive it, and this time there will be no survivors."[47] And, should Masbury object that Muldoon is usurping the place of God, the scientist responds that it may be that Providence had arranged for him to pull the trigger. Masbury appeals to the Tao, to eternal values, and the scientist answers, "Oh, yes; honour and truth and artistic integrity and the rest of them—a man must have some compass to steer by. . . . When you call them *eternal*, you only mean that they will appeal to the human race as long as it exists. When it dies, they will die with it."[48] The dilemma for Masbury is that his own understanding of eternal values prevents him from using force on Muldoon; his sense of honor will keep him from going to the police, and Muldoon knows it.

Following this conversation, the two men retire for the night, and Masbury has a dream that he relates to Muldoon the next morning: he found himself walking in the countryside; sheep are grazing in the meadows, and he comes upon a pub (the Carpenter's Arms), from which lights shine and the sounds of talking and laughter can be heard. For some reason, Masbury cannot get in. Then everything seems to go backward—he likens it to the experience when, as a boy on the train, he would watch the reflection of the countryside zooming by in reverse on the corridor window of

[46] Ibid., p. 332.
[47] Ibid., p. 333.
[48] Ibid., p. 334.

the compartment. Looking down, he sees a red figure of an Infant wrapped in linen bands stamped on the inside of his hand. Then he sees this Donatello image everywhere, and it creates an impression of *ownership*. A series of confused adventures follow, including a nightmarish Christmas party. Finally, he finds himself in a car driven by Muldoon, speeding faster and faster down a narrow country lane; he hears a voice insistently repeating, "Bought with a price! It isn't yours!" A road sign appears with the bambino in red, and Muldoon slams on the brakes. And Masbury awakes.

After hearing this account, Muldoon asks, "Did what I propose last night strike you as a kind of trespassing?" "Desecration would be a better word", Masbury replies, and adds, "Perhaps the dreamer of last night was not myself as I am now, but myself as I was twenty years ago, when I wasn't much more than a boy, and believed firmly in much that now seems doubtful. It might have been a young man's vision; it is only an old man's dream."[49] Muldoon then admits that he was only pulling Masbury's leg—there really is no such device as the one he described the evening before. But such was his trust in Masbury's sense of honor that he did not lock up the room with the telephone; he knew his guest would not call the police to report him.

The story ends on an ambiguous note. Muldoon, the man of science and facts, and Masbury, the man of classical learning and values, bid farewell to each other: "And Muldoon, as he waved his hand from the doorway, said to himself, 'I wonder if he ever had that dream.' And Masbury said to himself as he turned into the main road, 'I wonder if he *was* pulling my leg.'"[50] The tale is tantalizingly inconclusive:

[49] Ibid., p. 338.
[50] Ibid., p. 339.

Masbury senses that doubt has eroded the vision of virtue from his younger days into an old man's dream, and Muldoon wonders whether even the dream is true.

Ronald Knox wrote *Broadcast Minds* in 1932, just a year before Adolph Hitler assumed the post of chancellor in Germany. Ten years later, Lewis gave his lectures on *The Abolition of Man*, while both the Allies and the Axis powers were employing scientific advances to win the war. The final act of that war unveiled a weapon of unparalleled force, and the shadow of this weapon looms over Knox's 1956 short story. The confident assurance that science held the key to a future world in which human misery would be banished was shattered: "Are we really expected to go on bothering about Utopia, when we have to allow for the possibility that modern weapons, used indiscriminately, might make of the world a Utopia in the literal sense, a nowhere?"[51]

Two Loves, One City

A criticism leveled against Christianity by some is that it is "otherworldly", unconcerned about the welfare of this world in its longing for "the City of God". According to its opponents, Christian writers like Lewis and Knox do not live in the real world; they have retreated into the past and do not deal with the complexities of modern life. If modern critics even listen to the recital of their dreams, they wonder, like Muldoon, if they are being honest. Both of our authors passionately believed in what they professed, and they also felt that what they believed held out hope, not only for the world to come, but for this world. A remarkable expres-

[51] Knox, *God and the Atom*, p. 117.

sion of this is a little book by Knox, prophetic and sadly neglected, called *God and the Atom*.

It has been said that this was the last thing one would have expected Ronald Knox to write. It was also composed very quickly, something unusual for an author who customarily devoted considerable time and energy to polishing his phrases and choosing just the right word. It appeared first serially in the *Tablet*, but it made little impact; one friend reading it there wrote to ask if Knox had lost his reason, or if the friend had lost his. Evelyn Waugh judged that the work came too soon after the end of the war—people were worn down by the years of carnage and violence and were unreceptive to a philosophical reflection at a time of pressing practical issues. It repays study now as a frank appraisal of the condition of the modern world and how the horizon of faith can speak to that condition.

The development of atomic energy and its application to warfare provokes three "chills": doubt, because the randomness of the atom strikes at our sense of cosmic discipline; despair, because optimistic confidence in progress has been dashed in the horrors of this war and its weapons; and guilt, because the production and use of this kind of weapon calls into question the validity of our moral judgments. In the first part of his book, Knox analyzes these three conditions, and in the second half, he offers some responses from a religious perspective.

The first chill is doubt; not doubt about philosophical or moral truths, but doubt about our perception of the world around us. The eighteenth century bequeathed us the laws of nature, and the nineteenth the law of progress; the twentieth century has ushered us into the realm of relativity, "bred in a culture of terms we could not understand, and calculations we could not follow".[52] (Lewis once wrote to a friend that Humphrey Havard tried to explain to him on a train journey what he understood of Einstein, and how everyone else left the compartment at the next stop; "Of course it *may* have been a coincidence", he added.[53]) Where formerly science presumed the trustworthiness of our tools of observation, now it seemed to negate them: our ten spies had described physical reality as made up of hard, material particles; now our two spies were saying that such reality consists of mathematical relations between electric charges and that anarchy reigns among the electrons.

The second chill is despair, brought on by the violent and tragic events of the twentieth century. In the decades between Waterloo and the First World War, at least in England, "You could almost hear the dawn breaking."[54] Scientific advances, new inventions, and theories of evolution all pointed to an age of peace and progress, but such optimism could no longer be sustained. Europe, in Knox's opinion, mistook a fleeting foretaste of a civilized world order for one already firmly established.

The final chill is one of guilt, because of the magnitude of the destruction wrought by the bomb together with the enormity of violence throughout the war. (Knox does not spend a great deal of time discussing the morality of the bombings of Hiroshima and Nagasaki, although his personal position was that, right or wrong, it would have been better not to have used the bombs on cities.) His concern is not so much this isolated instance but the symbolic significance the use of such a weapon has on our sense of self-restraint. The atomic bomb raises the ante on the will

---

[52] Ibid., p. 32.
[53] Lewis, *Letters* II, p. 638.
[54] Knox, *God and the Atom*, p. 125.

to power: "World-domination, after all, belongs not to the cause which has right on its side, but to the cause which has the best-equipped laboratories on its side."[55] The bomb has ushered in a new age, the atomic age, but our situation is more precarious than ever: "And at the moment of victory, a sign appeared in heaven; not the comforting Labarum of the Mulvian Bridge, but the bright, evil cloud that hung over Hiroshima. In this sign we were to conquer. It hung like a mocking question-mark over the future of our race."[56]

What to make of our predicament? Knox proposes two myths, one pagan and the other Christian. The pagan myth would see atomic energy as a Nemesis sent from the gods to rebuke us for our folly, punishing our hubris with a weapon of our own devising. It is the pattern of Greek tragedy. The second myth is Christian, the pattern of the *Divine Comedy*, in which the human race is on a pilgrimage to God, a journey marked by trial and error. Knox compares this pilgrimage to the spiritual journey of an individual. For humanity, as for the individual, there are alternatives of light and darkness, consolation and desolation, presumption and despair: "And should we not rightly conclude that, for the race as for the individual, the secret of progress lay in fighting down those tendencies, each as it came?"[57] In response to doubt, despair, and guilt, the Christian myth suggests faith, hope, and charity.

Of these three virtues, the one Knox underscores is hope. He rejects the idea that Christian hopes are for the next world only, and he appeals to his fellow believers to resist this temptation:

[55] Ibid., p. 95.
[56] Ibid., p. 127.
[57] Ibid., p. 124.

It may be that mankind is being called upon to exercise the virtue of hope, and, if so, Christian people must think twice before they abandon themselves to the luxury of world-despair; before they wash their hands of our communal guilt, and betake themselves, singing "O Paradise, O Paradise!" to the hilltops. We shall do better, I think, to help man the pumps of the labouring ship, and let the world see that hoping is one of our specialties.[58]

The hope that religion offers is the power of integration. Knox takes the splitting of the atom as emblematic in physical terms of interior disintegration. We need a unifying motive that is a spiritual force: what Lewis means by the Tao. The fusing force must come from outside us and usually takes one of three forms: "A man will give up his darling vices because he is in love, will ruin his prospects for the sake of a cause, and will go without food or sleep because he is too busy arguing to attend to them."[59] Love for a person, loyalty to a cause, conviction about a system of thought—these are the integrating forces in our lives, and in its pure form, religion provides all three. By a "pure form", Knox means religion when it is neither reduced to a conventional code nor "miscanalized" into fanaticism. Inspired by the dynamics of atomic energy, he says, "amid the whirling stream of impulses that is our nature, religion becomes true to its name; it binds."[60]

Lewis also recommends this understanding of religion, which holds out hope for both this world and the next. The Christian alternative is not either natural or supernatural but is *both* natural *and* supernatural: there are responsibilities to

[58] Ibid., p. 128. Or, as Lewis would put it, "The fact that the ship is sinking is no reason for allowing her to be a floating hell" (*Christian Reflections*, p. 59).

[59] Knox, *God and the Atom*, p. 140.

[60] Ibid.

be met on each plane. This explains the paradoxical relationship between Christianity and the world. On the one hand, it can be seen as world-denying: the centrality of the crucifix, the exaltation of martyrdom, asceticism, and contempt for "worldliness". On the other hand, it is a world-affirming faith: care for the sick and the poor, the arts and philosophy, architecture, laws, and literature. As an example of this double purpose, Lewis refers to what is done every day in Lourdes Hospital: "to fight against death as earnestly, skillfully, and calmly as if you were a secular humanitarian while knowing all the time that death is, both for better and worse, something that the secular humanitarian has never dreamed of."[61]

Both secular and religious people can be altruistic, but they have different understandings of what it means to do good to others: "To the Materialist things like nations, classes or civilizations must be more important than individuals, because individuals live only seventy-odd years each and the group may last for centuries. But to the Christian, individuals are more important, for they live eternally; and races, civilizations and the like are in comparison creatures of a day."[62] If earthly life is all there is, happiness is to be attained by social programs and political organization, and everything else—"vivisection, birth control, the judicial system, education"[63]—is judged to be good or bad insofar as it produces material benefits. Knox sums up the two attitudes with a lapidary phrase: "Our work is to colonize heaven, theirs to breed for Utopia."[64] He and Lewis recognized that these conflicting approaches would provoke

---

[61] Lewis, *God in the Dock*, p. 149.

[62] Ibid., pp. 109–10.

[63] Ibid., p. 109.

[64] Knox, *Belief of Catholics*, p. 212.

persecution, because the Church stands for something other than mere earthly security and progress. Lewis predicted that Christianity would be treated as an enemy of the state, since it gives a standing ground against the omnipotent government; Knox foresaw a future Armageddon between Catholicism and some form of humanitarianism bent on attaining perfect humanity through the external pressures of eugenics, schooling, and legal controls.

We should not exaggerate these dire predictions: both of our authors made them, but they were not preoccupied with them. The supernatural horizon that led them to critique a benevolence limited to this world also gave them confidence in the ultimate triumph of God's goodness. They had serious reservations about what the future might hold, and they sought to alert their fellow believers to the dangers; but they were also convinced that more-than-worldly problems call for more-than-worldly solutions. Knox expresses these hopes eloquently at the conclusion of *God and the Atom*:

> I am not advocating world-movements or public meetings . . . My appeal is rather to the individual conscience than to the public ear; my hope is rather to see the emergence of a Saint, than that of an organization distinguished by initials. For the Saint . . . is, like the atom, incalculable in his moment; holds, like the atom, strange forces hidden under a mask of littleness; affects the world around him, as atomic energy does, not in an arithmetical but in a geometrical ratio—his is a snowball influence. No harm in besieging heaven for the canonization of such and such holy persons now dead. But should we not do well to vary these petitions of ours by asking for more Saints to canonize?[65]

[65] Knox, *God and the Atom*, pp. 165–66.

CHAPTER SIX

Evil and Suffering

Sometime in 1934, Ronald Knox was invited to give a series of talks to a non-Catholic audience, and he devoted one of his lectures to the problem of suffering. In it he recognized what a profound challenge to belief in God the reality of suffering is:

> I should say that nine in every ten of the people who describe themselves as atheists ought really to be described, more accurately, as pessimists. They have not examined the proofs for the existence of God, and found them wanting. They have simply looked round on the world, with all its tragedies, its miseries, its inequalities, and asked themselves how such an organization of the world can possibly be consistent with the rule of an all-powerful and beneficent Providence. They have found no means of reconciling that apparent inconsistency; and they have proceeded from that to infer that there is no God.[1]

As Christians, both Knox and Lewis had to grapple with this fundamental obstacle to belief. Their reflections can be considered under three headings: the problem of evil, the origin of evil, and the meaning of suffering. Lewis devotes far more attention to the first two questions than Knox does. Why does Knox say so little and Lewis say so much?

---

[1] Ronald Knox, "Suffering", unpublished conference, 1934, Knox Papers, Mells, Somerset; in Milton Walsh, *Ronald Knox as Apologist* (S.T.D. diss. Gregorian University, Rome, 1985), pp. 448–61.

Knox takes his cue from Saint Thomas. In *Difficulties* Knox frankly admits that the existence of evil is the last thing we shall ever understand, and he notes that the Angelic Doctor, after offering proofs for the existence of God, adduces evil and suffering as reasons for believing the contrary. Knox then points out that Thomas does not refute these objections: Thomas leaves them to refute themselves because they are in contradiction with something that has already been proved. This may be seen as begging the question—perhaps begging *the* question—but it illustrates Knox's way of engaging what he calls "the orbit of mystery": "My approach, which may seem to you a cowardly and perhaps even a dishonest one, is to stick firmly to that end of the mystery which seems to me lucidly obvious, and tell the other end of the mystery that it has jolly well got to square with that somehow."[2] For him, the "lucidly obvious" end of the mystery is that God exists; this has been demonstrated by reason's reflection on creation. At the "other end", the issue of suffering raises questions about the omnipotence and goodness of God, and Knox says something about these questions. Most of his energies are directed to what Christ reveals about the meaning of suffering.

If Knox is Aquinas, Lewis is Augustine. Lewis' personal struggles colored the issue for him, since he had found his way back to Christian faith from an atheism engendered in part by the scandal of evil. For Knox, the question of the existence of God is approached from "the crossword of creation"; for Lewis, it is inextricably linked to God's goodness. If Knox is reticent on the question of evil, Lewis is fascinated by it. The theme runs through his science fic-

[2] Ronald Knox, *Off the Record* (New York: Sheed and Ward, 1954), pp. 163–64.

tion and Narnia chronicles and is the central issue in several books. By contrast, apart from commentaries on some biblical events, Knox hardly mentions Satan.

The Problem of Evil

It is curious that in his two collections of Oxford conferences, delivered before and after the most horrific war in European history, Knox never explores the problem of evil. We should not assume that such a crucial topic was ignored. It may be that he chose not to publish his lectures on this question; more likely, he may have invited another speaker to address it, perhaps his good friend Martin D'Arcy, whose book *The Pain of this World and the Providence of God* he warmly recommended (along with Lewis' *The Problem of Pain* and Dorothy Sayers' *The Mind of the Maker*).[3] The topic does come up in his conferences to schoolgirls, *The Creed in Slow Motion*. He begins his lecture on "the Father Almighty" with the confession that to him this is the most difficult article of the Creed. He recognizes that misfortune is the thing that tempts most people to give up their religion, and (in a sadly familiar example in wartime England) he imagines the state of mind of a young wife who has lost her husband: "Could God have prevented this happening? If not, he is not Almighty. Did God, then, *want* this to happen? If so, he is no Father of mine. Father if you will, but if so, he is powerless to help those who trust in him. Almighty if you will, but if so, he is cruel. One or the other, but not both; an Almighty Father would not treat me like that."[4] The problem of evil

[3] Cf. Ibid., pp. 19–20.

[4] Ronald Knox, *The Creed in Slow Motion* (New York: Sheed and Ward, 1949), p. 19.

does not lead Knox to deny the existence of God, but it raises questions about God's attributes: it seems that God is either omnipotent but not good, or good but not omnipotent. Regarding omnipotence, Knox observes that if there are limits to God's activities, they are self-imposed limits: "You mustn't think of him as a kind of amiable Official up in heaven who is really very sorry about it, but he's afraid nothing can be done."[5] One divine self-limitation is tied to our free will: if free will is not to be a sham, God must allow us to choose evil, and this will be a source of suffering. What happened in the primeval catastrophe of the Fall is that "God created the possibility of evil and we actualized it."[6] This revolt tainted all of creation, so we live in a fallen, imperfect world.

That may be so, but could not God with fatherly care shield us from suffering? Our sense of justice can accept the consequences of an evil choice redounding on its perpetrator, but this does not account by any means for all the suffering in the world. Speaking of the Fatherhood of God, Knox points out that good parents discipline their children, because otherwise they become spoiled: their essential nature is pushed out of a healthy pattern and they become selfish, conceited, and lazy. Through the difficulties of life, "God is altering our natures all the time, turning us into the kind of people he wants us to be; he wouldn't be our true Father otherwise."[7] This, too, is only a partial explanation, and Knox does not pretend that it completely solves the problem. It seems that on this issue, Knox offers his own version of "Pascal's Wager": one can start with the convic-

[5] Ibid., p. 20.

[6] Philip Caraman, ed., *Occasional Sermons of Ronald A. Knox* (London: Burns and Oates, 1960), p. 333.

[7] Knox, *Creed in Slow Motion*, p. 23.

tion that God exists, and is all-powerful and all-good, and then strive to believe in Providence in the face of suffering; or one can start with the reality of suffering and conclude that there is no God—but does this make the mystery of suffering any more comprehensible? He chooses to invest his energies into describing what we are to make of suffering in the light of Christ, by which he means, not how we are to understand it, but how we are to give a positive meaning to something that in itself is evil.

Many of Knox's contemporaries found it difficult to accept his wager. For example, Bertrand Russell: "Lord Russell has been cramming up his argument against the Goodness of God before he will consider any proofs of his existence; he will not look for God in the things that are made, because he is terrified of finding him."[8] Another person who could be described as a pessimist before he was an atheist was the young C. S. Lewis, who struggled throughout his life with the idea of the goodness of God. For this reason, he devoted much more attention than Knox to the question of evil.

Lewis' first explicitly apologetical book was *The Problem of Pain*. The idea was not his own: he was asked in 1939 to address the topic as part of the "Christian Challenge" series. Lewis was uncomfortable because he felt he would have to enunciate principles that he himself failed to live out; he even asked if he could publish the book under a *nom de plume* (a strategy he was to follow years later in a far more personal reflection on suffering, *A Grief Observed*). In the event, the book was well received, although Lewis was amused to see it occasionally catalogued as a medical book; one advertisement for it appended the initials "M.D." after his name!

---

[8] Ronald Knox, *Broadcast Minds* (London: Sheed and Ward, 1930), p. 257.

In dealing with the question of divine omnipotence, Lewis echoes the traditional Christian view stated briefly by Knox: if we have free will, God must choose to limit the exercise of his power. Lewis draws out certain corollaries to the doctrine of free will: it implies a multiplicity of beings that exist in a world of stable laws. God *can* overrule such laws, but miracles by definition are exceptions—and rare exceptions—to the rule. Lewis uses the analogy of a chess game: it is possible for the players to agree to an occasional exception to the rules, as when a superior competitor voluntarily plays without one of his pieces; but if the rules are set aside each time a player finds them not to his liking, it is impossible to play the game.

What of divine goodness? Lewis sees the matter to be much more than a matter of "kindness"; what some people seem to want is not a heavenly Father, but a heavenly Grandfather—but love is much more than that:

> You asked for a loving God: you have one. The great spirit you so lightly invoked, the "lord of terrible aspect", is present: not a senile benevolence that drowsily wishes you to be happy in your own way, not the cold philanthropy of the conscientious magistrate, nor the care of a host who feels responsible for the comfort of his guests, but the consuming fire Himself, the Love that made the worlds, persistent as the artist's love for his work and despotic as a man's love for a dog, provident and venerable as a father's love for a child, jealous, inexorable, exacting as love between the sexes.[9]

He goes on to suggest that the problem of human suffering is irreconcilable with the idea of a loving God only so long as we attach a trivial meaning to the word "love" and hold that man, not God, is the center of things.

[9] C. S. Lewis, *The Problem of Pain* (London: Fontana Books, 1957 [1940]), p. 35.

This "God-centeredness" is a critical point for Lewis, because it reflects his personal resolution to the objection that evil in the world proves that there is no God. While Lewis himself once held this view, he came to believe that it was illogical: the very appeal to a concept like justice implies an objective order of right and wrong, and that order must have an origin. Our sense that we ought to do some things and avoid others derives from something or someone outside of ourselves. The very fact that we can call something evil suggests for Lewis two alternatives: either the world was created good and has been tainted somehow; or there are equally powerful spiritual forces of Good and Evil at war. We will consider Lewis' response to the second alternative later. But if the first explanation is true, our sense of good and evil derives from the Creator, and this presents a paradoxical situation. Our notion of the good derives from God, but since we are finite creatures, it cannot be equal to his; Lewis suggests it is like the difference between a perfect circle and a small child's crude drawing of a circle. Our moral sense can be outraged at an evil, but it may be that God permits it for a higher good; on the other hand, something may seem good to us, but God knows better. The loving mother gives her children, not always what they want, but what they need; and this is how God acts with us. More profoundly, Lewis points out, God himself is our greatest good, and much of our suffering is brought on by our efforts to substitute something else for God. But in the end nothing can be, apart from God: "God gives what He has, not what He has not: He gives the happiness that there is, not the happiness that is not."[10]

The moral sense, for Lewis, is universal, even if people

[10] Ibid., p. 42.

of diverse cultures disagree in some particulars. What is also common to all human beings is the awareness that we do not always do what is right and, indeed, seem to be incapable of doing it. Why is this?

The Origin of Evil

"The problem of pain" is a perennial challenge, but Lewis was examining it in a particularly painful time—during the Second World War. Various strands of his personal and professional life led him to address the question of evil more deeply. The success of *The Problem of Pain* prompted an invitation from the BBC for a series of radio broadcasts, and Lewis chose as his topic "Right and Wrong: A Clue to the Meaning of the Universe". In these and subsequent programs, later published as *Mere Christianity*, he explored the religious significance of evil. In a more scholarly vein, he was invited to give a lecture series at the University College of North Wales and spoke on Milton's *Paradise Lost*; his analysis was subsequently published as *A Preface to "Paradise Lost"*. On a more personal level, he had a disquieting experience while listening to a speech by Hitler over the radio: "I don't know if I'm weaker than other people, but it is a positive revelation to me how *while the speech lasts* it is impossible not to waver just a little. I should be useless as a schoolmaster or a policeman. Statements which I *know* to be untrue all but convince me, at any rate for the moment, if only the man says them unflinchingly."[11] Reflection on this reaction inspired an imaginative consideration of temptation from the demonic point of view, Lewis' *Screwtape Letters*. Thus, in the space of three years, Lewis probed the question of evil

[11] Walter Hooper, ed., *The Collected Letters of C. S. Lewis*, vol. II (San Francisco: Harper, 2004), p. 425.

in four different genres: apologetics (*The Problem of Pain*), theological fantasy (*The Screwtape Letters*), radio broadcasts (*Mere Christianity*), and literary criticism (*A Preface to "Paradise Lost"*).

In these writings, Lewis presents the traditional Christian doctrine of the Fall, which holds that in a primeval revolt, human beings used their free will to choose evil. The problem as Lewis sees it is that most people today do not advert to the reality of sin in their lives; this requires him to confront us with the bad news of our wounded, sinful condition before presenting the good news of the healing offered to us by Christ. In fact, Lewis suggests, Christ takes it for granted that people are bad and that until we accept the truth of Jesus' assessment, we will be unable to understand anything about him. Throughout history, Christians have debated how gravely human nature was wounded in the Fall. Lewis explicitly states that he rejects the doctrine of "total depravity", which holds that human nature experienced a radical corruption of its nature—but the very fact that he needed to do so suggests that he considered the impact of the Fall on human nature to be very serious. In part this is due to his own personal struggle with sin, and the way Protestant theology helped him interpret that experience; but it is also true that he felt the need to emphasize the corrosive power of sin precisely because the idea was minimized or rejected entirely in the culture of his day.[12]

In *The Problem of Pain* Lewis enumerates many factors that blind us to the seriousness of our fallen condition:

---

[12] Writing about *The Problem of Pain*, Knox noted that Lewis' view that the whole of existence was impregnated with evil as a result of the Fall has been criticized on the ground that this doctrine is not found in Saint Thomas. Knox had heard that Lewis got the idea from Milton, "But obviously the idea has a more respectable parentage than that" (*Off the Record*, pp. 19-20). It would seem, however, that Knox did not consider the effects of the Fall to be as catastrophic as Lewis did, nor would Catholic theology in general.

1. We find it hard to face the truth about ourselves, and so we take refuge in comparing ourselves with others whom we *perceive* to be worse than ourselves; judgment of good and evil tends to be based on appearances.

2. In order to avoid facing our personal failings, we focus on *social* wrongs.

3. We think the mere passage of time removes sin, where in reality it affects neither the fact nor the guilt of sin.

4. We seek safety in numbers, holding that because selfishness is widespread, it is normal; but it is not normal, as the behavior of generous people demonstrates.

5. We practice "chronological snobbery" by emphasizing the more humane aspects of our culture in contrast to past societies; but this attitude overlooks the fact that they excelled in virtues that we do not practice.

6. Highlighting certain virtues ignores the fact that, as Plato taught, all virtue is one; you cannot really be kind (the virtue of choice in our age) without practicing other virtues as well.

7. While it may be correct to protest against reducing Christianity to "moralism", this can also be an evasion: God is more than moral goodness, but he is not less.

8. Because it is common human experience that we are unable to keep the moral law perfectly, this is used as an excuse to avoid the responsibility of keeping it at all.

Such is Lewis' diagnosis, and if the reader squirms (and who honestly would not?), then he has succeeded in making his case. But toward the end of the chapter, he states that his desire is not to provoke an emotional twinge of shame but an intellectual conviction that human nature is deeply flawed.

It is often said that Christianity lays a "guilt trip" on people; this is like saying that the doctor lays a "sickness trip" on his patient. It is only when we become aware of our illness that we will seek a cure. The recognition of our sinfulness is the first step in our recovery, and while the process is demanding, it is not grim: "Humility, after the first shock, is a cheerful virtue".[13] Paradoxically, the saints are the most joyful people because they are the most humbled: they really believe that they are base in the sight of God, but they accept the gift of God's love precisely in their brokenness. And the closer they come to the goodness of God, the more clearly they see the imperfections and flaws in their humanity. Knox agrees: "Just as a person who has never felt acute pain is no judge of pain (he knows the meaning of the word, but cannot appreciate its content), so an outlook which is imperfectly supernatural is no judge of sin."[14]

The way we came to be in this predicament is related in the first pages of the Bible. How should we read the story of the Fall of Adam and Eve? Knox tells the schoolgirls that we can discuss how literally to accept its details, but we are not tempted to doubt that the story itself is true because we relive it many times ourselves. With his fascination for myth, Lewis suggests that there is probably *more* truth to the story than the doctrinal lessons Christianity draws, but the basic idea is that by some heinous act of disobedience the first human beings broke off their relationship with God. In his analysis of *Paradise Lost*, Lewis notes that Milton presumes the basic meaning of the story that is the common patrimony of Christianity, especially in its interpretation by Saint Augustine. He agrees with Addison that "the great moral which reigns in Milton is the most universal and the

---

[13] Lewis, *Problem of Pain*, p. 55.

[14] Ronald Knox and Arnold Lunn, *Difficulties* (London: Eyre and Spottiswoode, 1952 [1933]), p. 67.

most useful that can be imagined, that Obedience to the will of God makes men happy and that Disobedience makes them miserable", and concludes, "If you can't be interested in that, you can't be interested in *Paradise Lost*."[15] This act of revolt is rooted in pride, the desire to usurp the place of God. In their disobedience, Adam and Eve sought to call their souls their own and to have a world without God. Here we should recall that Lewis himself sought precisely this as a young man.

The result of this disobedience was catastrophic: "Man has called for anarchy: God lets him have it."[16] Adam and Eve move from happy dependence to miserable self-assertion, and their revolt against God poisons their relationship with him, with one another, and with the world in which they live. We can only guess what was lost in the Fall. Lewis agrees with Milton's portrayal of the prelapsarian couple as majestic, mature, and ceremonial. He suggests that their organic processes obeyed their wills and not the laws of nature and that they had a mysterious power over animals; he bases these guesses on the rare manifestations of paranormal powers that occur even in our fallen world. We may not know what our first parents forfeited, but we know what they bequeathed: we are a "spoiled species". While it can be said of a badly raised child that it is not his fault that he has turned out to be a liar, a thief, and a coward, that is in fact what he is. Even when we begin with good intentions, it is so easy for selfishness to taint what we do. Thoughts undertaken for God's sake end in pride and the hunger for celebrity:

[15] C. S. Lewis, *A Preface to "Paradise Lost": Being the Ballard Matthews Lectures Delivered at University College, North Wales, 1941, revised and enlarged* (London: Oxford University Press, 1942), p. 70.

[16] Ibid., p. 68.

Thus all day long, and all the days of our life, we are slid-
ing, slipping, falling away—as if God were, to our present
consciousness, a smooth inclined plane on which there is no
resting. And indeed we are now of such a nature that we must
slip off, and the sin, because it is unavoidable, may be venial.
But God cannot have made us so. The gravitation away from
God, "the journey homeward to habitual self", must, we
think, be a product of the Fall.[17]

Knox agrees that after the Fall, man became a "misfit"
in creation. To find yourself always doing what you do not
approve of is a "ludicrous destiny"—"You might as well be
a carnivorous rabbit. Man is a fallen creature; the freewill
he enjoys, which was meant to be a kind of parachute that
would enable him to float among the clouds, has turned
inside out, and is no better than an umbrella to keep the
rain off him here and there."[18] He shares Lewis' sense of
the gravity of the offense ("infinite in its malice, infinite,
but for divine mercy, in the consequence it entails"[19]) but
not his pessimistic view of its impact on human nature, con-
fessing himself to be more sympathetic to the Pelagian end
of the grace—free will mystery. Knox describes the effects
of the Fall less in terms of a punishment and more in terms
of the withdrawal of certain supernatural and natural privi-
leges: "To give a very crude parallel; it is not as if a schoolmaster said, 'You will write 200 lines every day this term,
to punish the insolence of last term's sixth form (who have
now left) in writing their names on the seats of my garden.'
It is rather as if he said, 'I am not going to let you wander

---

[17] Lewis, *Problem of Pain*, p. 64.

[18] Ronald Knox, "Why Does God Make Sin So Easy and Goodness So
Difficult?" in Ronald Selby Wright, ed., *Asking Them Questions: A Selection
from the Three Series* (London: Oxford University Press, 1953), p. 165.

[19] Philip Caraman, ed., *University Sermons of Ronald A. Knox* (New York:
Sheed and Ward, 1963), p. 409.

about in my garden in future, because when I gave that privilege to your predecessors they misused it.' "[20] He also notes that, apart from the story of Adam and Eve, there is hardly any reference to the Fall in the Old Testament, nor is there any allusion to it in the Gospels. It is Saint Paul who gives the Fall its place in Christian theology, and he does so when speaking of human solidarity in relation to Adam and Christ. By virtue of our descent from Adam, we inherit his flawed condition; by virtue of spiritual adoption in Christ, we acquire the status of people reprieved.

In the story, Adam and Eve enjoy the companionship of God, of each other, and of the creatures in Paradise. God allows the Tempter, a fallen angel, to approach Eve and entice her into the companionship of sin. God permits this because free will demands an alternative. What motive has the Tempter? Knox replies, "Why, none; but malice needs no motive; it cannot see innocence without labouring as if from some perverted sense of duty, to defile and trample on it."[21] While Knox is reticent about the interaction between Satan and the human race, Lewis devotes a great deal of attention to it, especially in *A Preface to "Paradise Lost"* and *The Screwtape Letters*. Central to Milton's depiction of Satan is "a sense of injur'd merit"—Lucifer resents the fact that the Messiah is the head of the angels. Lewis says, "This is a well known state of mind which we can all study in domestic animals, children, film-stars, politicians, or minor poets; and perhaps nearer home."[22] This pique leads Satan to revolt against his Creator, thereby sawing off the branch he is sitting on, since all his powers are a gift from his Maker. Lewis offers a sketch of Milton's portrayal of Satan's

[20] Knox, *Off the Record*, p. 26.
[21] Knox, *University Sermons*, p. 406.
[22] Lewis, *Preface to "Paradise Lost"*, p. 93.

dissolution: "From hero to general, from general to politician, from politician to secret service agent, and thence to a
thing that peers in at bedroom or bathroom windows, and
thence to a toad, and finally to a snake."[23] Satan engages in
incessant and subtle intellectual activity, but he understands
nothing; Screwtape laments the failures of "our Intelligence
Department" to figure out what the Enemy (God) is up to.
This lack of understanding is due to Satan's solipsism: while
Adam is interested in everything, Satan is interested only in
himself; his is a life of incessant autobiography. It could be
said of Satan in *Paradise Lost* what Knox observed of one
of the leaders of the Jansenist movement: "No note can be
struck in conversation or in correspondence which does not
bring him back to the enthralling topic of himself."[24] Satan
succeeds in alienating Adam and Eve from God but not in
attaching them to himself; at the end of the drama, our fallen
parents reconcile themselves to a lesser happiness, but Satan
stews in isolation.

Lewis rejects the suggestion that Milton presents a sympathetic picture of Satan, but he does recognize that he is
the best drawn of all the characters in *Paradise Lost*. According to Lewis, this tells us more about ourselves than it does
about the figures in the drama: "A fallen man *is* very like a
fallen angel",[25] and the Satan in us resonates with the figure in the poem. Lewis accepts the traditional teaching that
Satan is an angel and as such possesses a nature substantially
superior to ours: "A cow cannot be very good or very bad;
a dog can be both better and worse; a child better and worse

[23] Ibid., p. 97.

[24] Ronald Knox, *Enthusiasm: A Chapter in the History of Religion, with Special
Reference to the XVII and XVIII Centuries* (Oxford: Clarendon Press, 1950),
p. 193.

[25] Lewis, *Preface to "Paradise Lost"*, p. 99.

still; an ordinary man, more so; a man of genius, still more so; a superhuman spirit best—or worst—of all."[26] As fallen angels, devils are not what Wormwood calls the *comic* figures of modern imagination, but they are in fact creatures of immense subtlety and power, and one of Lewis' purposes in writing *The Screwtape Letters* was to examine the true nature —and the true danger—of demonic temptation. In a preface to the paperback edition, Lewis admitted that he had never written anything so easily, nor with less enjoyment: the strain gave him a spiritual cramp.

In that same preface Lewis felt it necessary to clarify that, while angelic and satanic power is significantly greater than ours, it is infinitely less than God's. The adversary of Satan is Saint Michael, not God, although in his pride, Satan flatters himself that he can challenge God on equal terms. This brings us to Lewis' evaluation of an alternative to the Christian explanation of the presence of evil in the world, dualism. While Christianity affirms that a good God created everything and that evil came about through a misuse of the gift of free will, dualism maintains that the world is the arena of a struggle between two equal and independent powers. Lewis rejects dualism for two reasons. First, our very designation of "Evil Power" and "Good Power" implies the existence of a standard beyond, and therefore greater than, these powers: "In fact, what we meant by calling them good and bad turns out to be that one of them is in a right relation to the real ultimate God and the other in a wrong relation to Him."[27] Second, goodness can be sought for its own sake, whereas evil can be sought only because it is perceived (wrongly) to be good: "In order to be bad he must

[26] C. S. Lewis, *Mere Christianity* (New York: Macmillan, 1943), p. 53.
[27] Ibid., p. 49.

have good things to want and then to pursue them in the wrong way: he must have impulses which were originally good in order to pervert them."[28]

More fundamentally, Lewis points out, in order to be bad, a being must possess existence, intellect, and will—and these are all good things. Evil has no existence of its own; it is merely a parasite living off of goodness. For this reason, in *Out of the Silent Planet*, the only word Ransom can find for "bad" in the lexicon of the unfallen hrossa is "bent". In a sermon on Providence, Knox makes the same point:

> Long ago, in a book which nobody reads now, I did write an essay in the character of a Modernist clergyman, which was called "Canon Dives' explanation of the existence of Good". And he explained, of course, that without the existence of good there would be no possibility of evil. It worked out right on paper; why is it nonsense? Because whatever else we are certain about, we are certain that good is the positive thing, and evil the negative thing, just as light is the positive thing and darkness is the negative thing; evil does not exist in its own right, but only as a privation of the good. And because God *is*, God is good and not evil.[29]

The Meaning of Suffering

In the traditional Christian understanding, God's good creation has been spoiled by angelic and human rejection of his sovereignty. Lewis envisions this as a civil war, in which we

[28] Ibid., p. 50.
[29] Knox, *Occasional Sermons*, p. 334. Knox is referring to a piece in *Essays in Satire* entitled "The New Sin", in which a Professor Laileb (Belial?) fills the Albert Hall with an audience anxious to learn about the new sin he has discovered. They find out the new sin is the very old sin of prurient curiosity.

find ourselves living in enemy-occupied territory. Because we human beings are the linchpin joining the spiritual and material orders of creation, our revolt infects the whole creation. This is how Knox understands what Saint Paul wrote in the Letter to the Romans: "Created nature has been condemned to frustration; not for some deliberate fault of its own, but for the sake of him who so condemned it" (Rom 8:20). While most modern exegetes hold that "him who so condemned it" refers to God, Knox prefers Saint John Chrysostom's interpretation that it refers to Adam. That the world around us is condemned to frustration is a matter of observation: "The material world, with its apparent waste and cruelty, its constant alternation of growth and decay, etc., can give no satisfactory account of itself; it can only provide the background to a spiritual interpretation of existence."[30] If the whole world is a misfit, like a squeaky drawer which does not fit quite properly, it seems to Knox more reasonable to lay the blame for this at the feet of Adam and Eve rather than with the God who created everything and saw that it was good: "When man fell, he was driven out of Paradise, a sensible kind of place in which there was no death and no suffering, and found himself an exile in this world of striving and frustration, in which he has been living ever since."[31]

This being the case, what are we to make of suffering? Both of our authors are clear that suffering in itself is evil, but they believe that we can draw good out of it. First of all, Lewis notes, our true happiness is to be found in conform-

[30] Ronald Knox, *A New Testament Commentary, vol. 2: The Acts of the Apostles, St. Paul's Letters to the Churches* (New York: Sheed and Ward, 1954), p. 98.

[31] Ronald Knox, *The Gospel in Slow Motion* (New York: Sheed and Ward, 1950), p. 172.

ing our wills to the will of our Creator, and in our fallen condition of self-absorption, this is a painful process. Within the mystery of the Trinity, the Son eternally renders filial obedience to the Father, and we are made in the Son's image. In Paradise, such an attention on the Other was pleasant, but not in this fallen world: "But to surrender a self-will inflamed and swollen with years of usurpation is a kind of death. We all remember this self-will as it was in childhood —the bitter, prolonged rage at every thwarting, the burst of passionate tears, the black, Satanic wish to kill or die rather than to give in."[32] With maturity, we leave behind (perhaps) the histrionics, but we still want things our own way, and so we repeatedly have to endure the death of our self-will. We are rebels who must lay down our arms, sailors who must give the order "Full speed astern!" to counteract the centrifugal force of selfishness that pulls us away from God. This is difficult, but Knox points out that in this world, most worthwhile things in life are—games, creative arts, falling in love: "Under our present conditions of living there is no value without struggle. All the ardours and splendours of life are mixed up with doing things that are hard to do."[33]

Our highest good is God, and the sufferings and disappointments of the world can help us free ourselves from the encumbrances that distract us from him. Everything in this world passes away, and Lewis suggests that one effect of the vicissitudes of life is to help us realize this and to seek God more earnestly. Pain shatters the illusion that all is well and that this world is our permanent home; in Knox's felicitous translation of Hebrews 13:14, "we have an everlasting city, but not here; our goal is the city that is one day to be." Our

[32] Lewis, *Problem of Pain*, p. 79.
[33] Knox, "Why Does God Make Sin So Easy?" in Wright, *Asking Them Questions*, p. 167.

illusions of self-sufficiency must be shattered, so even good people need to undergo these losses. In fact, "good" people may need to learn this lesson more than others, which is why Christ was more lenient with the vices of the dissipated than with those that lead to worldly success: "Prostitutes are in no danger of finding their present life so satisfactory that they cannot turn to God: the proud, the avaricious, the self-righteous, are in that danger."[34] Does God then send afflictions so that we can prove to him that we are obedient? Lewis considers the story of the sacrifice of Isaac, and he answers in the negative. God knows Abraham's obedience —it is Abraham who must learn of what obedience he is capable.

Suffering can wean us from our attachments, and it can also purify our motives. In this context, Lewis draws an interesting comparison between Immanuel Kant and Aristotle. Kant taught that an act is moral in the highest sense when the sole motivation is that it is the right thing to do; if a person *likes* doing the moral thing, it is not as selfless. Aristotle held that the more virtuous acts a person performs, the more he takes pleasure in virtuous acts; good acts become second nature to such a person, so that the element of sacrifice is mitigated or removed altogether. Sufferings that befall us, and that we would rather reject, offer an opportunity to embrace something that is not of our choosing, something that is not a good in itself but that provides an occasion for us to curb our self-will. The matter of motivation also sheds some light on the perennial problem of why the wicked prosper and the good suffer. Knox believes the question of motivation is at the heart of the Book of Job: if prosperity were proportioned to our deserts, would we

[34] Lewis, *Problem of Pain*, p. 86.

love God because it paid? On the other hand, if divine pun-ishment were meted out every time someone did a wicked deed, this would produce a "slave morality" among most people: "We should behave like schoolboys (to use a very crude illustration), who cannot indeed *see* that the master is in the room, but know that he is in the room because he always hits them on the back of the head if they try to look up from their books."[35]

The puzzle of the prosperity of the wicked suggests an-other value of suffering that seems universal in human expe-rience: pain as an instrument of punishment. Lewis admits that it is not easy to disentangle "retributive punishment" from vengeance, but he suggests that the problem may be that revenge mistakes ends for means. The desired end is for the bad person to recognize the evil he has done by being on the receiving end and so to make amends for it. This is a tricky business, however. Because suffering is an evil thing in itself, we can inflict it on others only for a greater good (Knox suggests the example of the doctor or dentist who gives pain in order to heal), and the justice human beings mete out can be a very blunt instrument indeed. Knox adds that perfect justice will never be obtained in this world and that appeal must be made to a higher justice and a broader horizon: "Suffering, as we see it in this world, must be the wiping out of a debt; otherwise we should go mad thinking of it, so unevenly distributed. If some of us have to suffer so much more than most of us, there must be compensation for that in the world to come. If you will not grant me that, then I will go out into the street with the atheists and rail at my God."[36]

---

[35] Knox, *Difficulties*, p. 211.
[36] Knox, *Pastoral Sermons*, p. 466.

Suffering as the payment of debt and as a path to detachment from the passing things of this world are insights common to many religious traditions. Does Christianity have anything to add to these basic intuitions? The short answer is yes—Jesus Christ. But this is an answer that calls for serious reflection. In *The Problem of Pain* Lewis suggested that Christianity makes the doctrines of punishment and nonattachment more tolerable because "the terrible task has already in some sense been accomplished for us—that a master's hand is holding ours as we attempt to trace the difficult letters and that our script need only be a 'copy', not an original."[37] At this point, fairly early in his Christian discipleship, Lewis understood the role of Christ in relation to suffering primarily in terms of an example. Christ is certainly an example, but he is much more.

Knox observes that the usual explanations that make some sense of suffering collapse when we consider the sufferings of Christ. Had he ever sinned? No. Did his motivation for loving his Father require purification, or did his character need perfecting? Again, no. If ever in human history there was an example of undeserved suffering, it is the agonizing death of Jesus. And yet he not only endured it but welcomed it: "From first to last, you have to remember, there is one Accomplice who co-operates more effectively with the plans of our Lord's persecutors than any other, and that is our Lord himself."[38] He could have eluded his enemies in any number of ways: by leaving Jerusalem that last evening, as he had left it the evenings before; by avoiding the place where Judas knew to look for him; by keeping silence before the high priest; by disowning a royal title before

[37] Lewis, *Problem of Pain*, p. 92.
[38] Ronald Knox, *A Retreat for Lay People* (New York: Sheed and Ward, 1954), p. 132.

Pilate, as he had done when the crowds wished to make him their king. These were the human means at his disposal, but Knox reminds us that this was also the Son of God; he could call upon twelve legions of angels, but he did not; less spectacularly, Providence could have arranged in a hundred less dramatic ways for him to be spared. He wanted to die, and not only to die, but to die a cruel, shameful, and agonizing death. He could have allowed the crowds to stone him when they sought to, but he did not; instead, he chose to endure the tragic drama of the Passion. It is no wonder that, from the first century to our own, the Cross has been the great scandal of Christianity.

In plumbing something of this mystery, Knox invites us to observe the three condemned criminals carrying their crosses to Calvary on Good Friday afternoon. The impenitent thief ("so we call him, though it is not for us to know in what dispositions of mind his death agony found him")[39] carries his cross in resentful protest. He bears the yoke because he must, the victim of a social order that protects the rich and has turned against him; he would escape if he could —and considers the so-called prophet from Galilee a fool if he does not call on his supposed miraculous powers to escape this cruel death. The good thief bears his cross with resignation, admitting that this punishment, cruel as it is, has been brought upon him by his own misdeeds. And the third Figure? Knox invites us to imagine his thoughts:

"Blessed above all the trees of the forest be these rough planks I take on my shoulders, the balance on which my Passion is to be weighed against the sins of the world! This is the moment to which I looked forward when I first learned my trade at Nazareth, which I decreed at the dawning of creation, when I

[39] Ibid., pp. 142–43.

bade the trees bring forth fruit of their kind. Here is Noe's ark, the refuge of drowning humanity; here is the rod of Aaron, ready to blossom with the flowers of salvation; here is the trunk on which Moses set up the brazen serpent for the healing of my people. Welcome the weight that bears me down, and the roughness that galls my torn flesh, and the shame it bears; for this is my Father's Will, this is the token of his Love, this is the stroke of Divine Justice, canceling the debt due from a guilty race. Welcome every painful step, the hard road I tread and the stones my feet stumble over; this journey is better than my entry into the Holy City a few days past, more triumphal still, for it is the pageant of self-immolated love. It was Jacob [who] boasted long ago, he had nothing but a staff with him, when he crossed the Jordan, and now he had come back with two companies behind him. And I, who set out with this Cross of mine now, will return to my Father's kingdom at the head of a great army, all the faithful souls who will love my Cross and carry it in their own lives. This is the scepter with which I will rule the world; this is the magnet by which, when I am lifted up, I will draw all men unto me." [40]

There are three ways to accept suffering: with resentment, with resignation, and with rejoicing. The inequities and tragedies of life can school us in the first, and the great masters of philosophy and religion can initiate us into the second —but only Christ crucified can teach us the third. Somehow he unites two contrary images: the "Man of Sorrows", scourged, bleeding, despised; and the victorious Hero, bearing his bejeweled Cross like a trophy.

The link between the Man of Sorrows and the victorious Hero is found in the love with which Jesus embraces the Cross—love for his heavenly Father who has asked him to carry the Cross, and love for us, for whose sins he bears it.

[40] Ibid., p. 144.

This charity has a transforming effect, which Knox likens to the filament in a light bulb. When it is not burning, you see only dull, dark wire; the electricity transforms it into a glowing mass: "So it is with suffering in human lives; an evil thing in itself, it becomes a good thing when it is transmuted, by the love of God, into a glowing focus of charity."[41] By his loving acceptance of the Cross, Christ has transformed "passion" and "suffering" from the passive to the active voice: they are no longer things you endure, but they are things you *do*. At the heart of Christ's Passion is generosity, a spirit that seeks more than duty, a response that is more than mere obedience: "who, being rich, became poor for our sakes, walking on earth as a man; who, as a poor man and homeless, had nothing to give for us except himself, his life and his blood; who gave that self, that life, that blood freely and to the utmost for the salvation of the world."[42] Love transforms resignation into rejoicing, duty into generosity.

If love of God changes our attitude toward suffering, love of neighbor changes our valuation of it through our awareness of the solidarity of the human race. Knox holds that all suffering is expiation for sin but that the one who commits the sin is not necessarily the one who suffers for it. This solidarity is revealed most clearly in the case of Jesus, the Sinless One who lays down his life for sinners. Here is the answer to the question raised by the young C. S. Lewis: How could the suffering and death of someone two thousand years ago affect me? It can because the whole human race is one body, and as head of that body, Christ, the new Adam, has borne the punishment due to us.

---

[41] Ronald Knox, *Creed in Slow Motion*, p. 76.
[42] Knox, *University Sermons*, p. 370.

Were we merely the recipients of this grace, it would be a tremendous thing; but Christ makes us more than recipients—he makes us active participants. In his Passion, he has paid off the whole debt of our sufferings, and he invites us to pay him back by our willingness to unite our sufferings to his. Knox thinks that there is a lesson here that many neglect: that in his Passion, the Lord did not spare himself pain, but he also did not spare pain to others. He did not go off bravely to face death alone, but he associated others with his sufferings—the disciples in Gethsemane, Simon of Cyrene under the weight of the Cross, Mary and the beloved disciple on Calvary. The solidarity goes both ways, from the head to the members, and from the members to the head: "As he covets suffering for himself, so he will allow his best friends to share it; their watchfulness, their sighs, their tears shall be privileged to co-operate with him in the work of the world's redemption."[43] This is because "sacrifice is not only the currency in which the debt of sin has to be paid; it is the currency in which Love loves to squander itself, by which love is attested, and by which love is called forth in return."[44]

Knox did not claim that meditation on the mystery of the Cross would offer an intellectual solution to the problem of suffering; for example, he noted that it sheds no light on the question of the suffering of animals, and he referred people to Lewis' views on this topic.[45] He did hope it would

[43] Knox, *Retreat for Lay People*, p. 139.

[44] Knox, "Suffering", unpublished conference, Knox Papers, Mells, Somerset; in Milton Walsh, *Ronald Knox as Apologist* (S.T.D. diss. Gregorian University, Rome, 1985), p. 456.

[45] Knox's interpretation of Romans 8 that "frustration" in creation is due to Adam's sin fits in, he notes, with Lewis' suggestion in *The Problem of Pain* that animal suffering may be related to human sin, but Knox owns that he finds the problem insoluble. Lewis got his idea from Milton, but Knox

offer people inspiration to bear suffering and, through the alchemy of charity, to transform something that in itself is evil into a source of good. Because suffering is evil, it is justifiable for us to seek to avoid it. Lewis frankly admits, "If I knew a way of escape I would crawl through sewers to find it",[46] and Knox tells us that one lesson of the Agony in the garden is that it is legitimate to pray to be spared suffering. Both our authors discouraged people from going out of their way to seek suffering, such as by adopting exaggerated ascetical practices. They also underscored the paradox that, like their Master, Christians have devoted their energies to alleviating the sufferings of others even as they have joyfully welcomed suffering when it was clear that this was God's will for them.

We should strive to lessen the suffering in our world, but since it is a fallen world, we will never fully succeed. When the shadow of the Cross falls upon our own lives, we can meet it with resentment, railing at the injustice of the world, or we can accept it with resignation, recognizing that we all need salutary chastisement. But Christ calls us to embrace the suffering we cannot avoid, not merely with resignation, but with joy, for it is the medicine of immortality: "If we have learned in our adversities, in sickness, in sorrow, in bereavement, in anxiety, in desolation, yes, even in doubts and scruples, to unite ourselves with his Passion, ours is the pain that heals: the more to suffer, the more to offer, that is the first principle of the Christian medicine."[47]

---

does not know where Milton got it from. Knox adds, "There is no trace of it in the schoolmen; they are content to avert their eyes from the sufferings of the rabbit and dwell on the satisfaction afforded to the weasel" (Knox, *Occasional Sermons*, p. 333).

[46] Lewis, *Problem of Pain*, p. 93.

[47] Knox, *Pastoral Sermons*, p. 86.

"The more to suffer, the more to offer" is strong medicine; many would add, bitter medicine. But it speaks to the
generosity that Christ calls forth in us, and which he can
call forth because of his generosity to us. And for both C. S.
Lewis and Ronald Knox, the Christian life is far more about
generous living than it is about simply making the most of
the tragedies of life. Lewis wrote to his friend Sister Penelope that "*cheerful insecurity* is what Our Lord asks of us",[48]
and both he and Knox believed that only the costly generosity of following Christ would make us happy here as well
as hereafter.

[48] Walter Hooper, ed., *The Collected Letters of C. S. Lewis*, vol. III (San Francisco: HarperCollins, 2007) p. 79.

CHAPTER SEVEN

The Way of Love

"Cheerful insecurity" sounds like a contradiction in terms: our instinct for self-preservation and the desire to protect ourselves at all costs make insecurity anything but cheerful for us. Anxiety was the first fruit tasted after the Fall: Adam and Eve became aware that they were naked and hid themselves. Lewis urges us to be cheerful because we come from a God who is good, and we are journeying to a God who is good; we should be insecure precisely because we *are* on a journey, and this earth is not our true home. We are tourists, not expatriates.

In a later chapter, we will examine our authors' views on the goal of our pilgrimage; here we will consider their understanding of the good God as our origin and what this teaches us about the way of love. Both men were impatient with the tendency to reduce the Christian religion to a matter of avoiding sin—they were generous spirits, and their generosity was fueled by an awareness of God's mercy toward them.

We recall that it was important for Lewis that there be an Arbiter of right and wrong outside of creation. But is this Arbiter arbitrary? Lewis asks if something is good because God commands it, or does God command it because it is good? Knox considers this dilemma on one occasion and affirms that "good" and "bad" are not labels God attaches to one thing and another, like conductors designating different carriages on the train as "smoking" and "nonsmoking"; rather, goodness is God's own nature, and he cannot be false to it. Knox suggests the example of a good artist who is asked his opinion of a bad painting—he simply *cannot* pretend it is good.[1] Lewis notes that the Israelites praised God for being "righteous" and in so doing recognized that his laws have a rock-bottom reality rooted in God's own being: "Their delight in the Law is a delight in having touched firmness; like the pedestrian's delight in feeling the hard road beneath his feet after a false short cut has long entangled him in muddy fields."[2]

The issue does raise difficult questions for Lewis: if something is right simply because God commands it, then goodness is emptied of intrinsic meaning: might makes right. If, on the other hand, God commands something because it is right, this implies that God executes laws that are external and antecedent to himself. This dilemma leads Lewis to suggest that God neither ordains nor obeys the moral law; in the Christian understanding, God is not a Person (the author or agent of laws) but a Trinity of Persons in the unity of Deity. Thus, although the Tao is found in all religions, Christian revelation offers a unique insight into the nature of God's goodness: "What is the ground of all existence, is not simply a law but also a begetting love, a love begotten, and the love which, being between these two, is also imminent in all those who are caught up to share the unity of their self-caused life. God is not merely good, but goodness;

[1] Cf. Knox, "Why Does God Make Sin So Easy?" in Ronald Selby Wright, *Asking Them Questions* (London: Oxford University Press, 1953), p. 162.

[2] C. S. Lewis, *Reflections on the Psalms* (New York: Harcourt, Brace and World, 1958), p. 62.

goodness is not merely divine, but God."[3] The goodness of God is fundamentally a communion of mutual love, and Lewis shows how the dogma of the Trinity, which to many seems an arid metaphysical speculation, is in reality the fundamental dynamic of the moral life.

The Trinity is a community of love that Lewis likens to a dance; and we are invited to take our place in that dance. The Triune God is not three individuals who merge into one nor one unity that splits into three—he is eternally one and eternally manifold. This infuriates Screwtape, who sees the Trinity as a violation of the most fundamental principle of Hell: one self is not another self, and thus one's gain must be the other's loss. In violation of this "obvious truth", Screwtape's Enemy aims at a contradiction: "Things are to be many, yet somehow also one. The good of one self is to be the good of another. . . . He is not content, even Himself, to be a sheer arithmetical unity; He claims to be three as well as one, in order that this nonsense about Love may find a foothold in His own nature."[4] This trinitarian communion is at odds with two popular alternatives: individualism and totalitarianism. Individualism leads to isolation, while totalitarianism overcomes isolation at the expense of personality. In contrast, Lewis suggests the image of the household, a community in which each member is valued because each is unique: grandfather, parents, grown-up son, little girl, and even the dog and cat are all true members precisely *because* they are not interchangeable. In this understanding, rivalry disappears because God loves each creature differently, uniquely . . . and infinitely. Similarly, in a series

[3] C. S. Lewis, *Christian Reflections* (Grand Rapids: Eerdmans, 1967), p. 80.

[4] C. S. Lewis, *The Screwtape Letters* (New York: Macmillan, 1973 [1942]), pp. 81–82.

of sermons on the parables of Jesus, Knox devoted one to the subject inequality of merit and another to equality of reward. The equality consists in the fact that each soul is fulfilled to its full extent with the delights of God's house.[5]

A crucial element of being-in-relation is the idea of sacrifice: the self exists to be abdicated and so to become truly itself. The Son of God laid down his life on the Cross; but Lewis points out that from the foundation of the world, the Son has surrendered his begotten divinity back to the begetting divinity of the Father in obedience:

> The golden apple of selfhood, thrown among the false gods, became an apple of discord because they scrambled for it. They did not know the first rule of the holy game, which is that every player must by all means touch the ball and then immediately pass it on. To be found with it in your hands is a fault: to cling to it, death. But when it flies to and fro among the players . . . and the great master Himself leads the revelry, giving Himself eternally to His creatures in the generation, and back to Himself in the sacrifice, of the Word, then indeed the eternal dance "makes heaven drowsy with the harmony".[6]

As Knox would say, "You see, sacrifice is the food of love. The lover is always wanting to send some present, perform some service. . . . Love that never finds an outlet grows stale and dies away."[7]

Our origin in the Triune God provides both a way of affirmation and a way of negation: affirmation, because every-

[5] The series was originally published in 1928 as *The Mystery of the Kingdom* and is included in *Pastoral Sermons*.

[6] C. S. Lewis, *The Problem of Pain* (London: Fontana Books. 1957 [1940]), p. 141.

[7] Philip Caraman, ed., *University Sermons of Ronald A. Knox* (New York: Sheed and Ward, 1963), p. 329.

thing that God has made is good, and we should rejoice in it; negation, because we are to receive things as gifts, not cling to them as possessions. In our fallen condition, it is easy to forget that everything should be cherished as coming from God and pointing to God; furthermore, if for the Creator the way of love is the way of sacrifice, this also is true of the creature. Screwtape cautions Wormwood to tread carefully when seeking to ensnare his "patient" in pleasures, because pleasures are the Enemy's invention: "He made the pleasures: all our research so far has not enabled us to produce one. All we can do is to encourage the humans to take the pleasures which our Enemy has produced, at times, or in ways, or in degrees, which He has forbidden."[8] The way of goodness is the way of love, but we face the challenge of competing and contradictory loves. Lewis sought to untangle this confusion in *The Four Loves*.

Lewis' Fourfold Love

As with some of his other popular books, *The Four Loves* began life as a series of radio broadcasts. In this case the invitation came from an American woman named Caroline Rakestraw, on behalf of the Episcopal Radio-TV Foundation of Atlanta, Georgia. Allowed to choose his own topic, Lewis decided to address four different meanings of the word "love": affection, friendship, romantic love, and charity; he felt that this provided a vehicle to consider the whole vista of Christian ethics. It turned out that there was one part of the vista that was decidedly unwelcome—Lewis' discussion of erotic love—and the series was not broadcast because it was considered "too frank for the American

[8] Lewis, *Screwtape Letters*, pp. 41–42.

people". Looking back from the other side of the sexual revolution of the 1960s, it is surprising to us that an author as conservative as C. S. Lewis would be considered risqué, and we smile at Lewis' exasperation when it was objected that he had brought sex into his talk on Eros: "My dear Mrs. Cartwheel, how can you talk about Eros and *leave it out?*"[9]

As Lewis reviews each kind of love in turn, he presents its distinguishing characteristics and then indicates the dangers associated with it. The solution to the potential danger is to see each variety of love in relation to the others: it is when one form of love is exalted to the detriment of the rest that we run into problems. Because love is good in itself and exercises a great influence over us, it is easy for a particular kind of love to become "inordinate", that is, excessive and unbalanced. The Christian understanding of love, far from being a religion of "thou shalt not's", offers a very positive vision of the various facets of love, and a path to their healthy integration.

Before examining the four kinds of love, Lewis presents a fundamental distinction between "Need-love" and "Gift-love", since both are at work in each of the four loves. Gift-love is the generous impulse to sacrifice oneself for the sake of the beloved, and it is the hallmark of divine love. Need-love, the desire to *be* the beloved, is a fundamental part of our human nature, and Lewis objects to it being dismissed as selfishness. As human beings, we come into this world in a state of total dependence; as creatures, we are always dependent on our Creator. Even as we seek to imitate the Gift-love

[9] Walter Hooper, *C. S. Lewis: A Companion and Guide* (San Francisco: Harper, 1996), p. 90. Lewis consistently referred to the woman as "Cartwheel", although her name was Rakestraw.

of God, it remains true that we draw closest to him through the exercise of our Need-love: in fact, the more aware we are of our total dependence on God, the freer we become to bestow Gift-love.

The first love Lewis considers is affection, the feeling we have for what is familiar to us, simply because it *is* familiar. It is said that you can choose your friends but you cannot choose your family; affection is what we feel toward people, places, and things that are homey: "Affection almost slinks or seeps through our lives. It lives with humble, un-dress, private things; soft slippers, old clothes, old jokes, the thump of a sleepy dog's tail on the kitchen floor, the sound of a sewing-machine, a gollywog left on the lawn."[10] Like gin, affection can be enjoyed "neat" or in mixed drinks, that is, as an accompaniment to the other loves.

There are dangers to this domestic virtue. Precisely because it is unmerited, it can come to be expected, even demanded. And this presumption can lead to unwarranted liberties: "Old clothes are one thing; to wear the same shirt till it stank would be another."[11] Another pitfall is jealousy: because affection relies on the old and familiar, it can resent any change in the beloved. A new interest or a religious conversion is perceived as desertion or robbery—how can he change like this? The unfamiliar threatens the familiar. The Gift-love side of affection can spoil, too. Lewis describes "Mrs. Fidget", who worked her fingers to the bone for her family but in such a way that her self-sacrifice suffocated them, drowning them in a torrent of unrequested (and unwanted) services. At her funeral, the vicar said that she was

[10] C. S. Lewis, *The Four Loves* (New York: Harcourt, Brace and Co., 1960), pp. 56–57.
[11] Lewis, *Four Loves*, p. 67.

now at rest; to this, Lewis added: "Let us hope she is. What's quite certain is that her family are."[12] What Mrs. Fidget did not realize is that the goal of giving is to put the recipient in a situation in which he no longer needs our gift. The need to be needed is powerful, in teachers and caregivers as well as in parents. They should rejoice when those in their care are able to stand on their own two feet; they will when affection does not reign in solitary splendor.

Lewis' next subject is what he considers the least *natural* love, friendship. It is not a biological necessity and can be viewed with suspicion by the community since it offers an alternative to "company loyalty". He suggests that it is a rather rare experience, although there can be no doubt that it was the most central human experience of love for most of Lewis' own life. His rather complex relationship with Mrs. Moore began in early adulthood (and may have inspired some of his reflections on the ambivalence of affection), and his romantic relationship with Joy Davidman came late in life; friendship was central throughout his life. This love grows out of shared interests and projects, but although companionship forms its matrix, friendship is something qualitatively deeper. Like companions, friends are doing something together, but it is a project that engages the depth of their being. Unlike lovers who stand face to face, friends stand side by side: "Eros will have naked bodies; Friendship naked personalities."[13] While the love of friendship is intense, it is not jealous—friends want others to enjoy their friends. This distinguishes friendship from something Lewis loathed, "the Inner Circle". Friendship is inclusive, the circle exclusive; the latter exists precisely for the purpose

[12] Ibid., p. 76.
[13] Ibid., p. 103.

of having an "in group" and an "out group". The deliberate informality of the Inklings offers an image of friendship: while a few members were regular participants, several others took part sporadically and were warmly welcomed.

What are the dangers in this kind of love? There can be the tendency for a circle of friends to devolve into a clique and presume superiority over others who do not share their tastes or interests. "A *coterie*", Lewis observes, "is a self-appointed aristocracy."[14] Also, as common wisdom teaches, "Show me your friends, and I will tell you who you are." Good friends make us better people, and bad friends make us worse. A safeguard against these corrosive tendencies is to see this kind of love, like every kind of love, in relationship to our love of God and God's love for us. If we recognize our friends as a gift from God, we will view our membership in the circle of friends with humility, not conceit. His Providence has brought us together and has opened our eyes to their beauties, which come from him. The laughter and loyalty that shine through the works of Lewis and Tolkien show that they understood friendship to be one of God's great gifts: "At this feast it is He who has spread the board and it is He who has chosen the guests. It is He, we may dare to hope, who sometimes does, and always should, preside. Let us not reckon without our Host."[15]

From friendship Lewis moves on to Eros, the state we call "being in love". While it discomfited Mrs. Rakestraw that the subject of sex be mentioned at all, Lewis recognizes that this is an important element in romantic love. However, he denies that it is *the* important element: "Sexual desire, without Eros, wants *it*, the *thing in itself*; Eros wants

[14] Ibid., p. 118.
[15] Ibid., pp. 126–27.

the Beloved."[16] Although we say that a lustful man "wants a woman", Lewis observes that in fact that is what he does not want: he simply wants pleasure, and he needs a woman as "a piece of apparatus". The lover, on the contrary, wants the beloved—this particular woman; Eros has elevated need to appreciation. Knox presents the difference between the sexual appetite and romance in this way: "Love is essentially the effort to sacrifice yourself, to immolate yourself, to another person. And passion is essentially the effort to sacrifice, to immolate, another person to yourself."[17] Sexual love can become a matter of conquest or surrender, and the ideal of communion is notoriously elusive in our human experience. What Lewis objects to in our contemporary society is the tendency to view the sexual aspect in isolation. On the one hand, this makes people take it too seriously: "All my life a ludicrous and portentous solemnization of sex has been going on".[18] He pictures a couple going to bed surrounded by the works of Freud, Kraft-Ebbing, and Havelock Ellis. Lewis warns, "Banish play and laughter from the bed of love and you may let in a false goddess."[19] On the other hand, treating the erotic in isolation gives leeway to sexual gratification that we do not allow to other drives. In an essay entitled "We Have No 'Right to Happiness'", Lewis notes that while progressive voices have urged that sexual impulses should be treated like any others, in fact they accord them the "preposterous privilege" of condoning behavior done in the name of love that would be condemned otherwise as dishonest, cruel, and treacherous: "It is like having a moral-

[16] Ibid., p. 134.
[17] Knox, *University Sermons*, p. 137.
[18] Lewis, *Four Loves*, p. 138.
[19] Ibid., p. 140.

ity in which stealing fruit is considered wrong—unless you steal nectarines."[20]

In the context of the "playfulness" of sexuality, Lewis describes the roles of "Sky-father" and "Earth-mother" assumed by the participants: along with something intensely personal, there is something primordial in the sexual act. For Lewis, "masculine" and "feminine" are roles that permeate reality: the masculine role is austere, penetrating, and possessing, while the feminine is warm, sensuous, and receptive. These traits are celebrated in sexual love, but they pervade everything in our experience. For example, he says that we all have the feminine role in relationship to God, since we are always the recipients of God's gifts. This is why Lewis opposed women priests: the priest at the altar represents sacramentally the Lord as Bridegroom of the Church. Although Lewis' own communion later rejected such a view, this understanding of the sacramental symbolism of the priesthood is maintained in Roman Catholic teaching. Fifty years ago some in the Episcopal Church considered Lewis' talk on Eros too daring; today many would consider it too conservative.

But even fifty years ago, Lewis was attentive to the problem of "male domination", and he tempered his assertion about dominant and submissive sexual roles with two countervailing ideas. First, this is "sacred play", and outside of this romantic context a woman who offered absolute self-surrender to her husband would be guilty of idolatry, and a man who demanded it would be guilty of blasphemy: only God can make such claims, and both parties remain equal before God. Second, in the context of *Christian* marriage,

---

[20] C. S. Lewis, *God in the Dock* (Grand Rapids: Eerdmans, 1970), p. 320.

the husband symbolizes the headship of Christ, but only insofar as he imitates the Lord, who gave his life for his Bride, the Church. Knox told the men at Oxford that in marriage, "what we have to imitate about our Lord's love for his Church is its unselfishness."[21] Lewis writes: "The sternest feminist need not grudge my sex the crown offered to it either in the Pagan or in the Christian mystery. For the one is of paper and the other of thorns. The real danger is not that husbands may grasp the latter too eagerly; but that they will allow or compel their wives to usurp it."[22]

The mention of marriage is a reminder that Eros should lead to a permanent bond, which in a way is contrary to its nature: romantic love is fickle; marriage makes it faithful. One of the great dangers of Eros, according to Lewis, is that it speaks like a god: it makes absolute demands on us, leading us to make promises of undying love for the beloved. But Eros cannot deliver on these promises: "Eros is driven to promise what Eros of himself cannot perform."[23] Like a godparent, Eros makes the vows—but we have to keep them. Here again, the answer lies in not allowing romantic love to exclude the other loves, and it is often the most jealous of loves. The alchemy that transforms passionate desire into lifelong commitment demands the rejection of self-sufficiency by the couple; like the other human loves, if Eros does not lead to a love beyond itself, it dies—or worse: "But he may live on, mercilessly chaining together two mutual tormentors, each raw all over with the poison of hate-in-love, each ravenous to receive and implacably refusing to give."[24] Knox says that when it comes to weddings, it is the

---

[21] Knox, *University Sermons*, p. 289.

[22] Lewis, *Four Loves*, p. 149.

[23] Ibid., p. 159.

[24] Ibid., p. 160.

Church, not the world, that is realistic; she thinks, not of the fun you will have, but of the virtues you will need: "She says, 'Oh, you want to get married, do you? That means, you want to imitate the action of Jesus Christ in his Incarnation. Well, God bless you; you will want all the grace I can rout for you if you are to do that, a whole trousseau of graces.' "[25] Eros must lead to, and be fed by, the fourth love —charity.

The crowning chapter of *The Four Loves* deals with charity. It is crowning not simply because it is the last in the series of loves but because Lewis believes that it purifies, preserves, and perfects the natural loves. Even *with* divine love, our human loves involve suffering; witness Our Lord weeping over Jerusalem or before the tomb of Lazarus. But if the natural loves are allowed to stand in the ultimate place that only the love of God can rightly hold, they will be distorted and destructive. The rivalry comes, not because we cherish these human loves too much, but because we do not love God enough. This love cannot be measured by emotional feelings but by the intention of the will. Lewis asks, "Which (when the alternative comes) do you serve, or choose to put first? To which claim does your will, in the last resort, yield?"[26] Aware of our human frailty, Knox urged people not to ask what would happen if they had to choose between the love of God and the love of some creature. Rather, he suggested, "Ask what you would *wish* to happen; if your *will* is to love God above all things, you do love him above all things; you are still responding, however unfeelingly, to the unfelt influence of his love."[27]

[25] Knox, *University Sermons*, p. 287.

[26] Lewis, *Four Loves*, p. 171.

[27] Ronald Knox, *The Layman and His Conscience: A Retreat* (New York: Sheed and Ward, 1961), p. 39.

Knox's reference to our response reminds us that our love for God is a response to God's love for us; indeed, in all of our human loves, we are also receiving and bestowing the love of God. Lewis reflects on how divine love purifies, strengthens and elevates our natural Gift-love and Need-love. Our Gift-love is *purified* because, even at its best, natural love is not devoid of self-interest; it is *strengthened* because grace allows us to love even those whom we do not find "naturally" lovable; it is *elevated* because it enables us to exercise a Gift-love toward God, to whom as creatures we have only the relationship of Need-love. And that Need-love itself is changed, because the awareness of God's love for us allows us to experience a joyful dependence, unhindered by any reserve, and to accept the love of others even when we feel we do not deserve it. Divine love offers what we most want—freedom—and from an unexpected source: Someone outside ourselves. Drawing on the dogma of the Incarnation, Lewis says: "As Christ is perfect God and perfect Man, the natural loves are called to become perfect Charity and also perfect natural loves."[28]

It is this transformed love, and it alone, that survives the grave. With death, nature passes away, and so do natural loves, unless they have been transfigured by charity. They are transformed when they are united to, and take their place beneath, the ultimate love for God, the source of life. Lewis ends his book with an appeal: the greatest gift is to love God in himself, and it is this we should pray for. This is not easy, since "perhaps for many of us, all experience defines, so to speak, the shape of that gap where our love of God ought to be. It is not enough. It is something."[29]

[28] Lewis, *Four Loves*, p. 184.
[29] Ibid., p. 192.

The theme that our natural loves can function properly only when related to the love of God runs through many of Lewis' writings. All of the relations between characters in the Narnia stories depend on the characters' relationships to Aslan. Orual, the protagonist in *Till We Have Faces*, has to learn that her love for her sister has become possessive and destructive. In *The Great Divorce*, the puzzlement of the characters experiencing a holiday away from Hell is that they refuse to see how their choice to love creatures apart from God is the source of their misery. One of the most poignant incidents concerns a woman who wants to see her dead son. She cannot because her love for her son was so all-consuming that it killed every other love in her life. She rails against God: "No one has a right to come between me and my son. Not even God."[30] She will not, or cannot, see that her son was never her possession, that he was a gift from God. Lewis' fundamental ethical stance is captured in the response to the mother: "Pam, Pam—no natural feelings are high or low, holy or unholy in themselves. They are all holy when God's hand is on the rein. They all go bad when they set up on their own and make themselves into false gods."[31]

Preaching the Way of Love

Ronald Knox never produced a treatise on the nature of love, but he often discussed it in conferences to Oxford undergraduates, in retreat talks, and in sermons at weddings. His purpose was not to address the general public on the philosophical and moral aspects of love but to encourage his

[30] C. S. Lewis, *The Great Divorce* (New York: Macmillan, 1946), p. 95.
[31] Ibid., p. 93.

Catholic hearers to live generous lives of discipleship. The leitmotif running through his talks is the challenge to rise above the understanding of religion simply in terms of avoiding sin and instead to develop a zest for living that is shaped by a desire to please Christ. Knox the convert ordinarily did not criticize the practices and traditions of his fellow Catholics, but he did challenge them here. He frankly told a group of schoolboys: "The curse of the Catholic Church is want of generosity; always brooding about sin, instead of setting out to find what God's will is, and doing it."[32]

From his lifelong study of Christian religious movements, Knox recognized that one source of this timidity was the tendency of the Church not to set the bar too high for membership. The early Church had been more demanding for several reasons: the first Christians had a strong expectation of the imminent end of the world; most of them were converts, with the zeal of converts; and they lived their faith in a context of persecution. Over the subsequent centuries, these circumstances all changed, and part of what Knox chronicled in *Enthusiasm* was the efforts of charismatic leaders to rekindle the zeal of the first Christians. In Catholic life the tendency to spread the nets widely when combined with the desire for heroic discipleship could lead to a kind of two-tiered approach: commandments incumbent on all, evangelical counsels embraced by those in religious life. Knox disapproved of what he called "two sets of books", and he commented on how much unheroic advice passed daily through the screen of the confessional: "What a terrible lot of time we priests spend in telling people what they *needn't* do; 'Oh, no,' we find ourselves saying, 'you're not *bound* to do that,' and one sometimes longs to add, 'But you'll

[32] Ronald Knox, *A Retreat for Beginners* (New York: Sheed and Ward, 1960), p. 80.

be a skunk if you don't.' "[33] This minimalism could transform moral theology into "the Hireling's Handbook"—a Christian's guide to what he did not have to do.

In contrast to this two-tiered approach, Knox urged people to read the Sermon on the Mount with the Epistles of Saint Paul as their bookmark. The Apostle to the Gentiles exhorted *all* his disciples to live generous lives and not be content with mediocrity. True to his Evangelical upbringing, Knox did the same: he told his Catholic audiences that although the heroism of the saints might not be within their reach, their spirit was; they should do ordinary things in a spirit of love, not bondage. What Our Lord taught in the Sermon on the Mount was not the contrast between two moral laws, but the contrast between the way of duty and the way of love. Knox illustrates the difference with an image of two ships. The first is moored on the open sea; although it does not drift away, it is constantly buffeted by winds and waves; under constant tension, its ropes wear down from all the motion. This is the person who serves God out of a sense of duty: blown about by bad example and bad company but pulled back at the last moment by the rope of obedience. The second ship is moored in the harbor, protected from the surging of the sea and the blasts of the wind, its rope never taut: "Let that be our image of a soul which serves God by the way of love. The commandments are there, the spirit of obedience is there, but it is not called upon to act; the soul is no longer at the mercy of the wind or tide, that it should need the warning tug of the rope to keep it in position; it rides securely on that calm surface, the love of Jesus Christ."[34]

---

[33] Knox, *Layman and His Conscience*, p. 128.

[34] Ronald Knox, *A Retreat for Lay People* (New York: Sheed and Ward, 1955), p. 152.

Knox applies his vision of generous love to Christian marriage in several of his conferences to Oxford undergraduates and in sermons he preached at weddings. In these talks, certain themes recur: the interplay of physical attraction, romance, and spirituality; marriage as a "natural sacrament" that demands lifelong fidelity; and Christian marriage in relation to the life and mission of Jesus Christ. His wedding sermons illustrate his ability to adapt these principles to the particular circumstances of each couple. Twenty-four of these sermons were published under the title *Bridegroom and Bride*; each is only a few pages long (Knox followed the advice of one bridegroom who asked for "the kind of thing for which five minutes is too short, and ten minutes is too long"[35]), but in those few pages Knox provides a sound theology of marriage, a wealth of applications from Scripture, and frequent allusions to the liturgical feasts and seasons of the year.

Speaking to his charges at the Oxford chaplaincy before the Second World War (which means that only men were present), Knox told them that he considered women to be naturally more unselfish than men, primarily because women were engaged in the altruistic task of bringing up children, and that men often unfairly took advantage of this unselfishness. He viewed the growth of feminism not simply as the desire for many women to enter into professional life but as a revolt against the code that calls for the woman to be unselfish and so play up to the selfishness of the man. He felt that such selfishness was contrary to Christian life and suggested to them that marriage would remain a life-

---

[35] Ronald Knox, *Bridegroom and Bride* (New York: Sheed and Ward, 1957), p. 11.

long romance only on the condition "that the husband's attitude is one of lifelong courtship".[36] Years later he delivered another conference on marriage at Oxford, and this time women also attended. He noted their presence (and playfully tweaked the shadow of chauvinism in theological circles) by observing that if one consulted the index of the latest and most elaborate edition of the works of Francisco Suarez, under the word *mulier*, it read, "*vide: scandalum*"; he then added with his customary understatement, "the Fathers of the Church will have their little grouse now and again".[37] In this talk, too, he appeals for a spirit of generosity in marriage, challenging the men when they marry to imitate Christ's unselfish love for his Bride. Like religious life, marriage demands a certain abridgment of personality, "but the abridgement of your personality will, commonly at least, be the enrichment of your character."[38]

Knox recognizes the place of Eros in marriage; the spirituality of love coexists with the satisfaction of physical desire: "the angel in us and the animal in us are both at work, and not as contrasts or opposites".[39] Like Lewis, he sees passion transmuted into romance, and romance transformed into sacrificial love, ultimately, divine love in human terms. Marriage is beautiful in itself, but in the Christian dispensation it becomes something "infinitely more exciting" and is in fact the gateway of all the sacraments: "Baptism, after all, derives its efficacy from the Incarnation . . . the Mystical Body is the matrix of our spiritual rebirth. And the Church is the Bride of Christ; the wedding comes before the

[36] Knox, *University Sermons*, p. 141.
[37] Ibid., p. 283.
[38] Ibid., p. 289.
[39] Ibid., p. 284.

christening."[40] Is this kind of language metaphorical? No, Knox insists, the New Testament constantly reverses our presumption that "the material" is more real than "the spiritual": it is not that Mr. Jones is really a father, and that we apply the word to God in a metaphorical sense; on the contrary, it is God who is truly a Father, and we apply the term to Mr. Jones by extension. Similarly, it is not that marriage gives us some idea of the love between Christ and the Church; rather, it is when we contemplate Christ's love for the Church that we get some idea of what Christian marriage is.

Regarding the question of divorce, Knox insists that (contrary to the opinion of many of his students' contemporaries), monogamy is God's will for the human race, not "a Catholic stunt".[41] When Christ forbade divorce, he appealed to the natural law in force before the Law of Moses. In Knox's lifetime, views about divorce were changing dramatically, and Catholics could not help but be influenced by these currents. Theologians and biblical scholars examined critically the variant wordings of Jesus' teachings as they are recorded in Mark 10:11–12 and Matthew 5:31–32. Drawing on his years of biblical research, Knox devoted an entire conference to these two passages. He reviews the various interpretations offered by scholars and recognizes the ambiguities surrounding these sayings. Then, in the final paragraph, he steps back from this microscopic analysis of a few verses and challenges his listeners to look at Christ's teaching in a broader context:

[40] Ibid., p. 285.

[41] Ibid. In *Mere Christianity*, Lewis noted that, although there existed some disagreement between Churches on the matter of divorce, they all viewed it as an extreme measure, either not to be done at all or only in the gravest of circumstances (p. 96).

Meanwhile, what *was* our Lord's teaching about marriage? This. "I tell you that he who casts his eyes on a woman so as to lust after her has already committed adultery with her in his heart." That is, the dangerous moment in a dangerous intimacy is not the one we think; it is several moments earlier. "It is not what goes into his mouth that makes a man unclean; what makes a man unclean is what comes out of his mouth . . . his sins of murder, adultery, fornication." That is, it is we who shape our destinies, not they us. "If I have washed your feet, I who am the Master and the Lord, you in your turn ought to wash one another's feet." That is, you cannot stop giving, and continue to possess. If people would live by *that* part of our Lord's teaching, there would be no divorces, and no need for them.[42]

In his wedding sermons, Knox exhorted couples to practice mutual unselfishness and invited them to see their marriage in light of their relationships with other people and with God. For people in love, unselfishness is spontaneous, and Knox prays that it will always remain so: "God knows we wish you happiness, but we wish you first unselfishness, and happiness as the fruit of it."[43] The lesson that we attain happiness only when we aim at the happiness of another is the lesson of a lifetime. This lesson comes easily to the couple on their wedding day, but it will not always be so. For this reason, the priest blesses the wedding rings with the sign of the cross, tracing over the symbol of perfect happiness the sign of sacrifice.

The friends and family of the newlyweds offer their prayers and support, but Knox suggests that they also receive a gift from the couple: they can draw warmth for their own charity from the watch fire of the couple's love.

[42] Knox, *University Sermons*, pp. 295–96.
[43] Knox, *Bridegroom and Bride*, p. 25.

And if it is true that people in love see the world through rose-colored glasses, such love can inspire others to catch a glimpse beyond their own jaundiced view of fallen creatures in a fallen world: "If only we had the magic of your clear vision, to . . . see men and women as they really are, splendid and lovable! It is given to you, at this moment, to see human nature as God sees it, to love it as God loves it."[44] On the other hand, it is important that the couple not be so caught up in love with each other that they live in "a world of make-believe, a little isolationist republic of two";[45] their love for one another should widen their sympathy for others. Christians, although freed by Christ, remain the slaves of charity; whoever has need of our help becomes by that very fact our master.

Finally, the couple should see their marriage in light of their relationship with God. Unlike the pagan god of love, who was blind, our God sees everything, and in his Providence, he has intended this couple for one another. When the couple say "I will", it should be with the spirit of the "*Fiat*" of Mary at the Annunciation: they should embrace enthusiastically God's will for them. Since marriage mirrors Christ's love for the Church, their nuptial love should deepen and strengthen their love for Christ. With his wonderful ability to draw out subtle connections, Knox links the command of Jesus for us to take his yoke upon us with the commitment of marriage. The Latin language describes husband and wife as yoked together, and the yoke of Jesus is not one he imposes on us—it is one he shares with us. Christ, bride, and groom are yoked together, and they must keep in step with one another.

---

[44] Ibid., p. 116.
[45] Ibid., p. 72.

Reference to the love of God brings us to one of Knox's favorite themes in his retreat conferences: the depth of God's love for us and how we should respond to it. He confided that he was tempted to translate the verse in the First Letter of John "God showed his love for us first" (1 Jn 4:10) as "God fell in love with us", but he did not have the courage to do so. He also noted that one of the things many people find off-putting in the devotion to the Sacred Heart was the sense of Jesus pleading for our love; and yet this too spoke of the passion of God's love for us. For Knox, Christians are the "spoiled children" of revelation: "we take it as the most natural thing in the world that God should want us to love him, instead of reminding ourselves that it is the most amazing act of condescension on his part."[46] God's generous love for us should incite a desire to love him in return to the best of our ability, but Knox cautions us not to measure the depth of our love by the intensity of our emotions—it is a matter of the will. He distinguishes between "spontaneous love", which is a matter of our feelings, and "deliberate love", which involves our choice. We may think that the saints experienced a passionate love for God, while our relationship to him strikes us as a marriage of convenience, but we should recall that the saints themselves endured periods of intense desolation. More importantly, Knox offers a piece of sound psychology: it is a mistake to try to turn deliberate love into spontaneous love. On the basis of his own spiritual experience, and from his work as a spiritual guide for others, Knox suggested a new beatitude: "Blessed are those who have not felt, and yet have loved."[47] He also was suspicious of those who were so caught up in their

---

[46] Knox, *Layman and His Conscience*, p. 34.
[47] Knox, *Retreat for Lay People*, p. 81.

desire for union with God that they neglected their neighbor. He urged people to be practical in their asceticism: "Don't aspire to become the sort of piebald saint who sleeps on a board and is not on speaking terms with his sister-in-law."[48] Love for God gives an appetite for love of neighbor, just as taking a walk gives an appetite for food.

Knox wanted people to be "alive to God" but recognized that we cannot always be thinking about him. The presence of God should be like a taste in the mouth or a perfume in the nostrils, which conditions our whole experience without our noticing it is there. He illustrates this attitude of habitual attention with the example of a dog: the presence of the master makes all the difference, even when it seems the dog is not apparently paying him any attention. A dog does not enjoy going for a walk without a human being to accompany it: "It wants, you see, a centre of reference. It is preoccupied with its own canine interests, and yet all the time it is half thinking of its master; if he finds some treasure in the hedgerow, an old boot, for example, *that* must be brought for the master's inspection and approval. . . . If he whistles, how it pricks up its ears! Everything must be referred to him."[49] If only we could be more like that, "walking through the world at God's heels"—sharing everything with him, every moment of sunshine or shadow of uncertainty. How to attain this? Knox admits it is a rare grace and urges us to pray for it. In terms of our own effort, he proposes that we cultivate short periods of silence in our day; just a few minutes here and there to call God to mind.

[48] Ibid., p. 198.
[49] Ibid., p. 20.

Conclusion

For both Knox and Lewis, the Christian life was an adventure that engages the whole of our being. Physical attraction, affection, friendship, romantic love, love of God—all of these have their part to play, and the key to happiness is to integrate them. They urged people to live generously and to see all human loves as grounded in God. The school of this love, the clinic in which we convalesce, the band with which we make earth's pilgrimage to Heaven is the Church. That the community intended by God as the meeting place of all human and divine loves should also be the source of discord and animosity was a source of great suffering for both Lewis and Knox and may have been the principal impediment to their becoming "Second Friends".

CHAPTER EIGHT

The Church

We come now to the most tantalizing issue in an imagined friendship between C. S. Lewis and Ronald Knox: the nature and place of the Church in their thought. For Knox, this was *the* defining matter of his personal pilgrimage; he struggled for years about this question, and when he came to the conclusion that the Roman communion was the Church founded by Christ, he joined it at great personal cost. When Lewis rediscovered the Christian faith, he returned to the Anglican communion of his childhood and was content to remain in it for the rest of his life. Knox wrote a great deal about the Church for several reasons: as a prominent figure in the Anglo-Catholic movement and as the son of an Anglican bishop, he felt his conversion called for some public explanation; as a writer and speaker, he was asked to defend the Catholic claims; and as a priest, he was charged with equipping Catholic students to profess their faith in a hostile environment. Lewis, for his part, did his best to avoid the subject of the Church. On a variety of topics, he was, in Austin Farrer's words, Oxford's "bonny fighter", but the question of Church membership was one he chose to steer clear of. As far back as 1934, he told his friend Bede Griffiths that he did not wish to correspond about Catholic-Protestant differences; and, when preparing the radio broadcasts that were to become *Mere Christianity*, Lewis had to be urged by the producer to say *something* about the Church.

Lewis' reticence is reflected in the scholarship about him. The subject of Lewis' ecclesiology is not addressed in Protestant studies of his thought, and the two major Catholic books (*C. S. Lewis and the Church of Rome* by Christopher Derrick and *C. S. Lewis and the Catholic Church* by Joseph Pearce) are concerned primarily with why he did not become a Catholic. Lewis' own response was characteristically direct: "The question for me (naturally) is not 'Why should I not be a Roman Catholic?' but 'Why should I?'"[1] Since Knox says so much and Lewis so little, how can we approach this vital issue?

A good starting place is to consider, not what they wrote, but what they did: how did our two authors practice their religion? Here, in spite of significant theological differences, we find important common ground. Both grew up in Evangelical families but came to appreciate more Catholic expressions of the faith. In Knox's case this led to the Roman Catholic Church (although it did not for his brother Wilfred, who remained an Anglican priest). Lewis felt no need to leave the Church of England, but throughout his life he identified increasingly with the more sacramental, Catholic elements of Anglicanism. Viewed from the Catholic perspective, it is understandable that the question is posed in terms of what prevented Lewis from "going all the way"; from the Protestant point of view, it is surprising that he went as far as he did. Tolkien believed that "Ulsterior" motives kept Lewis from becoming a Roman Catholic—but to begin life in "Puritania" and end up as a weekly communicant who went to confession, advocated prayers for the dead, and referred to the Eucharist as "the Blessed Sacra-

[1] Walter Hooper, ed., *The Collected Letters of C. S. Lewis*, vol. III (San Francisco: HarperCollins, 2007), p. 106.

ment" demonstrates how Catholic Lewis became in many ways. Both he and Knox never lost touch with the fervent, biblical roots of their Evangelical upbringing, and in spite of their differences about the "Roman claims", they might have recognized one another as kindred spirits. They each had close friends in the other's communion and would have respected one another's consciences on the matter.

It is also noteworthy how ordinary Knox and Lewis were in their church membership. They were two of the most articulate and popular spokesmen for their faith in the first half of the twentieth century, and yet they were happy to identify with the majority of their coreligionists. Although in *Surprised by Joy* Lewis confessed to a certain "antiecclesiastical" bias that made communal worship a bit wearisome to him, he willingly took part in daily chapel services at Magdalen College and in Sunday worship at his parish church. He liked the parochial setting because it did not lend itself, as congregationalism might, to factions; it created a community of place, not of tastes. He opposed both the liberal modernists and the conservative Anglo-Catholics on either end of the Anglican spectrum. Ronald Knox avoided championing any particular school of thought or movement in the Catholic Church and was content to enter into the life and worship of those with whom he lived, be it the community of Saint Edmund's College, the students at the Oxford chaplaincy, the schoolgirls at Aldenham, or the neighbors at Mells. Although of rather conservative tastes, Knox and Lewis were not preoccupied with liturgical minutiae, preferring simple, low-key services. They wanted to be "merely" Catholic and Anglican.

The Nature of the Church

When C. S. Lewis recovered belief in God (but was not yet a Christian), he felt the need to manifest this by attending church; he celebrated his return to Christian faith by receiving Holy Communion. Lewis described such activities as "flying the flag"—publicly expressing his belief. But he saw the Church as something far more than simply a meeting place for believers: she is the Bride of Christ and his Mystical Body. Lewis' rather high ecclesiology peeps out of his writings and led some readers to assume that he had become a Roman Catholic. Although he was reticent about the subject, we can gain some appreciation for his understanding of the Church when we examine the writings of one of his favorite theologians, Richard Hooker.

Hooker (1554–1600) was one of the principal architects of Anglican theology, and his book *Of the Laws of Ecclesiastical Polity* represents one of the first theological justifications for the Elizabethan Settlement. Hooker sought to articulate a position that avoided what he considered to be the excesses of Puritanism on one side and Papistry on the other. Because the war with Spain had put English Catholics under a cloud of suspicion, Hooker's *Ecclesiastical Polity* was directed primarily at Puritan objections to the Church of England. In contrast to the contention of some Reformers that the true Church consists only of "the elect" known to God alone, Hooker held that the Church is a visible community and that this community and the commonwealth were intimately connected. As a visible community, the Church has structures and institutions, and, again in contrast to the more extreme Reformers, Hooker stated that not all of these needed to be found explicitly in the Bible. He made two assertions that became fundamental to Anglicanism and help us to understand Lewis' conception of the Church. First, while truths of the faith that pertain to salvation are all to be found in Scripture, there are many matters of governance and ceremony that are not explicitly found there but that are permissible and may indeed be necessary. Second, reason and custom provide guidance in identifying these secondary matters. Provided that a particular custom or structure is not explicitly condemned in Scripture, it may be employed. He would not, with some Reformers, reject certain practices simply because they were "Romish". Nor, on the other hand, would he accept that ecclesial structures pertained to the essentials of the faith required for salvation; rather, they were part of the secondary "polity" of Church governance and could be accepted, rejected, or adapted as the judgment of reason, guided by tradition but always essentially grounded in Scripture, dictated.

Hooker describes the Church as the Mystical Body of Christ and his Bride, born from him as Eve was from Adam. But she is also a visible community with observable structures and an integral connection to the commonwealth: the universal Church is for Hooker comprised of national churches whose structures may vary provided that they institute nothing explicitly condemned in Scripture. Anglican scholars today debate whether Hooker was a Reformed theologian, a crypto-Catholic, or one of the first exemplars of the "via media" approach, which sees Anglicanism as a bridge between Protestant and Catholic doctrines. Given Lewis' reliance on him, it is not surprising that some readers presumed that Lewis had become a Roman Catholic and others wondered why an author with such an elevated ecclesiology was unconcerned about the structures of the Church. What did Lewis himself say about the Church?

In his first explicitly religious book, *Pilgrim's Regress*, a

central character is a woman identified as "Mother Kirk".
She is a mysterious figure, appearing both as an old crone
and a glorious queen; anyone who wishes to find Christ
must go to her, and she commands obedience. Given her
pivotal role in John's pilgrimage, it is understandable that
many readers saw this as a Catholic vision of discipleship;
when we note that Latin is her language, it is not surprising
that some people assumed the author had become a Roman
Catholic. One person who was greatly surprised by this assumption was Lewis himself. He felt the need in a subsequent edition to assure readers that his story favored no particular denomination and that he chose the name "Mother
Kirk" because "Christianity" did not seem to be a very con-
vincing name. No doubt a term like "Christianity" would
seem too cold and abstract in an allegory like this, but some
Catholic scholars suggest that a man of Lewis' imagination
could have devised a less "ecclesial" name if he had wished.
"Kirk" is a Middle English word for "church", and to be
sure, "Mother Church" is a Catholic expression; on the
other hand, "Kirk" also refers to the (Presbyterian) Church
of Scotland, so it could be argued that Lewis was uniting
Catholic and Protestant images in a very Anglican manner.

Whatever the precise attributes of the Church, however,
it is clear that for Lewis she is essential to Christian discipleship and can command obedience. Participation in the
life of the Church is not optional: "For the Church is not
a human society of people united by their natural affinities
but the Body of Christ, in which all members, however different (and He rejoices in their differences and by no means
wishes to iron them out), must share the common life, com-
plementing and helping one another precisely by their differences."[2] In a talk entitled "Membership", Lewis devel-

2 Ibid., p. 68.

ops this idea of the corporate nature of the Church, which he calls the Bride of Christ. The different members of this Body are distinguished first of all by their union with Christ himself, the Head of the Body, but they also have particular roles to play within the Body, which is a hierarchical community: "It delights me that there should be moments in the services of my own Church when the priest stands and I kneel."[3] This Church will outlive the universe, and in her each member also shall live forever. Organic images such as "Mother", "Body of Christ", and "Bride" suggest that for Lewis the Church is intimately involved in the saving mission of Christ, and our connection with her is an indispensable element of Christian life.

Lewis' reference to "my own Church" raises a crucial question: given the centrality, indeed the necessity, of the Church, where is she to be found? The devil Screwtape describes the Church as "spread out through all time and space and rooted in eternity, terrible as an army with banners."[4] The best weapon the demons can employ is factionalism, and although their efforts can never succeed in destroying the unity of the Church (for that unity comes from Christ, her Head), they can wound and weaken the Church. For this reason, Lewis always sought to avoid "denominational" arguments and felt that his proper provenance as a layman was to present the core beliefs of Christianity and not delve into confessional differences. While he did not simply identify "the Church" with the Church of England (for he recognized that his denomination, too, had its peculiarities that went beyond "mere Christianity"), he believed that Anglicanism was a viable expression of "the Church spread out through space and time" and that it avoided what he consid-

---

[3] C. S. Lewis, *The Weight of Glory* (San Francisco: Harper, 1980), p. 171.

[4] C. S. Lewis, *The Screwtape Letters* (New York: Macmillan Paperbacks, 1973 [1942]), p. 12.

ered the more extreme positions of Protestantism and Roman Catholicism. When addressing a gathering of Anglican clergy in Wales, he described liberal Protestantism and Roman Catholicism as two "unorthodox" extremes.

While Lewis had very close friends who were Catholics, he viewed Roman Catholicism as a faction. When his friend Alan Griffiths became a Catholic and wrote to Lewis about the "Roman claims", he responded: "You think my specifically Protestant beliefs a tissue of damnable errors: I think your specifically Catholic beliefs a mass of comparatively harmless human traditions which may be fatal to certain souls under special conditions, but which I think are suitable for you."[5] Years later he expressed his position more sharply, writing to an inquirer from the United States: "In a word, the whole set-up of modern Romanism seems to me to be as much a provincial or local variation from the central, ancient traditions as any particular Protestant sect is. I must therefore reject their *claims*: tho' this does not mean rejecting particular things they say."[6] He goes on to make a remarkable assertion: "But the great point is that in one sense there's no such thing as Anglicanism. What we are committed to believing is whatever can be proved from Scripture."[7] A disciple of Hooker, Lewis saw the Church to be comprised of all believers who assent to the saving truths to be found in the Bible; all other issues are a matter of "polity".

Lewis envisioned the various denominations as rooms in

---

[5] Walter Hooper, ed., *The Collected Letters of C. S. Lewis*, vol. II (San Francisco: Harper: 2004), p. 178.

[6] Ibid., pp. 646–47.

[7] Ibid., p. 647. The correspondent was not content with Lewis' reply and wrote again, but Lewis chose not to respond. H. Lyman Stebbins was received into the Catholic Church in 1946 and later founded Catholics United for the Faith.

a great house, and his desire in *Mere Christianity* was to lead the reader into the hall from which the doors open into these various rooms. Because the Christian faith is not simply a philosophy, it is necessary to enter one of the rooms, to participate in the life of an actual Christian community. However, although for Lewis any of the rooms is preferable to the hall, he concludes his description with a thought-provoking statement: "And above all you must be asking which door is the true one; not which pleases you best by its paint and paneling. In plain language, the question should never be: 'Do I like that kind of service?' but 'Are these doctrines true: Is holiness here? Does my conscience move me towards this? Is my reluctance to knock at this door due to my pride, or my mere taste, or my personal dislike of this particular door-keeper?' "[8] These were the questions Ronald Knox had wrestled with, and he too had envisioned the Church as a great house. But he came to believe that this one great house was the Catholic Church, of which the Church of England was an outbuilding, and that its door-keeper was the successor of that Apostle to whom Christ first had given the keys.

Knox begins his exploration by opening the New Testament and asking if Christ intended to found a Church, that is, a visible society of believers with a particular organization. He believes this was Jesus' intent and that the nature of this community is found in his teaching, above all in the parables. In these Christ speaks of "the Kingdom" of which the community of disciples is the nucleus, and Knox discerns three important characteristics in the Kingdom proclaimed by Jesus. First, although it is founded upon the existing Assembly of Israel, it embraces Gentiles as well as Jews:

[8] C. S. Lewis, *Mere Christianity* (New York: Macmillan, 1943), p. 12.

the latecomers to the vineyard receive an equal wage, the elder son should welcome the prodigal. Second, the Kingdom does not appear suddenly in its full splendor; rather, its final manifestation is preceded by gradual growth—leaven working in the dough, seed sprouting the field before the final harvest. Third, before its final manifestation, the Kingdom will not be perfect: tares grow among the wheat, there are foolish bridesmaids in the wedding party, and the dragnet takes in refuse along with the catch of fish.

Turning to the Acts of the Apostles, Knox finds there a self-contained and self-conscious body that seems able to face every situation with a wonderful sureness of touch: a replacement for Judas is chosen, deacons are designated to assist the Apostles, and a council is held, all on its own responsibility. Knox asks: "Is it credible that this peaceful, orderly development should not have been in line with the expressed intention of their Founder? Is it not plain that the Acts form a history spiritually continuous with the Gospels; and that the continuity of a single organized body, the Christian Church, which can easily be traced to the period of the Acts, is thus traceable to our Lord himself?"[9] Finally, he notes that although Saint Paul had never heard the preaching of Jesus about the Kingdom, he describes the attributes of the Church in the same way: she is a visible body, made up of Jew and Gentile, containing within herself an organic vitality and making present, albeit imperfectly, Christ himself.

Then he observes: "This good wine Christ has given us —it is only natural, in an imperfect world, that there should be some confusion about the labels."[10] Granted Jesus' in-

---

[9] Ronald Knox, *The Belief of Catholics* (New York: Sheed and Ward, 1953 [1927]), p. 126.

[10] Philip Caraman, ed., *University Sermons of Ronald A. Knox* (London: Sheed and Ward, 1963), p. 231.

tention to found a Church, where is that community to be found today? Because on earth this must be a visible society, Knox examines the four "marks" of the Church that are professed in the Nicene Creed: one, holy, catholic, and apostolic.

To say that the Church is one holds a double significance for Knox: there is only one Church of Christ, and this Church can never be divided:

> The Church has to be one, in the nature of the case, if it is to be a visible Church at all. Our Lord made certain promises, of vast moment, to his followers and to their successors. If there are to be two bodies of people, claiming with plausible arguments to be the true Church, then one must be right and the other wrong. . . . If, therefore, schisms happen within the body of Christendom, the result of such schism is not to produce two Churches of Christ; what you have left is one true Church of Christ and one schismatic body; otherwise, after all these centuries, we should no longer be certain that our Lord's promises held good.[11]

For most denominations, ecclesial unity is something that once existed and may come into existence again; in the case of the Catholic Church, it is a living reality. However, Knox acknowledges that both in the past and in the present this Catholic unity is far less perfect than it should be—popes and antipopes, controversies between Catholic nations, and rivalry between religious orders remind us how imperfect this unity is.

The note of holiness is elusive. How can this be claimed as a mark of the Catholic Church, when it is evident that people of outstanding sanctity are found in all Christian confessions and that the Catholic Church has at times scandalized the world with corrupt leaders and resorted to

[11] Knox, *University Sermons*, p. 58.

violence when dealing with those who oppose her? Knox agrees with both points: heroic disciples are to be found in every denomination, and it may be that the Catholic Church has a large percentage of unheroic Christians in her fold. (He readily admitted that it was probably safer to leave one's umbrella at the door of a Methodist church than of a Catholic one!) He then makes an important distinction: "Christians of any other denomination, if they describe that denomination as 'holy' at all (which they very seldom do), are referring in fact to the individual holiness of its members. Whereas when we talk about the Holy Catholic Church we aren't thinking, precisely, of the holiness of its members. We think of the Church as sanctifying its members, rather than being sanctified by its members."[12]

Regarding the catholicity of the Church, Knox has more in mind than the fact that the Roman Catholic Church is a worldwide organization; she is also a community that creates supranational loyalties. He would agree with Hooker that being born an Englishman gave you a right to belong to the Church of England, but adds: "If you will; but the fact that you are born a human being gives you a right to belong to the Church of Rome."[13] This bond of communion even unites enemies, as he observed in a sermon on the Eucharist preached during the Second World War: "The Blessed Sacrament, the Jerusalem of our souls, stands apart from and above all the ebb and flow of world-politics, its citizenship a common fellowship between us and those who are estranged from us, those who at the moment are our enemies. Our friends yesterday, our friends tomorrow—in the timeless existence to which that altar introduces us, they are

[12] Ibid., p. 233.
[13] Ronald Knox, *Anglican Cobwebs* (London: Sheed and Ward, 1928), p. 23.

our friends today."[14] Furthermore, the Roman Church is catholic in the variety of people she attracts. Rich and poor, learned and unlettered all find a place within her, and she is not a foolish mother who tries to make all her children like everything she likes, but she seeks to meet individual needs and desires. The variety of tastes is bound to cause friction, and Knox advises a potential convert that it is better to join the Church knowing that you hate a dozen things about her day-to-day life rather than in "a love-sick admiration of everything and anything she sanctions".[15]

Finally there is the mark of apostolicity. To speak of the Church as both catholic and apostolic sets up a paradox: the Church is presented as universal in scope and yet as tied to a set of doctrines handed down centuries ago in an obscure Roman province. The essence of apostolicity for Knox is the faithful handing on of this doctrine, but it is also expressed in the continuity of ordained leadership in the Church. While the latter point raises the question of the validity of Anglican orders from the Catholic perspective, Knox approached this question not so much in terms of validity as in terms of "mission". During his conversion struggle, Knox asked himself how he as an Anglican priest shared in the mission Christ had entrusted to his Apostles, and which was continued in the Church through their successors, the bishops. He posed the question this way: "Matthew Parker had sent me; who sent Matthew Parker?"[16] Plainly, he recognized, neither the Pope nor the universal episcopate had sent him.

---

[14] Philip Caraman, ed., *Pastoral Sermons of Ronald A. Knox* (New York: Sheed and Ward, 1960), p. 210.

[15] Ronald Knox, *Off the Record* (New York: Sheed and Ward, 1954), p. 143.

[16] Ronald Knox, "Why I Am a Catholic" in Hilaire Belloc et al., *Why I Am a Catholic* (New York: Macmillan, 1932), p. 62. Matthew Parker was the first Archbishop of Canterbury in the reign of Queen Elizabeth I.

Since the Anglican bishops of the provinces of Canterbury and York had all been appointed by the Crown in the sixteenth century to replace bishops in communion with the Catholic Church, Knox argued that Matthew Parker and his colleagues owed their commission to Queen Elizabeth, the head of the Church of England. This led him to conclude the following: "That the Church of England possesses valid orders may, from the non-Catholic point of view, be arguable. That it possesses no commission handed down to it by direct succession from the apostles is a plain matter of history."[17] Thus for Knox the term "apostolic" refers both to the content of the faith and to the body that professes that faith. Here is how he explained the relationship between these two elements in a letter written a few years after his conversion:

> I think your real issue . . . is this: am I to find out what is the *fides* and thus be in a position to label the people *fideles* or not at my discretion? Or am I to find out who are the *fideles*, and learn my *fides* from them? If the former, then you will have to thresh out every possible article of belief in light of 3 or 4 different competing systems of religion. If the latter, then you must find a body of Christians which, without first inspecting its beliefs, you can see to be descended straight from the Apostles. At least, that was my conclusion, and I could find no Body (in that sense) except the Roman Church.[18]

Since the *fides* pertains to revealed truth necessary to salvation, Christ must have made provision to guarantee that this doctrine would be preserved in its essentials throughout the

[17] Ibid., p. 63.
[18] Ronald Knox to Laurence Eyres, Aug. 30, 1920; in "Letters from R. A. Knox to L. E. Eyres", ed. by L. E. Eyres (Typescript: University of London, n.d.)

ages. What are these essential doctrines, and how are they safeguarded? This is the crux of the disagreement between Lewis and Knox.

Doctrinal Authority

Although Lewis shied away from denominational controversies, the doctrinal expressions of "mere Christianity" were important to him. He held that the great religious divide in England was no longer between Catholics and Protestants but between those who professed a religion with supernatural content and the conviction of salvation on the one hand and the proponents of liberal modernism on the other. The fact that his traditional doctrinal writings were positively received by professing Christians of diverse communions suggested to him that these people had more in common with one another than with the members of their denominations who were willing to compromise on matters of doctrine in order to be more up to date, and that it was from them that Christian reunion would come: "The world of dogmatic Christianity is a place in which thousands of people of quite different types keep on saying the same thing, and the world of 'broad-mindedness' and watered-down 'religion' is a world where a small number of people (all the same type) say totally different things and change their minds every few minutes. We shall never get re-union from them." [19] Lewis found himself in a delicate position: he championed the cause of dogmatic Christianity in opposition to liberalizing tendencies that were eroding the convictions of many believers, but his desire not to aggravate

[19] C. S. Lewis, "Answers to Questions on Christianity", quoted in Hooper, *C. S. Lewis: A Companion and Guide* (San Francisco: Harper, 1996), p. 554.

denominational differences led him to avoid or ignore some important doctrinal questions. Those whom he dismissed as advocates of "Christianity and water" could rightly ask on what basis he had decided that a doctrine that they considered outdated was still essential to Christian faith, while Lewis himself disregarded important doctrinal issues because they were divisive.

And if the modernists could be criticized for holding too little doctrine, was it possible to hold too much? In Lewis' view, it was—and this was his principal objection to Roman Catholicism. He voiced it, not in any of his religious books, but in his study of Spenser's *The Faerie Queen* in *The Allegory of Love*. There he suggests that Catholicism is allegorical and that allegory consists in giving an imagined body to the immaterial; the problem begins when symbolic walls become real:

> Then we have reached that sort of actuality which Catholics aim at and Protestants deliberately avoid. Indeed, this difference is the root out of which all other differences between the two religions grow. The one suspects that all spiritual gifts are falsely claimed if they cannot be embodied in bricks and mortar, or official positions, or institutions: the other, that nothing retains its spirituality if incarnation is pushed to that degree and in that way.[20]

For Lewis, Catholics and Protestants disagree about the degree of incarnation or embodiment that can be given to spiritual realities in the world of matter. Addressing a group of Catholics, Lewis suggested that from the Catholic point of view, the weakness of Protestantism is a formless drift that seems unable to retain Catholic truths, whereas: "To us the

[20] C. S. Lewis, *The Allegory of Love: A Study in Medieval Tradition* (London: Oxford University Press, 1938 [1936]), p. 323.

terrible thing about Rome is the recklessness (as we hold) with which she has added to the *depositum fidei*—the tropical fertility, the proliferation, of *credenda*."[21] What further troubled Lewis was that to become a Catholic meant to accept not only everything the Church has taught but whatever she might teach in the future: "It is like being asked to agree not only to what a man has said but to what he's going to say."[22]

To which Ronald Knox might have responded yes, because you have recognized that since Christ came to teach saving truth, he guarantees that his Church is protected from doctrinal error—not only in the past and present but in the future. When facing serious dogmatic contradictions between various Christian bodies, Knox held that there were two options: either examine their doctrines and join the Church whose views one agrees with; or identify the Church that has consistently exercised teaching authority and learn one's doctrines from her:

> Intellectually speaking, the position of one who 'submits to the Church' is that of one who has reached a satisfactory induction—namely, that the Church is infallibly guided into all truth—and can infer from it, by a simple process of deduction, the truth of the various doctrines which she teaches. He does not measure the veracity of the Church by the plausibility of her tenets; he measures the plausibility of her tenets by the conviction he has already formed of her veracity. Thus, and thus only can the human intellect reasonably accept statements which (although they cannot be disproved) cannot be proved by human reason alone.[23]

[21] C. S. Lewis, *Christian Reunion, and other Essays* (London: Collins Fount Paperbacks, 1990), pp. 19–20.

[22] Ibid., p. 19.

[23] Knox, *Belief of Catholics*, p. 144.

Knox held that the core of the faith was entrusted to the first community of believers but that with the passage of time, and in the light of new situations, the implications of that faith became more apparent. The question is, how to decide between contradictory interpretations of the deposit of faith?

This was a decisive question for Knox, but it seems it was an issue that Lewis chose to avoid. Lewis recognized that "Scripture alone" could not break the impasse, since the disputing parties could each appeal to the Bible. He found his warrant in a consensus among Christians based upon the Fathers, creeds, eminent thinkers, and liturgical texts: "What is most certain is the vast mass of doctrine wh. I find agreed on by Scripture, the Fathers, the Middle Ages, the modern R.C.'s, modern Protestants. That is true 'catholic' doctrine."[24] His assumption was that he could learn "the mind of the Church" from Anglicanism (although not exclusively there), and he appealed to this authority against clergy who were introducing into their parishes the practice of the veneration of saints. Lewis spent most of his life at Oxford, which Knox once described as "the Paradise of Anglicanism",[25] and it would have been relatively easy to identify religion there with "true 'catholic' doctrine" as Lewis understood it. What Lewis called liberal modernism has become much more widespread in Anglicanism since Lewis' death: revisions in the Book of Common Prayer, which was for Lewis not only a liturgical resource but a theological one as well; the decision to admit women to the priesthood and episcopate; major changes on important moral questions— and for these reasons some people ask, "If Lewis were alive today, would he still be an Anglican?" Obviously any answer

[24] Lewis, *Letters* II, p. 646.
[25] Knox, *Off the Record*, p. 115.

is speculative; but it may be that these changes would have forced him to confront the question of where authoritative Church teaching was to be found.

It is true that the deposit of faith is handed on in many ways: through the Bible, the sacraments, the teachings of the Fathers, and so on. Within the community of the Church, bishops possess a unique teaching authority as the successors of the Apostles. Lewis had an appreciation for the hierarchical structure of societies, and as an Anglican, he affirmed that bishops had an organic function in the Church, although he described it in rather dismissive terms: "An ecclesiastical hierarchy . . . [is] like a skeleton, important but the most mineral and dead part of the body."[26] For Knox, the teaching office of bishops is linked to their role as witnesses to the received traditions in their communities. When it is necessary to resolve a doctrinal dispute and bishops gather in council, it is primarily as witnesses and not as theologians that they do so. Most of the Fathers of the Church were bishops, but most bishops were not Fathers of the Church; their teaching function came, not from their theological acumen, but from their role as spokesmen for the doctrine held by their sees. And among these sees, one holds a unique position:

> The tradition of those cities, like Ephesus, where apostles took up their headquarters, are particularly valuable, because there the tradition is likely to have survived in its purest form. But Rome stands altogether by itself; for Rome has the tradition of that apostle who was commanded to "confirm his brethren." Its Bishop has a tradition of doctrine which is, by divine guarantee, immune from error as is the general tradition of doctrine collectively given to the Church.[27]

[26] Lewis said this in a conversation that is quoted in David Wesley Soper, *Exploring the Christian Mind* (London: Vision Press, 1963), p. 70.

[27] Ronald Knox and Arnold Lunn, *Difficulties* (London: Eyre and Spottiswoode, 1952 [1933]), p. 126.

There must be a "last word" in serious doctrinal disputes, and for Knox this must be the Bishop of Rome. The only alternative authority would be an ecumenical council, but for Knox this creates a circular argument: the only way to determine which councils are ecumenical is to know which are accepted as such by the Bishop of Rome. He goes so far as to say: "In a word, the *main* function of the Papacy in connexion with Christian doctrine is not to define infallible truths which haven't been defined by any council. It is to tell us which of the councils are genuine and which aren't."[28]

Not surprisingly, Lewis had little to say about the papacy, apart from expressing the thought to Bede Griffiths that nothing would give more support to the papal claims than to see the Pope actually functioning as the head of Christendom. In 1947 he began a remarkable correspondence with an Italian priest who was greatly interested in the cause of Christian unity—remarkable because it was conducted in Latin and because the priest has since been canonized. Saint Giovanni Calabria wrote to Lewis after reading *The Screwtape Letters* and shared with him his passion for Christian unity. Most of his letters no longer exist, but in one of them he must have spoken of the Pope as a "point of meeting" for Christians, because Lewis responded that Don Giovanni was begging the question: "For we disagree about nothing more than the authority of the Pope: on which disagreement almost all the others depend."[29]

Given his background and upbringing, Ronald Knox knew that along with theological objections to the papal office, his countrymen harbored deep-seated suspicions of Rome, fed

[28] Knox, *Off the Record*, p. 69.
[29] Lewis, *Letters* II, pp. 815–16.

by tales in the nursery, inflammatory pulpit rhetoric, and
the like; for example, Lewis always used the disparaging
term "Papist" when referring to Roman Catholics. Knox
was aware that many people viewed his Church as "a con-
spiracy to set up an unholy Roman Empire over the consciences of an enslaved race",[30] and he strove to describe the
role of the Pope in the Church in moderate terms. Anglicans
hold that the apostolic ministry is continued by the bishops;
why could they not see that the leadership among the Apostles that Saint Peter exercised is continued by the Bishop of
Rome? Regarding papal infallibility, he stated that the First
Vatican Council did not establish a practice, but it simply
defended the principle of the Roman Church's inerrancy in
matters of doctrine: the Pope does not enjoy some kind of
special inspiration but is providentially guarded when in certain circumstances he needs to identify what authentic Catholic tradition is. Knox also warned against exaggerating the
extent of papal infallibility, telling his Oxford students of a
companion in his own college days who was so convinced of
the infallibility of the Pope that no Anglican bishop would
ordain him, while the Catholic chaplain told him he could
not become a Catholic because he left no room for faith in
his belief system. More importantly, Knox invited his countrymen to see the Bishop of Rome as something more than
a spokesman for magisterial teachings:

> Did it never occur to you that we call the Pope the Holy Father
> because we think of him as our father? That the unity of the
> Church is not the unity of a machine but the unity of a great
> family? That our obedience to the Holy Father in that very
> limited range of affairs in which he demands our obedience
> is not that of a workman towards the foreman who will sack

[30] Philip Caraman, ed., *Occasional Sermons of Ronald A. Knox* (London: Burns
and Oates, 1960), p. 358.

him if he doesn't work, but it is that of children towards their father—each eager to outdo the others in showing affection; each eager to outstrip the others in anticipating his slightest wish? That we obey him in effect not because we fear him as the doorkeeper of heaven, but because we love him as the shepherd of Christians, of Christ's flock?[31]

In a sense, Knox was attempting the impossible: to breast the tide of four centuries of propaganda that painted the Pope as a malicious foreign despot hatching plots against freedom-loving Englishmen. More Newman's follower than Faber's, Knox eschewed the baroque forms of continental Catholicism and presented himself as a very ordinary English clergyman but one who recognized that the authority of the Pope was an integral part of the Church's life. It was only many years after his conversion that he visited Rome, offering as his excuse that it was better for a poor sailor not to know what goes on in the engine room.

Roman Catholic "Excesses"?

Lewis spoke of the "tropical fertility" of Roman doctrines, which to his mind went beyond "mere Christianity". For Knox, on the other hand, it is for the college of bishops united with the Pope, the successors of the Twelve and Peter, to determine what "mere Christianity" is, and Lewis' "belief that has been common to nearly all Christians at all times"[32] is for Knox the Catholic faith. But undoubtedly there was something "foreign" about the feel of Catholicism to many Englishmen, and Knox feared that this allowed them to see conversion simply as a matter of temperament: "If you love to exaggerate, to proclaim defiant paradoxes, to swim with

[31] Knox, *University Sermons*, p. 379.
[32] Lewis, *Mere Christianity*, p. 6.

the tide of exuberant spirituality which foams down in flood from the Seven Hills, then the Church of Rome is the place for you. It is otherwise if you are critical in your outlook, guarded in your judgments, tender towards the inherited prejudices and the robust common-sense of Protestant England. Rome is for the Roman-minded."[33] But if there are, in the Catholic fold, those who seek to enlarge the province of piety, lavish new titles on Our Lady, and extend the sway of papal authority, "there are others who keep a jealous eye on the documents of antiquity whose concern is to safeguard the balanced edifice of Christian doctrine",[34] and Knox was counted himself among this group. For this reason, it is interesting to imagine him discussing specifically Catholic beliefs with Lewis, who certainly was critical in his outlook, guarded in his judgments, and tender toward the inherited prejudices and the robust common sense of Protestant England.

Lewis' spiritual pilgrimage led him to an increasingly sacramental expression of Christian faith. One senses that he felt an undertow pulling him in the Catholic direction, and he resisted this by distinguishing his position from Roman Catholic doctrine. For example, in 1940 Lewis began the practice of going to confession on a regular basis. He wrote to Sister Penelope that the decision to do so was the hardest thing he had ever done, but he felt he should take up the discipline on the principle laid down by Saint Vincent of Lerins that Christians should abide by what has been held "everywhere, always, by everyone".[35] Now, although the Book of Common Prayer makes provision for confession in the celebration of the visitation of the sick, auricular confession has always been a very unusual practice among

---

[33] Knox, *Occasional Sermons*, pp. 237–38.
[34] Ibid., p. 239.
[35] Lewis, *Letters* II, p. 452.

Anglicans. (Before going up to Oxford, the young Ronald Knox had asked his father's permission to adopt it; while unsympathetic to the idea, Bishop Knox respected his son's conscience in the matter.) Lewis encouraged the practice, although he was hesitant to recommend his own confessor to others because he was "too Roman". He also distinguished his understanding of the Anglican view from the Catholic position: "where Rome makes Confession compulsory for all, we make it permissible for any; not 'generally necessary' but profitable."[36] In response it could be pointed out that, while the Catholic Church urges frequent confession, it is "compulsory" only once a year, and, strictly speaking, only if a person is conscious of mortal sin. Knox saw in the Church's practice a desire to inculcate "abiding penitence, not an hysterical outburst now and again",[37] and observed that the Catholic Church is criticized for laxity toward sinners: "The criticism urged against our present practice is not so much that auricular confession has outlived public confession (if it has not actually replaced it); rather, what has to be admitted is that the primitive Church was more exacting in its moral attitude than ours; that penances were real and protracted; that the sinner might even be refused absolution until the approach of death made its bestowal urgent."[38] Historically, the Roman bishops have always opposed rigorism and advocated leniency; the "compulsion" to celebrate this sacrament is in reality an expression of mercy.

In regard to the Eucharist, Lewis believed that Christ was truly present in the Blessed Sacrament and that reception of Holy Communion represented a privileged encounter with him: "I find no difficulty in believing that the veil between

[36] Lewis, *Letters* III, p. 320.
[37] Knox, *Pastoral Sermons*, p. 23.
[38] Knox, *Belief of Catholics*, p. 181.

the worlds, nowhere else (for me) so opaque to the intellect, is nowhere else so thin and permeable to divine operation. Here a hand from a hidden country touches not only my soul but my body."[39] Yet he regrets that definitions in this matter are allowed to divide Christian communities, and he is impatient with arguments about the manner of Christ's presence: "The command, after all, was Take, eat: not Take, understand. Particularly, I hope I need not be tormented by the question 'What is this?'—this wafer, this sip of wine."[40] But Jesus did not just say, "Take, eat." He said, "Take, eat: this is my Body." When a woman wrote to ask Knox why the words of institution should not be taken in a metaphorical sense, he responded that when we employ metaphor, the literal description of the thing is the subject of the sentence and the metaphorical description is the predicate. Thus in sentences like "I am the Door, the Way, the Light of the World", we can see metaphor, and the same could be said of "I am the Bread of Life", if we did not have the words spoken by Jesus at the Last Supper: "But when he says, 'This is my Body', it is impossible on grammatical principles to suppose that he is using a metaphor. It is either the truth or a lie."[41] The Eucharist was at the center of Knox's life both as a Catholic and as a priest; far from being "tormented" by the question "What is this?" he rejoiced in exploring the significance of the Body and Blood of Christ. Among his pastoral sermons collected by Father Philip Caraman, thirty-one are dedicated to the Eucharist. In the first of an annual series of sermons preached on the feast of Corpus Christi in 1926, Knox, too, spoke

[39] C. S. Lewis, *Letters to Malcolm Chiefly on Prayer* (San Diego: Harcourt, 1964), p. 103.

[40] Ibid., p. 104.

[41] Knox, *Off the Record*, p. 170.

of the Eucharist as a "veil" but in a way that expresses the richness of Catholic faith:

> We all know what veil it is that covers him now; it is the mystery which occupies our thoughts this morning. In this mystery of transubstantiation, he has broken into the very heart of nature, and has separated from one another in reality two elements which we find it difficult to separate even in thought, the inner substance of things from those outward manifestations of it which make it known to our senses. Burn all the candles you will in front of it, call to your aid all the resources of science, and flood it with a light stronger than human eyes can bear to look upon, still that white disc will be nothing better than a dark veil, hiding the ineffable light of glory which shines in and through the substance of Christ's ascended body. A veil, that is what we look at, a curtain drawn over the window, as you may curtain the windows of a sick-room, because the patient's eyes are not strong enough to face the full glare of daylight. But behind that curtain, all the time, is the window which lets our world communicate with the world of the supernatural. As the angels ascended and descended on Jacob's ladder, so here our prayers go out into the unseen, so here grace comes flooding through, like a rushing mighty wind, into the stagnant air of our earthly experience.[42]

Knox's sermons on the Eucharist present the profound doctrinal teaching of the Church in an imaginative, biblical way. Lewis feared that asking what "this" is removes the Eucharist from its context, and he likened it to taking a red coal out of the fire to examine it—it becomes dead. It could be argued that when Knox directed the minds and hearts of his hearers to what "this" is, he was gently blowing on the coal to make its heat and light penetrate them more deeply when they received Holy Communion.

[42] Knox, *Pastoral Sermons*, p. 205.

One of the most notable instances of Lewis' Catholic leanings is his belief in Purgatory, a process of purification after death that involves some kind of suffering:

> Our souls *demand* Purgatory, don't they? Would it not break the heart if God said to us, "It is true, my son, that your breath smells and your rags drip with mud and slime, but we are charitable here and no one will upbraid you with these things, nor draw away from you. Enter into joy"? Should we not reply, "With submission, sir, and if there is no objection, I'd *rather* be cleaned first." "It may hurt, you know"—"Even so, sir."[43]

Here Lewis is on very thin ice from an Anglican perspective, and his defense of his position is strained. He claims that the Reformers were right to throw doubt on "the Romish doctrine" of Purgatory, because by the sixteenth century, it had become simply a place of punishment, not purification. Lewis praises Dante's theology of Purgatory and rejoices that "the right view" returns in Newman's *The Dream of Gerontius*. His implication is that the Reformers did not object to the doctrine of Purgatory as such but to Romish exaggerations, which he finds exemplified in the writings of Thomas More and John Fisher.[44] In fact, the "Romish doctrine" was stated very simply in the sixteenth century at the Council of Trent: "There is a purgatory, and the souls detained there are helped by acts of intercession of the faithful, and especially by the acceptable sacrifice of the

[43] Lewis, *Letters to Malcolm*, pp. 108–9.

[44] At the time of his Anglican ordination, Knox was aware that some attempted to reconcile the Thirty-Nine Articles with Catholic doctrine by examining them in a legalistic way, looking for a loophole by means of faulty wording: "Thus I think it is contended that the 'Romish' doctrine of Purgatory, relics, etc., can be distinguished from the 'Roman' doctrine—the contemptuous word implies that the reference is only to abuses—and so on" (*Spiritual Aeneid*, pp. 95–96).

altar."[45] Whatever the real or perceived exaggerations of that doctrine by More and Fisher, the Catholic doctrine itself has remained consistent over the centuries, and it is this doctrine that the Reformers rejected.

On this subject Knox was addressing Catholics who believed in Purgatory; his purpose was not to justify that belief but to explore something of its meaning. He believed in Purgatory while still an Anglican, and in his lectures on the *Aeneid* in 1912, he described book 6, which recounts Aeneas' visit to the underworld, as a pagan foreshadowing of the doctrine.[46] Like Lewis, Knox recognizes that Purgatory must entail some kind of suffering, since it roots out the harmful effects of sin on our character, even in this life an uncomfortable and painful process. Both authors recognize that while God forgives us as soon as we are sorry for our sins, there remains the need to undo the harm our sins have done to us, and those wounds can be very deep. Knox says that we sometimes forget this when we think of the dead, because we have a natural charity in their regard: "We have said so much about them behind their backs while they lived . . . that we try instinctively to make up to them for it when they are gone."[47] Even the good actions for which people might praise us after we are gone—Knox wonders how much these actions were prompted by self-love. The purification will be intense, penetrating the depths of our being; the image of purifying fire is traditional, but it is the white-hot charity of the Sacred Heart of Jesus that purges the dross of our sinfulness.[48] Yet Knox does not dwell on the punishments of Pur-

---

[45] "Decree on Purgatory", 1563 (DS 1820).

[46] These lectures have never been published. However, the chapter dealing with Virgil's religious ideas was published in the *Ampleforth Journal* XXXV.2 (Spring 1930), pp. 109–29.

[47] Knox, *Pastoral Sermons*, p. 467.

[48] Ibid., p. 428.

gatory, preferring to emphasize it as a transitory experience leading to the glory of Heaven. He draws his inspiration, not from Dante, but from the ancient prayer of the Church: "Grant them, O Lord, eternal rest, and may perpetual light shine upon them." At first this seems to be a paradoxical request: our natures require both rest and light, but ordinarily when we need rest, we draw the curtains. Then he invites us to see the interlude between earth and Heaven under the image of an uneasy night between two stretches of daylight:

> Just as the cares of yesterday haunt us with their echoes and deny us sleep, so we can think of the soul which has left this world full of imperfections as longing for the echoes of those imperfections to die down in it, and restore its nature to equilibrium. And just as the mounting light of day seems to heal us, we cannot tell why, after a sleepless night—first the pale streaks, then the growing distinction between light and shadow, and at last the sun—so we may imagine the light of heaven, in some dim reflection, dawning on and into those immortal spirits which have still their heaven to attain. An interlude in which yesterday is forgotten, and tomorrow, somehow, grows gradually more real.[49]

And the severity of Purgatory is also relieved by the influence of Christ, who on Holy Saturday passed through the place of departed spirits: "I like to think of purgatory, however long and however dreary it be, as consoled in some measure by the consciousness that *he* has been there before us; as a process of passing onwards from room to room, always with the sense that the presence of the one we love has only just been withdrawn. Not strong enough, yet, to follow him out into the sunlight, we shall follow him eagerly

[49] Ibid., p. 474.

through the dark."[50] Knox articulates "the right view" of Purgatory, which is the perennial doctrine of the Catholic Church.

Lewis' acceptance of Purgatory flows from his practice of praying for the dead: "Of course I pray for the dead. The action is so spontaneous, so all but inevitable, that only the most compulsive theological case against it would deter me. And I hardly know how the rest of my prayers would survive if those for the dead were forbidden. At our age the majority of those we love best are dead. What sort of intercourse with God could I have if what I love best were unmentionable to him?"[51] In this approach Lewis replicates the experience of the Church at large: the theology of purification after death developed over many centuries and took different forms in the East and in the West; but this theology sprang from the primitive Christian experience of offering prayers for the dead. At the core of that experience is the conviction that Christ has broken the reign of death and that those who have died in the Lord continue to live in him. It is in prayer that we are closest to them, as Knox wrote in one of his monthly sermons in the *Sunday Times*: "It is only when we forget the dead that they are absent; we have but to kneel down, and they are present."[52] And, while the month of

[50] Ibid., p. 384. Fr. Philip Caraman felt it necessary to make the following clarification on this point: ". . . strictly speaking a distinction should be made between the Limbo into which Christ descended *after* his death, and Purgatory. Mgr Knox's 'fancy' should not be taken for a suggestion that our Lord passed through the state of Purgatory" (*Pastoral Sermons*, p. xii). Knox took correction well from theologians; he also believed that our analogies of the world to come are always childish, because we are still children in relation to that reality. His basic point here is that by embracing death Christ triumphed over death, and the repentant sinner can never be separated from him.

[51] Lewis, *Letters to Malcolm*, p. 107.

[52] Ronald Knox, *Lightning Meditations* (New York: Sheed and Ward, 1959), p. 94.

November is especially set aside by Catholics to remember their dead, Knox suggests that such prayers are not unique to Catholics: "You are praying, perhaps, if you take off your hat before the Cenotaph."[53]

Prayer not only makes us more aware of the presence of the faithful departed, but it enables us to assist them in their purification. Speaking to the schoolgirls at Aldenham, Knox reminds them of the fable of the lion caught in the net that was freed by a mouse:

> You and I are like that when we pray for the souls of Christians departed. They are much more splendid people than you and I are; they are already on the last lap of their journey home. But they are held up on that journey, and they can't help themselves; we can help them, and it isn't presumptuous to think of ourselves as helping them, even splendid people who have fallen gloriously in battle—we are the mice nibbling away at the bonds which hold them, that is all.[54]

The allusion to those fallen gloriously in battle reminds us that Knox delivered this sermon during the Second World War; but it also conjures up the memory of the close friends he had lost in the First World War, whose letters scrawled in violet pencil he read each Armistice Day.

Just as we can assist the faithful departed on the last lap of their journey home, so we can be helped by the prayers of those who have arrived. Knox told the schoolgirls that the Church is made up of All Saints, All Souls, and All Sorts. The saints—the canonized saints, but also the vast company known to God alone—have reached their home, but they

---

[53] Ronald Knox, *An Open-Air Pulpit* (London: Constable and Company, 1926), p. 185. The Cenotaph was erected in London to commemorate the fallen of the First World War. Every year on the Sunday nearest November 11, a memorial service is held at the monument.

[54] Ronald Knox, *The Creed in Slow Motion* (New York: Sheed and Ward, 1949), p. 202.

have not forgotten us. The Letter to the Hebrews says that as we run the race of faith, they surround us as a cloud of witnesses, but Knox suggests that they are not content with simply watching:

> Do they simply look on, and wonder which side will win? Is that the common attitude of spectators, when they watch an athletic contest? That is not my memory of the days, nearer thirty years ago than I care to think, when I used to watch football matches at the Aston Villa ground. My memory is rather of a small boy, wearing a claret-and-light-blue favour, who stood up on the seat and booed the referee. They are witnesses of our race, these martyrs of ours, but something more than witnesses, partisans who can cheer us to victory with the breath of their applause. For the applause of the saints is that prayer which goes up day and night before the throne of God.[55]

The saints help us with their prayers, "strong prayers, wise prayers, when ours are so feeble and blind."[56] In the communion of saints, we behold the Church as Lewis portrayed her in *The Screwtape Letters*, spread out through all time and space and rooted in eternity. In *Mere Christianity* he wrote that men are the mirrors and carriers of Christ to one another: "That is why the Church, the whole body of Christians showing Him to one another, is so important."[57] Asking the prayers of the saints could be seen as an instance of Lewis' "principle of Vicariousness", which holds that others can do for us what we cannot do for ourselves. He also touches on a possible justification for prayer to the saints in *Letters to Malcolm*, in which he writes: "Creation seems to be delegation through and through. He will do nothing simply

[55] Knox, *Occasional Sermons*, p. 107.
[56] Knox, *Pastoral Sermons*, p. 463.
[57] Lewis, *Mere Christianity*, p. 163.

of Himself which can be done by creatures."[58] And yet, although Lewis was forthright about the value of our praying for the dead, he was very circumspect about our asking the saints to pray for us. He recognized that the idea was theologically defensible but argued that it was dangerous and that it was a controverted question in the Church of England. He could find no warrant that God had promised us certain knowledge of the state of individual departed souls, and he invoked "the mind of the Church" against Anglican priests who, having judged that "our fathers erred in abandoning the Romish invocations of saints and angels",[59] introduced devotions to the saints. But other Anglicans could just as well appeal to "the mind of the Church" against Lewis' acceptance of the doctrine of Purgatory; and Orthodox and Catholic Christians might ask how Lewis could simply dismiss a tradition as ancient and widespread as the veneration of the saints.

If Lewis was reticent on the question of the veneration of the saints, he was explicit in avoiding discussion of the greatest of them, the Blessed Virgin Mary. In the introduction to *Mere Christianity*, he states that he is going to say nothing about her, because there is no topic more likely to wreck a book about mere Christianity: Roman Catholic beliefs about Mary are held with such a chivalrous sensibility that to dissent from them makes one appear to be a cad as well as a heretic; Protestant beliefs call forth feelings that go to roots of monotheism. (Despite assurances to the contrary by his Catholic friends, Lewis always believed that Papists worshiped the Virgin Mary.) Given both the theological and the emotional weight of the issue, he suggests that there is

[58] Lewis, *Letters to Malcolm*, p. 70.
[59] C. S. Lewis, *God in the Dock* (Grand Rapids: Eerdmans, 1970), p. 333.

no controversial question that needs to be so delicately handled as this. In practice, this meant that Lewis simply ignored Mary altogether, not only in his theological works, but in his studies of medieval and renaissance literature. Catholic commentators have marveled at his ability to avoid a figure so central to the culture that was his field of expertise. He did speak of Mary's place in salvation history on a couple of occasions. In his discussion of the Incarnation in *Miracles*, he describes the progressive selection by which God prepared the world for the coming of his Son: "The process grows narrower and narrower, sharpens at last into one bright point like the head of a spear. It is a Jewish girl at her prayers. All humanity (so far as concerns its redemption) has narrowed to that."[60] He extends this line of thought in a talk on the Psalms, in which he relates the Psalms of Judgment to the Magnificat and the demanding teachings of Jesus. Given the doctrine of the Virgin Birth, there is only one source for the human nature of Christ: "If there is an iron element in Jesus may we not without irreverence guess whence, humanly speaking, it came?"[61] That is all Lewis says of her from a theological perspective, and although that is enough to justify much Catholic teaching about Mary, to say anything more would be, for Lewis, to venture in the direction of Mariolatry. So, although the Blessed Virgin was prominent in medieval and renaissance culture, stood at the heart of the work of redemption, and might be expected to find a place in his imaginative theological writings, Lewis avoided talking about her. He seemed to share the consternation Bishop Knox voiced to his daughter at the devotional leanings of his sons: "Between ourselves, Winnie, I cannot

[60] C. S. Lewis, *Miracles* (New York: Macmillan, 1948), p. 141.

[61] C. S. Lewis, *Christian Reflections* (Grand Rapids: Eerdmans, 1967), p. 121.

understand what it is that the dear boys see in the Blessed Virgin Mary."

In his *Spiritual Aeneid* Knox tells us that his devotion to Mary was kindled in his Eton days. This did not emerge from any doctrinal conviction but simply from a sense of her patronage of the school: "Her name was part of our title; her lilies figured on our coat of arms; the blue of her robe you could see daily on the blazers of the Eight and the caps of the Eleven."[62] He did not see her as differing in glory from other saints but thought of her as having a special interest in him. At the time of his Anglican ordination, he made a private vow always to make some reference to her in his sermons, to make amends for the neglect of other preachers. Not everyone welcomed the efforts of High Churchmen like Knox to foster devotion to Our Lady. In one of his Anglican sermons, Knox relates a discussion between a bishop and priest on the subject, at the end of which the priest said, "Well, my Lord, what it comes to is this: I regard the Virgin Mary as the Queen of heaven, and you regard her as a dead Roman Catholic."[63] After his conversion Knox continued to cherish devotion to the Blessed Mother but with his customary reserve. He confessed that much literature about her and many popular devotions left him cold, and he found the word "Mariology" singularly depressing. He no longer felt the need to mention Mary in every sermon, but on the occasions when he did speak about her, his preaching was, as always, theologically solid and biblically grounded.

Could devotion to Mary be exaggerated? Knox believed it could, and he warned a group of young students that

[62] Ronald Knox, *A Spiritual Aeneid* (London: Longmans, Green and Co., 1918), p. 46.

[63] Knox, *University Sermons*, p. 480.

there are limits to the compliments we should pay her. He recalled working on a committee to revise the *Westminster Hymnal*; they were reviewing a hymn to the Blessed Mother by Father Faber, and one of the members observed, "The second verse of this hymn begins with the question, And art thou really infinite? The answer to that is, No." and they chose not to include the hymn.[64] Some Catholics rejoice in exuberant piety, while others do not—in Knox's opinion, the Church jealously guards doctrine but tolerates "a jumble of prayer-attitudes, as a Universal Church must."[65] He counseled a potential convert who found popular Catholic devotional practices distasteful that she should be prepared to go her way and let others go theirs; but as a Catholic, she would have to accept certain doctrines even if they did not assist her in her prayer life. He gives an example:

> If you become a Catholic now, you *might* find that in a year or two the Holy Father would assert his privilege of defining doctrine by laying it down that our Blessed Lady is the Mediatress of all graces. That is to assert, really, no more than we all believe, viz. that it was through her our Blessed Lord claims his kinship with Humanity, and that whenever we avail ourselves of his merits we are, in the nature of things, her debtors for the *Fiat mihi secundum verbum tuum* which made her the Accomplice of the Incarnation. I hope there will be no such definition, because it will lead to a great deal of barracking on the part of unfriendly polemists. But I should find no difficulty in accepting the doctrine as doctrine, although it would make no addition to my own prayer-life.[66]

[64] Ronald Knox, *The Gospel in Slow Motion* (New York: Sheed and Ward, 1949), p. 22.

[65] Knox, *Off the Record*, p. 149.

[66] Ibid., pp. 149–50.

Catholic devotion to Mary is built on solid doctrinal foundations, but it is also an affair of the heart: "She permeates the art, the poetry, the lives of Catholics with radiance as of a spring day, or of good news heard suddenly."[67] To the objection that Catholics deify Mary, Knox responded that the problem is not that Catholics exaggerate the eminence of God's Mother but that modern-day Protestants belittle the eminence of God: they refuse to honor the God-bearing Woman because to them Christ is only a God-bearing Man. From the Catholic perspective:

> We, who know that God could (if he would) annihilate every existing creature without abating anything of his Blessedness or his Glory, are not afraid lest the honour done to his creature of perfect Womanhood should prejudice the honour due to him. Touchstone of Truth in the ages of controversy, Romance of the medieval world, she has not lost, with the rise of new devotions, any fragment of her ancient glory. Other lights may glow and dim as the centuries pass, she cannot suffer change; and when a Catholic ceases to honour her, he ceases to be a Catholic.[68]

As Lewis suggested, discussion of the Blessed Virgin Mary can wreak havoc with "mere Christianity", and we may conclude this section by imagining him saying to Knox, "This idea that the Pope might proclaim Mary Mediatress is precisely what I object to—the Roman tendency to pile doctrine upon doctrine!" and Knox responding that, while he would not favor such a definition, it would be asserting nothing more than what Lewis himself said about Mary in *Miracles*: she stands at the heart of the work of redemption in "the Great Miracle" of the Incarnation.

[67] Knox, *Belief of Catholics*, p. 194.
[68] Ibid.

Conclusion

As we conclude this chapter, it is appropriate to underscore how much Lewis and Knox had in common in their understanding of the Church—and how much they did not. To begin with what they had in common, here is how Knox described the Church in a sermon on the Good Samaritan:

> The Samaritan sets his patient on his own beast to bring him to the inn; see once more how helpless the wounded man is, how he has to have everything done for him. Grace comes to us, not we to grace. And the inn where he is to make his recovery can be nothing else than the Church which Christ our Lord left behind him. The Church triumphant is the home to which we look forward; the Church militant is the inn, the temporary resting-place in which we find shelter from the storms of this travel-stained and transitory world. Three things above all we shall look for in the inn—refreshment, good company, and repose. What refreshment this inn of the Church gives us, as we feed upon the body and blood of Christ! What company, as we are knitted together in its holy fellowship with all God's chosen people in this world and beyond—our boon companions at the divine altar! What rest for sin-worn consciences, when scruples and doubts and fears are lulled by the murmur of absolution, and we can draw free, deep breath once more! We are all convalescents, recovering by degrees from the terrible blow sin dealt to us, building ourselves up and making the most of our time till the good Physician gives us our discharge and we are fit to travel safely home.[69]

The themes and the imagery could be Lewis' own; but then Knox continues: "The innkeeper stands for St Peter and

---

[69] Knox, *Pastoral Sermons*, p. 84.

his successors. To them, as having the care of this inn, this convalescent home, his Church, he leaves the stipend that is to see us through our time there—bequeaths to us the inexhaustible treasure of his merits."[70] Here they part company: they had a similar understanding of *what* the Church is, but they disagreed about *where* the Church is.

The conversation has reached an impasse. It might be best to conclude by listening to our authors each praise one of his heroes, for in their praise they express how they view the Church. Here is what Lewis has to say about Richard Hooker:

> Hooker is never seeking for "the true Church", never crying, like Donne, "Show me, deare Christ, thy spouse". For him no such problem existed. If by "the Church" you mean the mystical Church (which is partly in Heaven) then, of course, no man can identify her. But if you mean the visible Church, then we all know her. She is "a sensibly known company" of all those throughout the world who profess one Lord, one Faith, and one Baptism (III.i.3). None who makes that profession is excluded from her. . . . In this Church we have always been and still are. We have not left her by reforming ourselves, nor have the Papists left her by their corrupt "indisposition" to do likewise (III.i.10). No doubt many of the questions which Hooker treats are what we should now call questions between "denominations". But that is not how he envisages the matter. He is not, save accidentally, preaching "a religion"; he is discussing the kind and degree of liberty proper to national churches within the universal, visible Church.[71]

[70] Ibid.

[71] C. S. Lewis, *English Literature in the Sixteenth Century, excluding Drama* (Oxford University Press, 1954) p. 454. Citations in parentheses refer to sections of Hooker's *Ecclesiastical Polity*.

Lewis' account of Hooker's ecclesiology is a description of his own. Although it satisfied him, it did not satisfy Ronald Knox, nor John Henry Newman before him. Hooker may not have felt the need to find "the true Church", but Knox and Newman did—and they found it in the Roman Catholic Church. Occasionally Knox preached about Newman's conversion, and although he rarely referred to himself in his sermons, one senses an autobiographical undercurrent in these talks. In one sermon, he describes Newman's losses, above all the sacrifice of prominence in an important intellectual movement and the loss of dear friends. What did he gain? "What he gained, the only thing he substantially gained, the only thing it mattered to gain, was the consciousness of telling, of living the truth. He went where he belonged; that is all the convert asks; all that the convert *can* ask with safety."[72] Knox concludes:

> And yet, for us Catholics, truth is something homelier and friendlier than bare intellectual conviction. Revealed truth does not merely claim the homage of our intellects, it satisfies the aspirations of our hearts. What Newman gained in 1845 was not the mere saving of his own intellectual honesty; it was a system of spiritual values which lit up the world for him; not a cold glare but a warm blaze, a kindly Light which made the darkness more congenial than the garish day he loved once. . . . He followed truth, not as one who demands mere leadership; it was a wine he thirsted for, he was love-sick for its romance. His great name live imperishable in the annals of the Church, a man who lived haunted by the truth, and died desiring it.[73]

[72] Knox, *Occasional Sermons*, p. 249.
[73] Ibid., p. 250.

CHAPTER NINE

Prayer

The little boy watched the elderly man walking back and forth in the garden, book in hand. "What are you doing, Ronnie?" the boy asked. "I'm praying", he answered. "No, *that's* not how you pray!" Kneeling down, the four-year-old folded his hands and said, "*This* is how you pray." Fifty years later, Raymond Asquith smiles at his boldness at giving spiritual pointers to one of the most eminent Catholic spiritual writers of the twentieth century. One suspects Knox himself admired the combination of solemnity and spontaneity in a child's prayers.

It could be argued that, whatever his other accomplishments, Ronald Knox's greatest desire was to deepen the spiritual life of his readers. He was first and last a priest and strove to speak of God's love for us and elicit our love for God in return. The audiences were varied: schoolgirls, university students, throngs in Westminster Cathedral, small gatherings at some parish church—and to them all Knox spoke of the love that is at the heart of the Christian life. Sermons, retreat conferences, and brief meditations in the *Sunday Times* were collected and published so that readers could avail themselves of the instruction others had been privileged to hear. These thousands of pages continue to provide solid, biblical, and insightful spiritual guidance.

His prodigious efforts as a translator were dedicated to the same purpose. At the forefront stands his translation of the

Vulgate Bible. Knox had imbibed a deep love of Scripture from his Evangelical upbringing, and he was concerned that many Catholics did not seem to share this: "In my experience, the laity's attitude towards the Bible is one of blank indifference, varied now and again by one of puzzled hostility."[1] As for his brother priests, he observed that when he asked to consult the Bible on some point, the request seemed to prompt a certain amount of rummaging around. The charge of Catholic ignorance of the Bible can be exaggerated, but Scripture has not held the place in most Catholics' devotional life that it does for Protestants, and Knox hoped that a modern version of the Catholic Bible would help change that situation. Although eclipsed by more recent translations, Knox's Bible was very popular in its day, and it was used in the production of missals, prayer books, and breviaries that also made the treasury of the word of God more accessible to Catholics. In addition, Knox's commentaries on the New Testament nourished the spiritual life of many. He translated the texts of the Holy Week liturgy in 1951, and the revised Easter Vigil texts several years later, as well as nearly fifty Latin hymns for the *Westminster Hymnal*. At the request of the English bishops, he produced a translation of the *Manual of Prayers* that contained the extraliturgical texts authorized for public services, although this turned out to be an ill-fated project and was withdrawn. His last published work was a translation of *The Story of a Soul*, the autobiography of Saint Thérèse of Lisieux; and he was still at work translating *The Imitation of Christ* when his final illness overcame him.

---

[1] Ronald Knox, *Trials of a Translator* (New York: Sheed and Ward, 1949), p. 21. Published in England as *On Englishing the Bible*.

It is not unusual for a priest to dedicate his energies to fostering the spiritual life of his people (although this should not be presumed: Knox observed in a retreat for priests, "The laity at large have the impression, and rightly, I think, that we priests know our job. I sometimes wonder whether they have the same confidence that we know our Employer"[2]); that a lay Oxford don should write about prayer is surprising. And yet C. S. Lewis wrote about the spiritual life, too, and his last book was *Letters to Malcolm: Chiefly on Prayer*. Although the book was published posthumously, Lewis began exploring the idea of a book about prayer as far back as 1952. His intended audience was primarily adult converts to the faith who did not have inherited habits and patterns of prayer. Although Lewis was not in Holy Orders, he felt that his "amateur" status could be a help rather than a hindrance: "The fellow-pupil can help more than the master because he knows less. The difficulty we want him to explain is one he has recently met. The expert met it so long ago that he has forgotten."[3] Knox, too, saw himself as a "fellow-pupil" with other Christians; both he and Lewis were able to offer helpful guidance in prayer because they could share their own spiritual struggles.

Most of this chapter will treat the topic of personal prayer, because that is primarily what our authors wrote about. Liturgical prayer was important to them, but they did not write much about it. One notable exception is Knox's *The Mass in Slow Motion*, a reflection on the various prayers and ceremonies of the Mass; but even here he offers the disclaimer that he knows nothing about liturgy and that his

[2] Ronald Knox, *The Priestly Life* (New York: Sheed and Ward, 1958), p. 29.

[3] C. S. Lewis, *Reflections on the Psalms* (New York: Harcourt, Brace and World, 1958), p. 1.

intention is simply to share ideas that might be helpful to
personal prayer. However, the patterns of liturgical prayer
shaped the spirituality of Knox and Lewis, and their reticence to write about it should not obscure this fact. The
Eucharist (weekly for Lewis, daily for Knox) was at the
heart of their spiritual lives, and the Psalter was their fundamental prayer book because of its use in the breviary and
the Book of Common Prayer. As a young Anglo-Catholic,
Knox prayed both the Latin breviary and the Offices from
the Book of Common Prayer, and in his *Spiritual Aeneid* he
says that during his struggles prior to becoming a Catholic, the Psalms were his principal spiritual reading; in 1919
he published a small collection of meditations about them.[4]
Lewis for his part attended matins every morning in term,
and by his constant use of the Psalter knew most of it by
heart; he also produced a book on the subject, *Reflections
on the Psalms*. They each translated Psalms—Knox for his
Bible, Lewis as part of a committee to revise Coverdale's
translation used in the Book of Common Prayer.[5]

At the outset of *Letters to Malcolm*, Lewis states that he
is not going to write about liturgical prayer (and then pro-
ceeds to address the rest of the chapter to the subject!); but
an important topic it brings up is the relationship between
"ready-made" and "homemade" prayers—that is, between
set prayer texts and one's own personal reflections. By their
very nature, public prayers are set texts, but it is also customary for many people to recite prayers privately. While

---

[4] Ronald Knox, *Meditations on the Psalms* (London: Longmans, Green and
Co., 1919). The brief meditations follow the pattern of three points, acts, and
a colloquy, and the arrangement of the Psalms moves to increasingly interior
levels of the spiritual life.

[5] Another member of the committee was T. S. Eliot, and the opportunity
to work together put him and Lewis on friendly terms with one another.

Lewis prefers praying in his own words, he sees several advantages to using set prayers as well: they keep us in touch with sound doctrine; they expand the horizons of our intentions; and they introduce an element of reverent ceremonial into our communication with God. Furthermore, they help us when our own abilities fail us. But the words are secondary: "They are only an anchor. Or, shall I say, they are the movements of a conductor's baton: not the music."[6] Knox makes a similar point about the Rosary, telling schoolchildren that the purpose of the beads is to occupy their fingers, and the Hail Marys to occupy their lips, so that their minds are free to meditate on the mysteries of the life of Christ. He also points to one of the pitfalls of set prayers when he suggests that for some people the temptation is not to say the Rosary but to get it said. The words of prayers are, or should be, a means and not an end. One helpful practice is what Lewis calls "festooning"—decorating the text of a prayer with personal reflections; he uses the Lord's Prayer as an example. Knox does something similar with liturgical hymns in some of his retreat conferences.[7]

Our authors devote little attention to techniques of prayer. Postures, such as kneeling, can aid in prayer; certain locations might be more or less conducive to creating a prayerful atmosphere. (Lewis found it difficult to pray in an empty church because invariably someone was practicing the organ or cleaning; Knox found praying in the presence of the Blessed Sacrament helpful.) They read spiritual books, but

---

[6] C. S. Lewis, *Letters to Malcolm* (San Diego: Harcourt, 1964), p. 11.

[7] For example, the *Salve Regina* in *Retreat for Priests*, pp. 177–79; the *Veni, Sancte Spiritus* in *The Layman and His Conscience*, pp. 60–63 and the *Rerum Deus tenax vigor* in *The Priestly Life* pp. 115–23. His own meditations on the Lord's Prayer can be found in a series of five talks in *Pastoral Sermons* (pp. 3–29).

both admitted to difficulties with formalized "meditations" because their imaginations tended to stir up what Knox described as "a hornet's nest of distractions"; and he added that "these considerations, which are so thoughtfully designed to set my intellect at rest, have the effect of making it romp about like a kitten."[8] Knox gave retreat conferences on prayer, but his concern is principally to encourage "liberty of spirit" in prayer rather than recommend particular methods. Again, it is a matter of means and ends, and Knox felt that the danger for many Catholics, especially those who went on retreats, was the temptation to become preoccupied with how they were praying. He counseled that if someone felt he had been distracted while saying a prayer, he should not say it again—simply offer the prayer to God and move on; the alternative approach could lead to scrupulosity. At Mass, he asked, is it better to exercise the mind and consider the meaning of the readings and prayers or to exercise the heart and simply enjoy being in the presence of God? Knox replies, "The golden rule is that there is no golden rule": what is best is what brings you closer to God here and now.[9] The way to deal with distractions is to treat them like wasps: the more you wave your arms around, the more they keep buzzing around; it is better just to ignore them.

Prayer is simply communion with God, and we should make use of whatever helps to attain that end. It is easy to say, "Put yourself in the presence of God", but our authors found that simple directive troubling. Lewis devotes the fifteenth chapter of *Letters to Malcolm* to this deceptively straightforward idea. His starting point is the consideration

[8] Ronald Knox, "Prayer: II: The Prayer of Acts and the Prayer of Stupidity" in *The Clergy Review* vol. XVII no. 1 (July 1939), p. 3.

[9] Ronald Knox, *Retreat for Beginners* (New York: Sheed and Ward, 1960), p. 117.

of two realities: "the bright blur" that is God, and myself. Then, he says, I must banish the blur, break the idol, and recognize that these seem to be phantasmal products of my own devising. Next I step back and consider the "reality" of my physical surroundings and myself sitting in this room. Yet there is more here than meets the eye: scientists tell us that the foundation of this resistant matter is mathematics, and psychologists tell us that there is a vast sea of unconsciousness beneath the being I call "me". Now, having plumbed something of these depths, Lewis says I am ready to put myself in the presence of God: either the mystery of the material world or the mystery of myself points back to the creative hand of God. It is this Creator I meet in prayer: "The two façades—the 'I' as I perceive myself and the room as I perceive it—were obstacles as long as I mistook them for ultimate realities. But the moment I recognized them as façades, as mere surfaces, they become conductors."[10] Prayer comes when I realize that this "real world" and "real me" are not the rock-bottom realities: beneath this stage set and my role on it, the real me addresses, "not the other actors, but—what shall I call Him? The Author, for He invented us all? The Producer, for He controls all? Or the Audience, for He watches, and will judge, the performance?"[11] Knox compares prayer to an aside made by an actor to the audience: while nothing seems real but the brilliantly lighted stage, in fact the real people are in the darkness, and the actor's asides bear witness to this truth. The purpose of prayer is not to escape from time and space but simply to become aware that I am a creature and that here and now, in this time and place, I am in communion with my Creator.

[10] Lewis, *Letters to Malcolm*, p. 80.
[11] Ibid. p. 81.

Knox offers a meditation on the presence of God, and although he follows a different path from Lewis', he reaches a similar conclusion. He first considers several dead ends. Does the instruction mean, "Put yourself in the presence of God"? No, because we are always in the presence of God. Does it mean, "*Feel* that you are in the presence of God"? This is very hard to do because it calls for imagination, and we cannot begin to imagine the infinite, creative presence of God. Knox's starting point then becomes, as for Lewis, somewhat philosophical: "We don't know much about the nature of God, and what we do know is terribly remote, terribly elusive. But still, we do know something, partly from natural philosophy, partly from revelation. Can't we somehow mobilize that knowledge, so that the idea of God, always present, will sink into us?"[12] Then he poses a simple question: Do you pray with your eyes shut, or with your eyes open? Both approaches are legitimate; the first seeks to focus on God without the distractions of creatures, while the second sees creatures as leading to God. Although both approaches have value, Knox suggests that most of us find it more helpful to find God *in* his creatures rather than by forgetting his creatures. This is partly because creatures are difficult to forget: even when we close our eyes, it is easy to conjure up mental images that are just as distracting as the pictures we receive from sight. More importantly, we find it hard to "face up" to the thought of God: "We have to think about something else, and look at God, as it were, out of the corner of our eyes."[13] On a lovely spring day we do not talk about how beautiful the sun is; we talk about how beautiful everything looks in the sun. Knox suggests

[12] Ronald Knox, *The Layman and His Conscience* (New York: Sheed and Ward, 1961), p. 46.

[13] Ibid., p. 49.

the following change in the formula: "Put yourself in the presence of something else, and find God there." In this way, even our distractions lead us back to God:

> For instance, your eyes are caught by the flowers on the altar, and you say to yourself, "Good gracious, here I am with only a few minutes to spend in church, and I start thinking about the flowers!" No, don't say that; think about the flowers and let them take you to God. That one on the left is drooping rather; they'll all be drooping soon—what a short time flowers last! Flowers? So do we, for that matter. . . . And then your mind travels back to yourself as part of the impermanent world, and then it travels off again outwards, and sees as the background, as the obverse of all this impermanence, that eternal being which is God's. Eternal God, brought near to me in the sight of a flower on the altar—you have not really been wasting your time. Your mind has only been like an aeroplane, taxiing before it can be airborne.[14]

Lewis echoes this advice when he thanks Malcolm for teaching him the principle of beginning where you are: "I had thought one had to start by summoning up what we believe about the goodness and greatness of God, by thinking about creation and redemption and 'all the blessings of this life.' You turned to the brook and once more splashed your burning face and hands in the little waterfall and said, 'Why not begin with this?' "[15]

Awareness of God brings in its wake adoration, gratitude, and sorrow for sin. Or it should prompt such reactions, but do they come naturally to us? Knox suggests that adoration must have been a spontaneous reaction for Adam when he first opened his eyes on the world God had made for him: "As the new-born child turns towards its mother, his soul

[14] Ibid., pp. 49–50.
[15] Lewis, *Letters to Malcolm*, p. 88.

will have turned towards the hand that had but now fashioned it—God, the source of all life and all being; how great, how wonderful, how worthy to be praised!"[16] Adoration and gratitude go together, and he urges us to strive for something of the simplicity of the saints like Francis and treat all of God's gifts as surprise gifts. Lewis for his part confesses that when he was going through his conversion, he was troubled by the talk about praising God because it seemed to suggest God was some kind of egomaniac, a dictator who had to be flattered and appeased. Later he came to see that we are called to *enjoy* communion with God and that enjoyment spontaneously overflows into praise; to fully enjoy is to glorify. But in our fallen condition, this takes effort: we can look back to Paradise before the Fall, or ahead to Heaven, where we will be "drunk with, drowned in, dissolved by"[17] the love of God. In our earthly state, we are still tuning our instruments, not riders yet but students in riding school. Praise is our duty, and it requires discipline; this is why, Knox points out, we have to be commanded to love God: it is not a question of feelings but of the will.

As to sorrow for sin, Lewis describes a spectrum from a "low" pagan wish to placate an offended divine power to an elevated desire to restore an infinitely valued relationship. But even the "low" expression finds its place in Judeo-Christian religion. The imagery of a vengeful God is the flip side of a loving, personal God: "Hot wrath, hot love. Such anger is the fluid that bleeds when you cut it."[18] Lewis admits that he is ambivalent about the Puritan tendency to dwell on one's corruption in the presence of God: it may be a helpful "spiritual emetic" occasionally but not as a reg-

[16] Knox, *Layman and His Conscience*, p. 112.
[17] Lewis, *Reflections on the Psalms*, p. 96.
[18] Lewis, *Letters to Malcolm*, p. 97.

ular practice. Knox suggests something akin to what Lewis speaks of, although he suspects that the theologians will haul him over the coals for it: "But I think the thing we love [in ourselves], the thing we ought to detest, is something of which we are only partly conscious, and our love for it is a partly conscious love. It is not an image which we set before our minds, it is an idol at the back of our minds, hidden away and swathed round with rags of pretence. And it is in the dark recesses of our minds that we go on worshipping it."[19] This is the part of ourselves that lashes out when we are annoyed or reaches out for some attraction to the senses —it is there all the time, only we forget we are adoring it. Most of us, he says, will probably never rid ourselves of this tendency, even as we fight against temptations. But some receive the grace of a "second conversion": "Whereas those who have crossed the line have achieved a kind of poise, a kind of equilibrium, that is quite different; they still have temptations, and sometimes yield to them, they still have sinful tendencies, but they have fallen out of love with their sins. Corrupt nature is no longer their romance."[20] This second conversion is God's gift, but the desire for it comes from spending time in his company.

The Prayer of Petition

The prayer of petition received a great deal of attention from both Lewis and Knox. In part, this is because it is such a common form of prayer: "I suppose about ninety per cent of our fellow-countrymen, when they talk about prayer, mean

[19] Ronald Knox, *A Retreat for Lay People* (New York: Sheed and Ward, 1955), p. 186.
[20] Ibid., p. 187.

asking God to give them things."[21] While it may be otherwise with the mystic, for the rank-and-file believer it is
important that God takes an interest in the welfare of his
creature; hope is the natural food of faith. It is more generous to love God for himself rather than for his gifts, but in
Enthusiasm Knox surveyed some of the vagaries in the history of Christian spirituality when that laudable principle is
carried too far. "Disinterested love" is a worthy ideal, but
when it leads to a desire to be damned if such be God's will,
it has broken out of the traces of Christian faith. On the
other extreme, Knox found personalities and movements
that were preoccupied with the desire for constant signs of
the divine will. Knox's study was an exploration of these
two extremes: "There are two spiritualities: one which is
too generous ever to ask, and one which is too humble ever
to do anything else."[22] Between these two extremes, most
people seek to live their lives to the best of their ability but
also turn to God in their needs. If to the mystic this is a
"low" form of prayer, it is not to be despised: both Knox
and Lewis point out that Christ taught the prayer of petition
by word and example.

While the prayer of petition is common to many religions
and was encouraged by Christ himself, it raises several questions. If God is omniscient, does he not already know what
we need? To be told to make our requests to God and to
pray, "Hear us", seems to suggest that either God does not
know what we need or he needs to be reminded. In answer to this objection, Lewis points out that we are always
known by God: prayer is the expression of *our* awareness of
that truth; it is an "unveiling" by which we assent to being

[21] Ronald Knox, "Prayer: I. The Prayer of Petition and the Prayer of Acts",
in *The Clergy Review*, vol. XVI, no. 6 (June 1939), p. 485.
[22] Ronald Knox, *Enthusiasm* (Oxford: Clarendon Press, 1950), p. 579.

known by God and acknowledge our personal relationship with him. Second, if God is good, and what we desire is good, will he not give it to us even if we do not ask for it? Lewis' response is that the logical conclusion of such reasoning would be to ask why we should do anything at all. Whether we act or pray, in either case we are cooperating with God's creative work. Knox responds to this objection by distinguishing between spiritual and temporal goods. As regards the former, God always gives us grace sufficient for salvation, but other spiritual blessings are granted to a greater or lesser degree, dependent in part on our ability to receive them; to ask frequently for spiritual gifts expands our capacity. As to temporal blessings, often there is more than one "best" course open to us, and prayer helps us to discern how to use the temporal gifts for which we ask.

Another question is this: Do my prayers "change" God? Some biblical language seems to imply this, but both Lewis and Knox hold that such a view labors under the misunderstanding that God is bound by time. But God is outside time altogether, so our prayers were heard "at the foundation of the world": the relationship between our prayer and the course of events is inherent in the very act of creation. While this might seem extraordinary, Lewis again draws the parallel with human actions. If we believe that God's Providence takes into account the actions of men, why can it not also take into account their prayers? The obstacle is the limitation of our imagination: we simply cannot conceive what it is like to be "eternal", that is, completely outside time. A related question is this: Do my prayers change the course of events, and if so, how? Lewis and Knox recognize that there is no empirical proof that they do and that our certitude in such matters is more psychological than logical. Lewis asks what kind of evidence could prove that prayer works, and he says that if someone were to conduct an experiment—for example, praying for patients in hospital A and not praying for them in hospital B—this would not be prayer at all: its real purpose would be, not to pray, but to find out what would happen.[23] From the Christian point of view, petitionary prayer is a request; it is neither magic nor medicine.

Such requests are based upon a personal relationship with God and the conviction that God has created rational beings to play an active role in his creation. His purposes take in the actions and prayers of his creatures. Knox says that this partnership is an expression of God's "courtesy" in our regard and compares our role in the world to the corner of a well-manicured garden that is left for the children to tend. As noted earlier, Lewis goes so far as to say, "For He seems to do nothing of Himself which He can possibly delegate to His creatures."[24]

These general questions about the prayer of petition take on a unique focus when we consider the experience of Jesus in Gethsemane. Before considering that event, however, we should advert to a particular problem with which Lewis wrestled. While Jesus taught us to pray for the Father's will to be done, there are several places in the New Testament where prayer is urged without this modification; rather, we

---

[23] Over the past several years, such experiments have actually been conducted. The results of one such project by the Mind/Body Medical Center near Boston concluded that petitionary prayer did not "work". The findings were hailed by the Episcopalian chaplain at Columbia University Medical Center as welcome news because it will discourage the "infantile" practice of intercessory prayer. Perhaps if the Mind/Body Center had taken Lewis' advice, they could have saved $2.4 million.

[24] C. S. Lewis, *The World's Last Night and Other Essays* (San Diego: Harcourt, 1960), p. 9.

are told that whatever we pray for—without condition—will be granted. The problem for Lewis is not that the refusals to our prayers are so frequent but that the promises are so lavish. Why does God make such promises and not deliver on them? It seems that the goods "look a little larger in the advertisement than they turn out to be".[25] He wonders if the promises are directed to a degree of faith that most of us do not possess: only exceptional figures such as Apostles, prophets, and healers have the confidence of friends that enables them to have their prayers answered in this way. Lewis tells us that he has consulted theologians in several denominations but has never found a satisfactory answer.

Both Lewis and Knox note several times that Jesus taught his disciples to offer petitions and that what he taught by precept he did by example in his Agony in the garden. In the Our Father, Christ instructed us to present our petitions only after we have prayed that the Father's name be hallowed and that his will be done. The pattern is reversed in Gethsemane, where Jesus first pleads that, if possible, the cup of suffering be taken away; and then he adds, "but your will be done". Several facets of the prayer of petition crystallize around this remarkable occurrence, and we will examine it at some length. Knox notes by way of introduction that there were many ways, both natural and supernatural, that Jesus could have evaded arrest and crucifixion; he knew where the path of his mission was leading and consented to journey to Jerusalem to die. Why now does he beg his Father to take the cup of suffering away?

Lewis' answer is that somehow the knowledge of his death must have been withdrawn from Jesus; otherwise, how

[25] C. S. Lewis, *Christian Reflections* (Grand Rapids: Eerdmans, 1967), p. 151.

could he have prayed for the cup to be removed and simultaneously know it would not be? He suggests that in his distress, Jesus recalled God's saving interventions in Israel's history and thought he might be spared: "But for this last (and erroneous) hope against hope, and the consequent tumult of the soul, the sweat of blood, perhaps He would not have been very Man. To live in a fully predictable world is not to be a man."[26] Knox would be uncomfortable attributing "erroneous hope" to the Son of God; from his early days, when he crossed swords with the authors of *Foundations*, he always espoused a high Christology. When he pondered such questions as Our Lord's temptation in the wilderness, his Agony in the garden, his dereliction on the Cross, and even his growth in human wisdom, he cautioned prudent reserve: "We don't know enough about relations between person and nature to be able to say how much and in what manner the divineness of our Lord would overflow, so to speak, into his human experience. It was his *human* nature that was tempted, and agonized; it was as Man, not God, that he learnt his alphabet. You've no apparatus, here, for deciding that such and such an experience was impossible to him."[27]

Knox offered some tentative reflections about the relationship between Our Lord's human and divine natures. He considered three divine attributes: omnipotence, omniscience, and holiness. Regarding the first, it is clear that Jesus experienced fatigue, hunger, and thirst, and, in Gethsemane, the extremity of nervous humiliation. At the same time, he performed miracles through his human nature. He did so by exception: once or twice, for example, he miraculously fed

---

[26] Lewis, *Letters to Malcolm*, p. 42.
[27] Knox, *University Sermons*, p. 105.

the multitudes; ordinarily, he acquired food and drink in the normal human ways. Was Jesus all-knowing? Again, there are two sides to the evidence: on the one hand, he possessed great insight, knew what was in men's hearts, and prophesied future events (including his Passion and death); on the other hand, he had experimental knowledge and learned things as we all do. How can we connect these diverse data? Knox says we cannot. As regards holiness, Knox points out a distinction made by theologians: for Adam and Eve before the Fall, and for Mary by virtue of her Immaculate Conception, it was possible not to sin; sin is a defect in the human condition, and Adam, Eve, and Mary were fully human. With Christ it is a different matter. Because he is the only begotten Son of God, it is not possible for him to sin: his human nature, while free, is always under the influence of his Divine Person. This brief digression into the theology of the Incarnation adds depth to the mystery of what took place in the Garden of Gethsemane: the paradox of the Son of God, who has come into the world precisely to lay down his life, praying to be spared; his request not being heard; and his resignation to the Father's will. As to what was "going on" in Jesus, Knox counsels prudence: "It seems clear that our Lord, in his perfect Humanity felt a nervous shrinking from death, and that his human Will rose superior to it; we shall not do well to pry more closely into the psychology of the Incarnate."[28]

While not presuming to pry into the psychology of the Incarnate, Knox recognized how the Agony in the garden highlights questions about the prayer of petition. During Holy Week in 1915 he preached four conferences at Saint

[28] Ronald Knox, *A Commentary on the Gospels* (New York: Sheed and Ward, 1954), p. 65.

Mary's (Graham Street) and All Saints (Margaret Street) on "impetrative prayer" that were published as *Bread or Stone*. In his *Spiritual Aeneid* he recalled: "My idea was that people were more than ever wanting to pray, yet more than ever being tempted by doubts about the efficacy of prayer."[29] The world around him was enduring the hardships and tragedies of the First World War; within his own soul Knox was grappling with a spiritual crisis. These conferences considered these difficulties in terms of the prayer of Jesus in Gethsemane, and they provide a useful structure for a deeper examination of what he and Lewis had to say about the prayer of petition.

The first conference deals with the goodness of God. In his Agony, Jesus prayed, "Abba, Father". God loves us and cares for us: "God's love, like woman's love, still clings to what you were, believes in what you might be".[30] To say "Our Father" is the first disposition required for prayer, but Knox realizes it is a bold avowal—man and nature, the sins of the ages, and the sorrows of the world seem to argue against it. He emphasizes our personal relationship to God in *Bread or Stone*: "Your name is perhaps little known in the world, and used, behind your back, in criticism and abuse; but there is a secret name by which God knows you and it rings in your ears with a princely dignity; in all your insignificance, you are still a person to him, in all your weakness, you have still power in his counsels."[31] Lewis seconds this attitude of personal confidence as a necessary prerequisite: "Prayer is either sheer illusion or a personal contact between

[29] Ronald Knox, *A Spiritual Aeneid* (London: Longmans, Green and Co., 1918), p. 164.

[30] Ronald Knox, *Bread or Stone: Four Conferences on Impetrative Prayer* (London: Society of SS. Peter and Paul, 1915), p. 9.

[31] Ibid., pp. 12–13.

embryonic, incomplete persons (ourselves) and the utterly concrete Person."[32] We can bear to be refused but not to be ignored: "The apparent stone will be bread to us if we believe that a Father's hand put it into ours, in mercy or in justice or even in rebuke."[33] Knox makes the same point in *God and the Atom*: "Let him punish them sevenfold for their sins; let him hide his face away for a time, so as to quicken their longing for him; let him deal out sorrow as well as joy, to show that he is Master still. But he must have a personal relation to them, somehow, if they are to have a personal relation to him."[34]

In his second conference Knox considers the omnipotence of God. This quality, like his goodness, is not immediately obvious from what we see around us—it is easier to believe in a limited God because it seems that the evil and suffering in the world would not be allowed by a God who is both all-powerful and all-good. Yet Jesus prayed in Gethsemane, "Abba, Father, all things are possible to thee". Knox brings home the force of this statement by pointing out that, however much the terrible war was due to human agents, "God could have prevented, if he had willed to prevent, that crime being carried into execution: he could have struck the German Emperor dead . . . he could have annihilated the army before Liége, as he annihilated the army of Sennacherib; he didn't, therefore he willed it—willed that the crime should be allowed to reap its own bitter fruits."[35] This is not pulpit rhetoric: some of Knox's closest friends were dying at the front.

The mind recoils from this conclusion about the omni-

---

[32] Lewis, *The World's Last Night*, p. 8.
[33] Lewis, *Letters to Malcolm*, p. 53.
[34] Ronald Knox, *God and the Atom* (London: Sheed and Ward, 1945), p. 55.
[35] Knox, *Bread or Stone*, p. 21.

potence of God. Some suggest that God's will is found in the larger picture, not in the details. He is like a general who is willing to sacrifice a battalion for the sake of victory. Knox does not agree: "And when he allowed a European War to break out, he didn't do it for one single purpose, regardless of the consequences: he foresaw every corollary it would involve; he foresaw how each soldier would fall, what effect that loss would have, or ought to have, upon those who loved him, how every single human soul living in the world would be affected by the upheaval; he foresaw all that, and, as at the Creation of the world, he pronounced it very good."[36] Lewis takes a similar position in reaction to Alexander Pope's assertion that "the first Almighty Cause acts not by partial, but by general laws": "The God of the New Testament who takes into account the death of every sparrow is not more, but less anthropomorphic than Pope's. I will not believe in the Managerial God and his general laws. If there is Providence at all, everything is providential and every providence is a special providence."[37]

This allusion to "special providence" raises a topic upon which Knox and Lewis seem to disagree; but the disparity is only apparent. Lewis wrote an appendix to *Miracles* in which he denies the existence of special providences. Knox, in *Some Loose Stones*, suggests that belief in them is a part of Christian revelation. He notes that there are coincidences that the devout would describe as "an intervention of Providence", and the untheological as "a lucky accident": the doctor happens to be passing by when the child is dying, the tree is struck by lightning after you have moved away from it, and so on. His concern here is to distinguish such happenings

[36] Ibid., pp. 23-24.
[37] Lewis, *Letters to Malcolm*, p. 55.

from miracles, because the authors of *Foundations* had tried to explain away miracles as special providences. But they are not the same: a special providence consists in the ordinary laws of nature working for our good, while a miracle is something that contradicts the laws of nature: "A thing may be 'marvellous' without in the least beginning to be 'miraculous' in any strict sense of the word. Raphael's Madonnas are marvellous, so are aeroplanes; but it is only by an avowed metaphor that we can talk of the former as artistic miracles, or the latter as miracles of modern science."[38] Years later, in *Difficulties*, Knox had to defend special providences on a different front. Arnold Lunn maintained that there were not special providences and that when we prayed, we were asking God to either influence the will of another person or perform a miracle. Knox disagreed: in his prayer for a sick friend, he is asking for more than an impulse of grace to help him bear up, and less than a miraculous healing: "I am hoping that my infinitesimal unit of prayer is going to have weight in the general scheme of things by which this bug got into my friend's system and, I hope, is going to get out again without damage."[39] Lewis' objection is different: he opposes the idea of special providences when Providence is limited to "marvelous events"—for him, as we have seen, everything is providential. Knox would agree with Lewis and simply suggests that when a person believes in a providential God, it is to be expected that he will perceive the hand of God in "coincidental" events. However, our judgments in such matters are notoriously imperfect: what seems a reversal of fortune can in fact be a source of great good, and what seems at first to be a blessing can in the event bring

[38] Ibid., p. 54.
[39] Ronald Knox and Arnold Lunn, *Difficulties* (London: Eyre and Spottiswoode, 1952 [1933]), p. 148.

great misery. For Knox, every event is providential, but we do not see, nor should we expect to see, the workings of Providence. What is certain, for him and Lewis both, is the goodness and the power of God. For this reason, if we pray for something and do not receive it, this is not because God is unable to do what we want, but it is because it is a stone we are asking for, and he wants to give us bread: "That wisdom must sometimes refuse what ignorance may quite innocently ask seems to be self-evident."[40]

Was the prayer of Jesus in the garden made in ignorance? This brings us to Knox's third conference, dedicated to the prayer of petition as such. The anguish of Jesus is palpable; dismayed and distressed, he prays, "Abba, Father, all things are possible to thee; take away this chalice from before me." Lewis views the scene from the perspective of Jesus' human nature: he is about to experience the indifference and cowardice of friends, the betrayal by one of his inner circle, the condemnation of leaders and people, and even a sense of abandonment by God. For Lewis, Christ is draining the dregs of human suffering: "Every rope breaks when you seize it. Every door is slammed shut as you reach it. To be like the fox at the end of the run; the earths all staked."[41] Knox views the scene from the perspective that this is the Son of God praying. Could he, who had come into the world to give his life as a ransom for the many, now be praying that redemption would be withdrawn? Certainly in his humanity Jesus experiences the distress of impending death, but Knox suggests that what prompted Jesus to pray that the cup be taken away was that it was mingled with human treachery and human sin. Christ did not only foresee

---

[40] Lewis, *Christian Reflections*, p. 142.
[41] Lewis, *Letters to Malcolm*, p. 43.

what he was about to endure, but he beheld all the sin of human history: "He saw it, and all his desires, thwarted by human wills, for human salvation and perfection, turned to prayer in the crucible of his burning Heart, and went up in agony to God."[42] The prayer seems not to be heard:

> But, you say, the prayer was never granted. Here is Almighty God wasting his time. Was it wasted? Surely as the desires turned into prayer, so the prayer turned into grace—a flowing tide of grace that surged up, eddy after eddy, into the hearts of a Judas, a Caiaphas, a Pilate, broke itself against the hard rock of their stony will, and fell back, but with force undiminished: with force undiminished entered the coward soul of Peter, forced him to his knees, and converted him into the stablisher of his brethren, washed away the sins of the penitent thief, and bore him into Paradise. The prayers of Jesus are meritorious, because they are the prayers of a human will, not one of them is unheard, not one unanswered.[43]

Is this human will of Jesus in conflict with the will of God?

In his final conference, on acceptance of God's will as the highest form of prayer, Knox answers that question in the negative. Although Jesus concludes his prayer, "Abba, Father, all things are possible to thee; take away this chalice from before me; only as thy will is, not as mine is", this is not a conflict between the will of Jesus and the will of God: it is the will of Jesus passing beyond itself, being universalized into the will of God. We are not to think that this means that the human will of Christ willed to live, and the divine will of the Son of God corrected it; Knox considers this theological heresy and psychological nonsense. What is called "the will to live" is in fact an instinct, and Jesus certainly felt the dread such an emotion creates; but

---

[42] Knox, *Bread or Stone*, p. 34.
[43] Ibid., pp. 34–35.

his human will was always in accord with the will of his Father. Here Knox makes a subtle but important distinction: "Jesus did not will the Crucifixion, did not will that Judas should betray, Caiaphas conspire against, and Pilate misjudge him—nor did the Father. God never wills what is evil. The Father did will the Passion, did will that Jesus should receive the kiss, stand before the tribunal, tread the way of the Cross, without complaining—so did Jesus. Jesus always willed what was good."[44] This is paradoxical, but what it indicates is that even circumstances that are evil in themselves can provide an occasion for good, if we seek the good. In the Agony of Jesus, we confront the challenges surrounding the prayer of petition in a particularly intense way, but we also find here a pattern for our prayer.

When we imitate this pattern, we too call upon God as "Abba, Father"; our petitions express our confidence in his providential care. Should we pray only about important matters? Lewis says that on the one hand, we should strive to develop what Saint Augustine would call an "ordinate love" and seek to get our priorities right; but on the other hand, we must lay before God what is truly in our hearts, not what "ought" to be there: "If we lay all the cards on the table, God will help us moderate the excesses."[45] He warns us not to be too "high-minded" in our prayer, observing that we are sometimes deterred from making small requests by a sense of *our* dignity rather than God's. It is worthwhile to build up a habit of reliance on God by turning to him in small needs as well as great. Knox notes that in the Lord's Prayer, we are taught to pray for the simplest thing—our daily bread—and that it is easy to take simple things for

[44] Ibid., p. 44.
[45] Lewis, *Letters to Malcolm*, p. 23.

granted. "We must be content with simple pleasures, before we can understand what it really means to ask God for our daily bread."[46] We must not despise the simplest petitions: Mary prayed for wine. Our prayer should be the measure of our concerns, and by instructing us to pray for our daily bread, Christ teaches us not to be preoccupied about next week.

The fact that we address God as "Our" Father reminds us that we are to pray for one another. It is good to bring to God the needs of those who are dear to us (although not as a substitute for actually helping them ourselves, Lewis cautions), but Knox suggests that we strive to make our petitions deeper and wider. Deeper, by praying not only for our friends' temporal needs but for their spiritual needs, too; wider, by moving beyond those we know to pray for others. For example, if we are praying for a friend who is ill, we might also remember in prayer all the sick. No prayer is ever wasted, and in this life we do not know our prayers' influence. Knox audaciously states, "The whole church of God is benefited when any little girl prays for a new doll."[47]

We need to pray with persistence. When something is not granted immediately, Knox urges us not to be discouraged: if we obtained cheap and easy results, there would be little place for faith. However, persistence does not mean agitation. It is wrong to assume that a request is not granted because we have not prayed hard enough; we should not think that the willpower we exert has a direct effect on the object of our prayer. This is not to exclude the natural emotions we feel, for example at the bedside of a sick friend; Jesus prayed with great emotion in Gethsemane. What Knox is

[46] Knox, *Pastoral Sermons*, p. 18.
[47] Knox, *Bread or Stone*, p. 51.

cautioning against is the temptation to artificially crank up a frenzy of prayer; we ought to pray with determination but also with a sense of calm confidence.

The two basic traits we need to foster are a spirit of faith and a desire to do God's will. For the first, our prayer life needs to be part of an attitude of reliance on God, which both Lewis and Knox recognize to be more a matter of *habit* than of isolated prayers. In Knox's words, "And when our Lord talks about having faith as a grain of mustard-seed, and so on, I cannot help feeling that He is thinking of faith as an abiding quality, not as a mere transient attitude of the will. That is the real reason for asking holy people to pray for us."[48] Here he seems to echo something of Lewis' reflection that truly holy people have a qualitatively deeper spirit of faith than most of us; and it is that deeper spirit for which we should hunger.

And just as faith should be an abiding quality, so attachment to God's will ought to be more than mere "resignation" when we do not receive what we pray for. Lewis observes that when he prays "Thy will be done", "the petition, then, is not merely that I may patiently suffer God's will but also that I may vigorously do it. I must be an agent as well as a patient. I am asking that I may be enabled to do it. In the long run I am asking to be given 'the same mind which was also in Christ.' "[49] When we turn to God in prayer, Knox says, we should strive to rise from our particular desires to a universal desire for God's glory in all things: "To will with your whole will the whole will of God; that is perfect prayer; that was the prayer of Jesus."[50] He describes in more detail this "perfect prayer" in a retreat for priests:

[48] Knox, "Prayer I: The Prayer of Petition and the Prayer of Acts", *Clergy Review*, June 1939, p. 490.

[49] Lewis, *Letters to Malcolm*, p. 26.

[50] Knox, *Bread or Stone*, p. 50.

The perfect prayer is that in us and in all those we love, in those who wrong us, and in those whom we have scandalized or offended, in those whose lives are committed to our care, and in those who have asked us to pray for them, in all the beneficent economy of creation, and in all the varied events which distract the annals of human history, in the saints glorified in heaven, in the souls waiting in Purgatory, yes, even in the punishment of the lost, in life, in death, and in every creature, God's most high, most holy, and most adorable will may be done.[51]

What he and Lewis both believed, and more importantly, lived, was the conviction that the chief purpose of prayer is not to bend God's will to mine, but my will to his. The questions still remain, and Knox says it is reasonable to ask them: even the sinless Mother of God asked, "My Son, why hast thou treated us so?" But having asked the question, "we must look steadily upon the perfection of the Divine Nature, the unforgetting Love, the indefectible Power, and find in the contemplation of it the necessary answer to our doubts. Jesus is about our Father's business, when he hides his Face."[52] There are times when God hides his face and our prayer is in the dark, but there is a communion in that obscurity. What Lewis wrote to the fictitious Malcolm he could have written also to the elderly priest walking up and down in the garden praying his breviary: "I think it is only in a shared darkness that you and I can really meet at present, shared with one another and, what matters most, with our Master. We are not on an untrodden path. Rather, on the main road."[53]

---

[51] Ronald Knox, *Retreat for Priests* (New York: Sheed and Ward, 1946), pp. 155–56.

[52] Knox, *Bread or Stone*, p. 41.

[53] Lewis, *Letters to Malcolm*, p. 44.

CHAPTER TEN

The Last Things

It has been said that those who embrace a secular view of life dwell in a world without windows. C. S. Lewis and Ronald Knox doggedly opposed such a perspective, and their vision of this world is suffused with a light from the world to come. Knox describes our earthly life as "this sluggish isthmus of dawdling minutes between the great ocean of eternity in which we had no existence, and that other ocean of eternity in which we shall live endlessly."[1] What are traditionally known as "the Four Last Things" (death, judgment, Hell, and Heaven) were for him and Lewis vivid realities. Breasting the tide of an increasingly secularistic world view, they devoted their considerable imaginative talents to making the Christian understanding of our final destiny something palpable here and now. The tide of secularism has only grown stronger over the past fifty years, so their views are both more challenging and more necessary than ever.

Death

As devout Christians, Knox and Lewis shared the conviction that Jesus Christ had broken the power of death; but this did not prevent them from tasting its bitterness in their

---

[1] Ronald Knox, *Retreat for Priests* (New York: Sheed and Ward, 1946), p. 87.

lives. Here we should recall that they both lost their mothers in early childhood and some of their dearest friends in the First World War. Knox once compared death to crossing the Jordan into the Promised Land: just as for forty years that goal was a mere three days' distance from the wandering Israelites, so death is always at our elbow. While he and Lewis had to face the reality of mortality from early childhood, it was only toward the end of his life that Lewis wrote his most heartrending meditation on death, *A Grief Observed*. It is unique among his works because it was not intended for publication: he wrote it as a way to cope with the trauma of his wife's death from cancer. He was persuaded to publish it under a pseudonym, and it was only after his own death that it was reissued in his name. The journal chronicles Lewis' inner struggle between his intense feelings of bereavement and his belief in the goodness of God. Some followers of Lewis have found the "anti-God" declarations so disturbing that they have suggested that this is a work of fiction, not an account of his own state of mind. The fact that he published it under another name suggests that Lewis himself was uncomfortable with some of the sentiments expressed but that they were not fictitious.

The opening chapter describes the physical and psychological sufferings of the grieving husband—the numbness, the tears, "the bath of self-pity, the wallow, the loathsome sticky-sweet pleasure of indulging it—that disgusts me."[2] When his good friend Charles Williams died unexpectedly in 1945, Lewis felt that he was closer to him than ever; but this is not true at the death of his wife Joy, even though he has prayed intensely for it. As to God, he fears that his temptation will not be to lose belief in God's existence but

[2] C. S. Lewis, *A Grief Observed* (New York: Seabury Press, 1961), p. 8.

to believe dreadful things about him. In the second chapter, Lewis battles his self-absorption but is troubled when he tries to think of Joy instead of himself: the sharp outlines of her image fade with each passing day. Friends assure him that she is with God, but this brings no peace: "Supposing the truth were, 'God always vivisects?'"[3] This image of a sadistic God is a "yell", not a thought, but it escapes Lewis' lips and it must be voiced. Against the idea of a cruel God, he can set the figure of Christ—but what if *he* had been mistaken? In the third chapter, the intensity of grief begins to wane, but this creates a new uneasiness: "Does grief finally subside into boredom tinged by faint nausea?"[4] His theological conviction in the goodness of God does not bring peace, since, if God hurts in order to heal, the "scouring" Joy is undergoing may be more thorough than any tortures inflicted by a sadistic god. "What do people mean when they say, 'I am not afraid of God because I know He is good?' Have they never been to a dentist?"[5] As to God's care for him, Lewis recognizes that his own distress may be impeding his awareness of God's presence, like the drowning man who cannot be helped because he keeps struggling. And he wonders if God separated husband and wife because he resented their happiness or because he knew that they had mastered what they needed to learn together and were now ready to move on to the next lesson. In the final chapter, Lewis comes to view grief as a process rather than as a condition. He also admits that his reflections have been about himself, Joy, and God—in that order. Better, he suggests, to reverse the order and to strive to praise God as the giver, and his wife as the gift: "Praise is the mode of love which always has some

[3] Lewis, *Grief Observed*, p. 26.
[4] Ibid., p. 30.
[5] Ibid., p. 36.

element of joy in it."[6] If his picture of Joy is becoming less distinct, this may be because she is *more* real, not less real, than his picture; and this is true of God, too. All reality is iconoclastic, always shattering our necessary but limited images. Lewis concludes that he is being invited to share a new kind of intimacy with his wife, even as she now shares a new kind of intimacy with God, and for this reason, he concludes: "How wicked it would be, if we could, to call the dead back! She said not to me but to the chaplain, 'I am at peace with God.' She smiled, but not at me. *Poi si tornò all' eterna Fontana.*"[7]

A Grief Observed is remarkable for its raw depiction of Lewis' emotions and reflections in the weeks following his wife's death. We have no such account in the writings of Ronald Knox (nor in the works of any other writer, either: Lewis' journal is unique). Knox's reticence about personal matters would have prevented him from writing such a book, but this does not mean that he was a stranger to the emotions Lewis describes. One of Knox's greatest tragedies was the death of his closest friend, Guy Lawrence, in the final weeks of the First World War. Lawrence was killed on August 28, 1918, during the "last push" near Arras (the same area, coincidentally, where Lewis had been serving when he was wounded in April of that same year). Knox was so numbed by the news that he could not even mention Lawrence's name in a letter he wrote to inform a mutual friend of his death, nor for several weeks afterward. Evelyn

---

[6] Ibid., p. 49.

[7] Ibid., p. 60. The last line is a quotation from the *Paradiso* of Dante's *Divine Comedy*: "And to the Eternal Fountain she turned her head" (Canto XXXI, line 93). In answer to Beatrice's prayers Saint Bernard comes to guide Dante on the final stage of his journey; she smiles to him, and turns to gaze upon God.

Waugh thought that the loss of Guy Lawrence created a void in Knox's affections that would be filled only two decades later by his friendship with Daphne Acton.

Knox's reflections on death are found primarily in his retreat conferences to priests, lay people, and children. It was customary in his day to devote at least one conference of a retreat to a meditation on death. Our discomfort about the subject is reflected in the fact that it would be very rare today to present such a conference to young people—or to adults for that matter. While Knox is forthright in addressing the subject, he sees no value in terrorizing the retreatants by making the meditation as fearsome as possible, with descriptions of rotting corpses and dirt rattling on our coffin lid: "When it is our coffin-lid, we shan't mind whether it rattles or not."[8] At times he dwells on the human and Christian consolations of death. Humanly, it means the end of our anxieties and worries; we have a foretaste of this in illness, when our weakened condition does not allow us to dwell on matters that normally preoccupy us. Death cancels all obligations and gives us the perspective to see how petty many of our concerns and grudges are. From a Christian point of view, birth and death are the two great reminders of our creaturely status. Death also brings us from the shadows of this world to the truth that hitherto has reached us in such a confused state; and it means our time of probation is over, and we can no longer sin. He suggests that dying is like letting a dog off its leash—we are now free to run about without constraint or fear of entanglement. Finally, it means we are closer to God and the saints.

This might be how we *should* feel, but is it how we do feel? He puts the question to a young audience: "Death means

[8] Ronald Knox, *The Priestly Life: A Retreat* (New York: Sheed and Ward, 1958), p. 158.

going home for the holidays; surely, there ought to be, about the very sound of the word, something to inspire and uplift us. Death, what a cheerful subject it is. You don't feel like that about it? Well, let me tell in the strictest confidence, neither do I."[9] The reasons for not seeing death as a holiday are twofold: the fear of dying and the fear of being dead. Regarding the first, Knox observes that even with the light of faith, we are like the Israelites contemplating the Promised Land from the wilderness side of the Jordan: "What lies on the farther side of it we know only by hearsay report, and such reports are now encouraging, now discouraging, like the reports which the Israelites received about the land of Chanaan."[10] As with the Israelites, the majority report of the spies who scout out the Promised Land can be dispiriting. Death feels too much like extinction for us to feel comfortable about it, and it is difficult to view the process by which our body and mind are increasingly weakened as the gateway to immortality. Is the fear of dying unworthy of a Christian, or does it suggest a lack of faith? Knox admits he is afraid of dying and considers the examples of John Wesley and Doctor Johnson. Wesley underwent a conversion experience that enabled him to face the prospect of death without a tremor, whereas Johnson refused to even discuss the subject. Both were devout Christians: what did Wesley have that Johnson lacked? Knox suggests Wesley's religious experience had given him an emotional conviction that made the things of eternity seem close at hand, whereas Johnson (like most of us) had to be content with the Christian faith

[9] Ronald Knox, *Retreat for Beginners* (New York: Sheed and Ward, 1960), p. 174. At the end of *The Last Battle* Aslan compares leaving the Shadowlands to the holidays after the school term.

[10] Knox, *Retreat for Priests*, p. 86.

embraced firmly in his intellect and will. "It is possible to argue", Knox suggests, "that the true business of faith is not to produce emotional conviction in us, but to teach us to do without it."[11] It is a comfort to the "unheroically minded" of us that the hallmark of the true Christian is not necessarily courage in the face of death but a willingness to offer our shrinking from it as a sacrifice to God. If it is true that cowards die many times before their deaths, Knox proposes that we can offer all those deaths to God.

As to the fear of being dead, Knox sees several reasons why this is not surprising. For one thing, the separation of the soul and body is not natural: they are made for each other, and their separation can be viewed only as a diminution. Knox addresses the immortality of the soul in his conferences to students at Oxford. What does reason, unaided by revelation, tell us about this question? He considers two popular ideas in this regard. First, the pantheistic idea that at death the soul returns to some kind of reservoir of spirit, like a drop falling into the ocean. In this view, death may not be annihilation, but it is like something getting lost in the wash. This does not tally with our experience, which is that the soul is something individual and indivisible. Although we talk of intellect, will, and memory as faculties, they are not "parts" of the soul: "Your will is you, the whole of you, willing; your intellect is you, the whole of you, thinking."[12] If the soul cannot be imagined as cut in half, it also cannot be imagined as merging with other souls; it is always a unique, individual experience of conscious life. A second

[11] Ronald Knox, *Retreat for Lay People* (New York: Sheed and Ward, 1955), p. 38.
[12] Philip Caraman, ed., *University Sermons of Ronald A. Knox* (New York: Sheed and Ward, 1963), p. 112.

popular idea is the transmigration of souls, or reincarnation. The great Western proponent of this doctrine was Pythagoras, who found a shield that had belonged to a soldier killed in the Trojan War, and the idea occurred to him that he had been that soldier in a previous life. (For this reason, Knox proposes reincarnation as a useful doctrine for those fond of collecting antiques!) Knox recognizes that reincarnation provides a way of addressing the inequities of this life but again holds that it is out of line with what we know about the human soul, because of the faculty of memory: "Now, this phenomenon of memory, linking up all our experiences and dividing so sharply the total of my experiences from the total of yours, has disappeared, it seems, when you and I find ourselves reincarnated in a different life. What confidence, then, are we to feel that some soul a hundred years hence will be identical with yours or mine, when the very hall-mark of conscious identity, namely memory, is absent from it?"[13] Christian revelation affirms that the soul will be united to a glorified body; any doctrine that envisions the soul existing forever apart from the body must mean less life than we experience now. And as such, it is understandable that we should fear it.

Another source of the dread of being dead is a relic from the pre-Christian world. The Old Testament says relatively little about life after death, and it seems to suggest mere existence in a world of shadows. By and large, for the ancient Jews, God's rewards or punishments were given in this life. Surveying the beliefs and funeral customs of the ancient world, Knox believes that the intuition of the human race was that if there is anything beyond the grave, it is a mode of being more uncomfortable than this life. Exceptions may

---

[13] Ibid., p. 114.

have been made for kings and heroes, but for most people, the next life did not hold much promise: "There may be heaven, there must be hell; such, on the whole, was the verdict of antiquity."[14] The contention of Spiritualists that the dead are uniformly happy is in fact a deformation of Christian teaching. It is with Jesus that the idea that the life to come as something far more wonderful than this one appears in the world. In Jesus' teaching, he promised rewards not in this life but in the life to come; and in his Resurrection, he has ratified those promises. By tasting death and rising in glory, Christ has delivered us from the reign of death. The fear of dying might still be there (Jesus himself experienced it in Gethsemane), but not the fear of being dead. Speaking to the schoolgirls at Aldenham, Knox likened Jesus' dying to a mother who takes a taste of bitter medicine before giving it to her child to assure her that it will be all right.

For Lewis as for Knox, it is the teaching and Resurrection of Christ that give us some knowledge of what awaits us after death. Jesus came into the world to share with us what Lewis calls "the good infection" of new life: "He is not merely a new man, one specimen of the species, but *the* new man. He is the origin and centre and life of the new men. . . . Everyone who gets it gets it by personal contact with Him. Other men become 'new' by being 'in Him.' "[15] In spite of the efforts of many to deny or ignore it, at the core of Christ's teaching is the doctrine that the stakes are supremely high: eternal joy or everlasting misery. Our authors took Jesus at his word and recognized that any theology that ignored or denied judgment, Heaven, or Hell plays false to what he taught and did.

---

[14] Knox, *Retreat for Priests*, p. 94.
[15] C. S. Lewis, *Mere Christianity* (New York: Macmillan, 1943), p. 186.

Judgment

We know about the Last Judgment, Heaven, and Hell only from Jesus Christ and the authors of the New Testament; these doctrines are accepted on the authority of Christ himself. Knox points out that these teachings are not theological corollaries but matters of divine revelation. Theological arguments cannot "prove" that these doctrines are true; they can merely demonstrate that they are not contrary to reason. Lewis for his part consistently defended the dogmatic nature of Christian faith against liberal theologians, because he maintained that Christ came to teach us realities that went beyond the limits of human reason. Thus, for example, Heaven is by definition something outside our experience, so any description of the world to come will necessarily be of limited value. Knox compares our efforts to describe the next world to trying to play Wagner on a toothcomb. Elsewhere, he notes that we can employ only metaphors when speaking of supernatural realities but that things can be objectively real even if they can be described only metaphorically. Thus, for both our authors, belief in the world to come is an essential part of the revelation of Christ—perhaps *the* essential part of his teaching—but our ability to comprehend the particulars of that existence is limited, because we must use the language of our experience to describe something that transcends experience. Knox admitted to one correspondent, "I thoroughly agree with you that any efforts we make to get our imaginative faculties to work on the prospect of a future life are curiously depressing."[16] Lewis, speaking of the biblical images of Heaven,

---

[16] Ronald Knox, *Off the Record* (New York: Sheed and Ward, 1954), p. 171.

concurs: "The natural appeal of this authoritative imagery is to me, at first, very small. At first sight it chills, rather than awakes, my desire."[17]

Why bother attempting to discuss such matters at all? While the first Christians were very concerned about the imminent return of Christ as Judge, this is not true of most Christians today. And yet the notion that the next life is what really matters and that everything on earth should be seen in the light of eternity has, or should have, a profound effect on how we live our lives here and now. Both of our authors hold that the "Last Things" run through the whole of the New Testament, and it is both dishonest and dangerous to ignore these doctrines. Many people might consider these beliefs childish or even repellent, but Lewis insists that it is precisely the puzzling or repellent aspects of our faith that conceal what we do not know and need to know. He finds an interesting parallel in scientific research: "The phenomenon which is troublesome, which doesn't fit in with the current scientific theories, is the phenomenon which compels reconsideration and thus leads to new knowledge. Science progresses because scientists, instead of running away from such troublesome phenomena or hushing them up, are constantly seeking them out."[18]

Lewis presented his thoughts on the Second Coming of Christ in an essay entitled "The World's Last Night". He begins by stating that you cannot maintain belief in the divinity of Christ or the truth of his revelation if you abandon or neglect the idea of his return as Judge. But he recognizes there are both theoretical and practical objections

[17] C. S. Lewis, *The Weight of Glory* (San Francisco: Harper, 2001), p. 33.
[18] C. S. Lewis, *God in the Dock* (Grand Rapids: Eerdmans, 1970), p. 91.

to this doctrine. For one thing, we live in a time when the eschatological elements in the Gospels are neglected, perhaps in reaction to the emphasis placed on them by Albert Schweitzer and his followers at the beginning the twentieth century. It is recognized that in the New Testament era, there was a great interest in apocalyptic writings, both within and beyond Christianity, but many today hold that such ideas "do not transcend past time" (by which, Lewis notes, people really mean "do not agree with our time"). But were the people of the first century wrong to expect an imminent catastrophic and divinely ordered end of the present universe? More importantly, was Jesus himself mistaken about this?

That the disciples expected Christ to return soon could have been inspired from his words "Believe me, this generation will not have passed, before all this is accomplished" (Mk 13:30), a sentence that Lewis calls "certainly the most embarrassing verse in the Bible".[19] The mystery deepens when Jesus next tells them, "But as for that day and that hour . . . they are known to nobody, not even to the angels in heaven, not even to the Son; only the Father knows them" (Mk 13:32). How can the Son himself be ignorant of the time of his return? This is a question that has puzzled scholars for centuries, but the common solution is that Jesus was speaking in terms limited by his human nature. The fundamental point beneath these paradoxical statements is that the first followers of Jesus did not know when he would return, but they were to live their lives in expectation of it.

Another difficulty this doctrine poses is that it is uncongenial to the evolutionary, developmental character of modern thought. "Progress" has been a byword since the

[19] Lewis, *The World's Last Night and Other Essays* (San Diego: Harcourt, 1960), p. 98.

nineteenth century, and the idea of the Second Coming "foretells a sudden, violent end imposed from without; an extinguisher popped onto a candle, a brick flung at the gramophone."[20] Here Lewis returns to a favorite theme of his: the fallacy of extending biological evolution to progress in general. Not all changes are for the better, and he argues that there is manifestly no law of progress in ethical, cultural, or social history. Some things get better, while some things get worse, and to those who regard the Second Coming as an "interruption" in the march of progress, Lewis responds that since we are players in the drama, we do not know whether we are in act 1 or act 5. We assume we know the script, but we who are "wholly ignorant of the future and very imperfectly informed about the past, cannot tell at what moment the end ought to come."[21] What is important is that we play our part as best we can. The doctrine of the Second Coming should not be dismissed because it contradicts the modern myth of progress; on the contrary, for that very reason, it provides a salutary antidote to overweening confidence in human abilities.

On the practical level, Lewis notes that for two thousand years, "prophets" have predicted the exact moment of the Lord's return. They have always been mistaken, and this has led people to downplay the importance of the Second Coming. But such predictions are contrary to Christ's own teaching: he assures us he will return, but we cannot know when—so we should always be ready and eager to welcome him. When we recall that we are speaking not only of the end of this world but of judgment, this preparedness should entail sober work within the limits of ordinary morality and

[20] Ibid., p. 101.
[21] Ibid., pp. 105–6.

prudence. Lewis likens our situation to a woman choosing a dress who sees it in the artificial light of the store but needs to consider how it will look in daylight: "That is very like the problem of all of us: to dress our souls not for the electric lights of the present world, but for the daylight of the next. The good dress is the one that will face that light. For that light will last longer."[22]

Ronald Knox devoted attention to questions surrounding the Second Coming throughout his life. From *Some Loose Stones* (published just a few years after Schweitzer's work that described Jesus as a misguided apocalyptic prophet), through his translation of and commentary on the Gospels, and in correspondence published toward the end of his life, Knox grappled with the issues of the Lord's return and the expectation of the first disciples in this regard. Like Lewis after him, Knox argued that liberal theologians were in thrall to the doctrine of "progress" and looked for a completion of God's purposes in this world: their quarrel is with the whole machinery of Gospel apocalyptic. More seriously, if Jesus were in error about the imminent end of the world, how can we put credence in anything else he taught? Knox suggests that in most of the apocalyptic discourses, what Jesus was speaking about was the imminent destruction of Jerusalem. Did he, or his followers, conclude that the world itself would end soon after that catastrophic event? Knox tentatively suggests that it may have been the antecedent will of God that this world would come to an end soon after the destruction of the Holy City but that this denouement was contingent upon the acceptance of Jesus as Messiah by the whole Jewish people. In the event, this did not take place,

[22] Ibid., p. 113.

and the mission to the Gentiles was launched.[23] Admittedly, this is a rather questionable thesis. More persuasive is Knox's point that we should not dwell on one or two statements by Jesus but look at the whole of his teaching. Here, especially in the parables, Knox finds that Our Lord describes the Kingdom in terms that suggest a long, slow period of growth preceding a dramatic fulfillment. And Knox asks, "Do not the words, 'Lo, I am with you always, even unto the end of the world,' lose their whole emphasis if the end of the world is explicitly dated for the day after to-morrow?"[24] Jesus was instilling in his disciples a psychological state of anticipation, of eagerness to welcome him when he returns —and that is, or ought to be, the perennial condition of the Christian life.

The Second Coming is the pattern of our own individual stories writ large: our personal histories, like all history, is the narrative of a probationary journey through this passing, precarious world leading to the final moment when our destiny is determined eternally, for good or ill. The question of John Donne that inspired the title of Lewis' essay, "What If the Present Were the World's Last Night?" can be addressed to each of us. We will be judged at the moment of our death, but the judgment of God differs from any earthly verdict: "When God judges man, the judge knows the truth already; it is the accused that has to learn it."[25] The particular judgment concerns our personal biography, whereas

[23] His most developed presentation of this hypothesis is "Eschatology: A Guess" in *The Month*, May 1950.

[24] Ronald Knox, *Some Loose Stones* (London: Longmans, Green and Co., 1913), p. 121.

[25] Philip Caraman, ed., *Pastoral Sermons of Ronald A. Knox* (New York: Sheed and Ward, 1960), p. 249.

the general judgment at the end of time will reveal our place in the whole drama of human salvation. Knox likens the general judgment to a good novel or detective story, at the end of which the reader sees how everything fits into place.

We will be judged by Jesus Christ, and our authors consider this to be very significant. Knox told the schoolgirls at Aldenham: "The *Credo* doesn't say God will judge us, it says Jesus Christ will come to judge us. And evidently it means Jesus Christ as man will come to judge us, because it is all part, as it were, of his human biography. Now what exactly is the point of that? Why, surely this, that what we shall be judged by is our reaction to the love of Jesus Christ and his offer of salvation. . . . According as we have accepted or rejected it, we shall be, in the hour of judgement, what we are."[26] In another retreat, he says we do not hope to go to Heaven because we have served the Church well or made the world a better place but simply because we are the personal friends of Jesus Christ. Lewis makes a similar point when he notes that many people think that by being good they can please God: "But the Christian thinks any good he does comes from the Christ-life inside him. He does not think God will love us because we are good, but that God will make us good because he loves us."[27]

With his vivid imagination, Lewis paints this crucial encounter with Christ in dramatic terms. At the end of *The Chronicles of Narnia*, all the creatures look Aslan in the face with either hatred or love, and their reactions determine whether or not they can pass through the Door leading to life. In *The Weight of Glory*, Lewis writes: "In the end that

---

[26] Ronald Knox, *The Creed in Slow Motion* (New York: Sheed and Ward, 1949), p. 141.

[27] Lewis, *Mere Christianity*, p. 64.

Face which is the delight or the terror of the universe must be turned upon us either with one expression or the other, either conferring glory inexpressible or inflicting shame that can never be cured or disguised."[28] Knox suggests that the idea that we are judged in terms of our relationship to Christ runs all through Saint John's Gospel: "We accept or reject him, and thereby betray ourselves as the kind of men we are; no more is needed for our condemnation or acquittal."[29]

This poses an obvious difficulty: what is the fate of those who are not followers of Jesus? We must not ignore an important thread in Our Lord's teaching: "Always, he represents it as a matter of urgency to become a genuine citizen of his kingdom before the moment of judgement overtakes you, and it is too late."[30] Is salvation then limited to baptized believers? Knox does not think so. Speaking of pagans who lived before the coming of Christ, he says: "Man can only be saved through the merits of Christ; what conception of a Redeemer or a redemption was it necessary for such a man to form, in order to be saved? I think we can only say that we don't know. We don't know how often the thing has happened, and we don't know what happens when it does. All we can be quite certain of is that we must never despair of a man's salvation for want of the outward signs of it."[31] Since a person can be damned only through his own fault, Knox argues that good people who did not reject Christ must be in Heaven. We do not know how such people are judged, but we believe that God is very merciful, is never unjust, and does not withhold his grace from those who do their best. Lewis agrees: "We do know that no man can

---

[28] Lewis, *Weight of Glory*, p. 38.
[29] Knox, *Pastoral Sermons*, p. 249.
[30] Knox, *University Sermons*, p. 239.
[31] Ibid., p. 243.

be saved except through Christ; we do not know that only those who know Him can be saved through Him."[32]

If salvation depends on our relationship to Christ and cannot be earned by good works, does this mean that our behavior has no impact on our destiny? Both Lewis and Knox reject a view associated with Calvinism that since salvation is a pure gift it is unaffected by our sin. We are saved by our union with Christ, a union that Lewis identifies with faith in Christ, baptism, and the Holy Eucharist. As members of his Body, this Christ-life is at work in us, but it is strengthened or diminished by our choices. Every time we make a moral decision, we change the core of who we are into something a little different than it was before: "You are slowly turning this central thing either into a heavenly creature that is in harmony with God, and with other creatures, and with itself, or else into one that is in a state of war and hatred with God, and with its fellow-creatures, and with itself."[33] It is possible, Knox warns, to reach a state such that the soul no longer responds to the love of God, and the love of God no longer acts upon it, "any more than a magnet would act upon a piece of wood. By its own fault, it has shut out God's mercies, and made for itself a godless universe."[34]

While all of these choices, good and bad, have their effect on us, Knox stresses that it is the attitude of the soul at the moment of death that has a decisive importance for all eternity. The Christian faith sees this life as a time of probation: there is a term to our efforts, a limit to the opportunities offered us. On the one hand, this serves as a warning: like the foolish virgins in the parable, "When once the terrible

[32] Lewis, *Mere Christianity*, p. 65.
[33] Ibid., p. 86.
[34] Knox, *Retreat for Beginners*, p. 210.

moment of decision has passed, not all the prayers of Paradise will avail us: as the tree falls it will lie."[35] On the other hand, we can see this as an expression of the mercy of God:

> But we do know that a soul can be saved by grace at the last moment of a mis-spent life; that is certain in the case of the Penitent Thief; and we may hope, please God, that it has been true in countless other lives, even where there was no external sign given of a death-bed contrition. . . . Life doesn't just depend upon being good and being bad; God's grace is what we want to pray for, and pray for all the more earnestly in proportion as we are humble enough to realize that we cannot do without it.[36]

Lewis was a disciple of George MacDonald, who was a Universalist (that is, one who believes that all men will ultimately be saved), and in *The Great Divorce* Lewis describes damned souls receiving further opportunities after death. They are allowed, if they choose, to leave Hell and dwell in "the Valley of the Shadow of Life"; but most do not want to because their self-absorption imprisons them. It is interesting to note that, although Lewis criticized Thomas More's *Supplication of Souls* because it made of Purgatory a temporary Hell, this is what Lewis himself does. One of the Bright Spirits informs a ghost: "You have been in Hell: though if you don't go back you may call it Purgatory."[37] Knox, on the other hand, describes Purgatory in relation to Heaven. Inspired by the imagery of the *Aeneid*, he envisions the overriding characteristic of Purgatory to be frustration, a desire to get somewhere and being unable to do so. In one sense, he says, the privations of Purgatory are more searing than those of Hell because in Purgatory we long for union with God; it

---

[35] Knox, *Pastoral Sermons*, p. 115.
[36] Knox, *University Sermons*, p. 115.
[37] C. S. Lewis, *The Great Divorce* (New York: Macmillan, 1946), p. 39.

is the intensity of our love that fuels the pain of separation. Lewis and Knox are agreed that Purgatory is transitory: the goal of purification is to prepare us for the bliss of Heaven.

Another facet of judgment is explored several times by Lewis: the question of seeing salvation in "mercenary" terms. He was grateful that for the first year after his conversion to theism he did not have any belief in immortality, since this helped him avoid this pitfall. Historically, he notes, the Jewish people throughout most of their history before the coming of Christ had little or no sense of reward or punishment in the life to come, and this may have been providentially done to preserve them from the temptation of serving God as a kind of bribe. Eternal rewards or punishments are integral to the teaching of Christ, as we have seen, so how can we deal with such a temptation now? Lewis reminds us that the root issue is motivation: a man can marry for love or for money; a general can fight for victory or for a peerage. "The proper rewards", he notes, "are not simply tacked on to the activity for which they are given, but are the activity itself in consummation."[38] Marriage is a fitting reward for a man who loves a woman; eternal life is a fitting reward for one who loves God. For this reason, the promises made by Christ, properly understood, do not encourage a mercenary attitude: "It is safe to tell the pure in heart they shall see God, for only the pure in heart want to."[39] Furthermore, part of our probation is the purification of our desires. This was a central theme in Lewis' life and writings: the pursuit of joy can eventually lead us to God, the source of joy. Throughout our earthly lives, we are seeking an ec-

[38] Lewis, *Weight of Glory*, p. 27.
[39] C. S. Lewis, *The Problem of Pain* (London: Fontana Books 1957 [1940]), p. 133.

stasy that is always just beyond our grasp; one day we will wake to find, beyond all hope, that we have attained it—or that it was within our grasp and we have lost it forever. The judgment of Christ is not some arbitrary verdict delivered upon us, but it is the logical conclusion of the choices we have made: "If we insist on keeping Hell (or even earth) we shall not see Heaven: if we accept Heaven we shall not be able to retain even the smallest and most intimate souvenirs of Hell."[40] Earth is the antechamber to either Hell or Heaven. Those are the only options open to us.

Hell

Many would agree with the sentiment of John Stuart Mill, quoted by Arnold Lunn in *Difficulties*: every other objection to Christianity is insignificant compared to the objection to the doctrine of eternal torment. Both Knox and Lewis felt acutely the challenge of this dogma, but they also insisted that it was an essential part of Christian revelation. Lewis said that there was no doctrine he would more willingly remove from Christianity if he could, but it was based on the teaching of Christ himself and the rest of the New Testament, it had been consistently held by the Church over the ages, and it is supported by reason. Knox admitted that it was the greatest stumbling block to his conversion and that, both as an Anglican and as a Catholic, he could accept Hell only on the authority of the Church, and behind that, on the authority of Christ himself. He once told Arnold Lunn that the doctrine of eternal punishment was like a bulky parcel that he could just barely squeeze into an overflowing bag, to

---

[40] Lewis, *God in the Dock*, p. 6.

which Lunn responded, "And then only because your bag is a *Revelation* bag."[41]

Did Jesus give us the doctrine of Hell? In *Broadcast Minds* Knox considers three alternatives. The first is the traditional Christian position:

1. Christ was a true prophet.

2. Christ believed in eternal punishment.

3. Therefore, eternal punishment exists.

The second is Bertrand Russell's view:

1. Eternal punishment does not exist.

2. Christ believed in eternal punishment.

3. Therefore, Christ was not a true prophet.

Finally, a third possibility:

1. Eternal punishment does not exist.

2. Christ was a true prophet.

3. Therefore, Christ did not believe in eternal punishment.

While he did not agree with Russell, Knox credits him with taking seriously the data of the New Testament; the third position, popular though it may be, can be held only by deliberately excising an important part of the teaching of Jesus. This avoidance is understandable: we do not want to think about Hell because we do not want it to happen. It is a revealed truth, and hence something that reason alone could not attain; but both our authors hold that it is not contrary to reason.

[41] Ronald Knox and Arnold Lunn, *Difficulties* (London: Eyre and Spottiswoode, 1952 [1933]), p. x.

In discussing the doctrine with Lunn in *Difficulties*, Knox offers three "suasions" that make the doctrine reasonable to himself:

1. Given the graces he has received, Knox would not think it unjust for him to suffer eternal punishment if he turned his back on God.

2. The saints saw sin to be something so hideous that Hell would be less hideous in relation to it.

3. If the possibility of eternal punishment is removed, the whole Christian system is radically altered: the sense of urgency and finality in the teaching of Jesus and the gravity of his atoning death make sense only if there is a terrible alternative.

These observations address the atmosphere of the question, but the logical foundation for the possibility of Hell is the sovereignty of free will, an idea captured in Lewis' lapidary phrase, "The doors of hell are locked on the *inside*."[42] True happiness for a creature is found in self-surrender, and one can refuse to make that surrender. Much of *The Great Divorce* is devoted to the theme that even if the damned were given the opportunity to escape Hell, most of them would not take it. Knox would add that the pride that rejects punishment makes the punishment harder to endure; the damned are in constant rebellion against the whole order of things in which they find themselves. The characteristic of a lost soul is that he rejects everything that is not himself. Lewis argues that a life of self-absorption destroys all taste for the *other*; when death cuts off his last rudimentary contact with this world, "he has his wish—to live wholly in the self and to make the best of what he finds there. And

[42] Lewis, *Problem of Pain*, p. 115.

what he finds there is Hell."[43] Knox says that it is possible
to lose sight of God in this life. After death, creatures vanish
and we are thrown back on God alone, but the lost soul has
fashioned for itself a godless universe: "It's as if a man who's
been playing blind man's buff should take the handkerchief
from his eyes and discover that he's gone blind."[44]

Granted that free will necessitates the possibility of damnation, why would God create an angel or man whom he
knows will suffer eternal punishment? In response to Lunn's
objection that he could not believe in a God who would
inflict pain on anyone, Knox makes a shocking statement:
"You see, *God does*. He does, in this world, give some of us
a load of suffering to bear which none of us would willingly
inflict on a fellow creature."[45] When considering this question, we enter into the shadowy world of God's antecedent
will. For example, Knox is certain that God created Satan
to be an angel of light, not a demon—but that God allowed
freedom to thwart that antecedent will. Damnation, Lewis
notes, represents a defeat of omnipotence, but this defeat is
in fact the miracle of God creating beings with free will,
with the power to resist their Maker. If someone were to
choose freely an eternity without God, and thus an eternity
of misery, would it not have been better for God not to
create such a being at all? Knox responds that "such a policy
would have eliminated the moral struggle altogether; or, if
we had had the sense of moral struggle, it would have been
illusory—we should have been like a man treading water
when he is not really out of his depth."[46] He goes on to
explain how he deals with this disturbing question:

[43] Ibid., p. 111.
[44] Knox, *Retreat for Beginners*, p. 211.
[45] Knox, *Difficulties*, pp. 52–53.
[46] Knox, *Off the Record*, pp. 164–65.

My vivid belief that God can do nothing which is not good is
the end of the mystery which I hang on to: how this is com-
patible with the creation of beings who will, in fact, refuse
God, is the blurred end of the mystery which I accept as best
I can, merely confident that there must be more in it than
I know. But my belief in God's goodness is so vivid that I
would hold on to it even if in fact the difficulty could only
be solved on the supposition that God has mercies for the
sinner which he has not revealed to us.[47]

To the objection that the awareness that some are damned
would taint the joy of the saved, Lewis responds that the idea
sounds very merciful but that something dreadful lurks behind it: "The demand of the loveless and the self-imprisoned
that they should be allowed to blackmail the universe: that
till they consent to be happy (on their own terms) no one
else shall taste joy: that theirs should be the final power;
that Hell should be able to *veto* Heaven."[48] It is important
to reiterate that damnation is not something God inflicts
on a person; he is merciful, but he will not violate the free
will of his creature, even when the exercise of that free will
brings misery.

What is the nature of this misery? Our authors maintain
that we are hampered in speaking about either the blessed-
ness or the suffering in the next life because they so transcend our experience. Interestingly, Lewis holds that we can
know more about Heaven than Hell because Heaven is the
intended home for humanity, whereas Hell is not; Knox, on
the other hand, believes we can know more about Hell than
Heaven because Heaven is so vastly better than anything we
can imagine, whereas the sense of abandonment and suffering we experience here on earth will be what we know,

[47] Ibid., p. 165.
[48] Lewis, *Great Divorce*, p. 120.

although to a degree beyond our comprehension now, in Hell. But what we know of either is little enough, guesswork based on what Christ has told us. Knox sums up the issue with admirable simplicity: "Eternity without God is hell; eternity with God is heaven; enough is said, if we know so much as that about eternity."[49]

What we know from what Jesus said, according to Lewis, is that damnation will entail privation, destruction, and punishment. The greatest privation, of course, is to be without God; and every other suffering derives from this. Knox describes the damned soul's condition in this way: "A soul, by its own sins, violently pushed out of shape, warped into a wrong pattern, giving a false reaction, eternally, to every stimulus which a providentially ordered universe can offer it."[50] This is a central theme in Lewis' *The Great Divorce*: for the damned, Heaven itself is Hell—they cannot bear to surrender their self-centeredness and enter into the communion of saints. One manifestation of this condition is discord, a lack of harmony. Screwtape rants against the music and silence of Heaven by rejoicing in the noise that fills the infernal regions: "Noise, the grand dynamism, the audible expression of all that is exultant, ruthless, and virile—Noise which alone defends us from the silly qualms, despairing scruples, and impossible desires. We will make the whole universe a noise in the end."[51] His tirade reaches such a fever pitch that he is involuntarily turned into a large centipede! This cacophony is endured in both the soul and

[49] Ronald Knox, *The Layman and His Conscience* (New York: Sheed and Ward, 1961), p. 213.

[50] Knox, *Retreat for Beginners*, p. 212.

[51] C. S. Lewis, *The Screwtape Letters* (New York: Macmillan, 1973 [1940]), p. 103.

the body of the damned. Knox suggests that we get a small taste of this in the experience of starting the day in a bad mood: everything gets on our nerves, each petty annoyance becomes an intolerable affliction; to the man who is not at peace with himself, there is no peace in his surroundings either. Lewis suggests that what casts itself into Hell is merely the "remains" of a man, banished from humanity.

While Lewis would not go so far as to describe this condition as "annihilation", there is a sense in which, just as evil is the absence of good, so Hell can be understood as the absence of Heaven. In *The Great Divorce*, the narrator is surprised to learn that he and his fellow passengers emerged from a tiny crack in the ground. Hell is cramped: "Their fists are clenched, their teeth are clenched, their eyes fast shut. First they will not, in the end they cannot, open their hands for gifts, or their mouths for food, or their eyes to see."[52] Here we should recall that, entertaining as *The Screwtape Letters* are to read, they took a toll on their author: Lewis complained of the dust, grit, thirst, and itch of the diabolical world. Hell is "the outer darkness" that lies at the border where being fades into nonentity. Lewis says that it is not a condition parallel to Heaven, and Knox agrees: "We mustn't think of heaven and hell as entirely symmetrical, like two china dogs on each side of the mantelpiece."[53] Perhaps it is most helpful to think of Hell as the absence of something, of something so glorious and beautiful that it defies description; and with that in mind, let us turn our attention to what Lewis and Knox have to say about Heaven.

[52] Lewis, *Great Divorce*, p. 123.
[53] Knox, *Layman and His Conscience*, p. 204.

Heaven

If the popular imagery of Hell is lurid, the picture of Heaven for many is vapid: a dreamy, indistinct place of clouds and harps, "pie in the sky". Lewis attacks this dismissive view with characteristic directness: "But either there is 'pie in the sky' or there is not. If there is not, then Christianity is false, for this doctrine is woven into its whole fabric."[54] What the Christian faith teaches about Heaven is that it is *more* real, not less real, than earthly life. Heaven is the substance, earth the shadow, Knox tells us, and our human nature needs to be transformed to enjoy the flavors of that sublime reality: "If you went to heaven just as you are, you wouldn't appreciate the happiness of heaven any more than a dog would appreciate Shakespeare."[55] How to describe something of a reality by its nature beyond our comprehension, a reality compared to which any other good upon which our desire fixes must be in some degree a mere symbol? This is what Lewis and Knox attempt to do when speaking of Heaven.

One approach is by way of what Lewis calls "transposition". Ordinarily, he says, we can understand a lower medium only if we have some experience of the higher medium it seeks to convey. For example, we appreciate a painting because we are familiar with the three-dimensional world it depicts. He then describes the imaginary example of a woman who has given birth to a child in a dungeon. The boy has never been out of the cell, and his mother tries to acquaint him with the world outside by drawing pictures. The child is confused when he learns that the real world is not full of pencil marks; from this he gets the idea that the

---

[54] Lewis, *Problem of Pain*, p. 133.

[55] Knox, *Layman and His Conscience*, p. 207.

outside world is somehow less visible than the pictures he has seen, when in fact it is incomparably more visible. So it is with us; what we will be in Heaven is more real than what we are on earth: "Our natural experiences (sensory, emotional, imaginative) are only like the drawing, like penciled lines on flat paper. If they vanish in the risen life, they will vanish only as pencil lines vanish from the real landscape."[56] Our limitation is that, since we have no experience of the higher medium, we can see only the lower medium, so the beauty of Heaven eludes us. Knox uses a similar image. He notes that our pictures of Paradise are inadequate because we do not have colors into which to dip our brush: "They are like those shaded lines by which heraldry represents colours —red represented by upright lines, blue by horizontal lines, and so on. Just so these phrases of ours stand, all of them, for a reality which we have no means of expressing."[57]

Another approach to Heaven lies along the path of desire, a favorite theme for Lewis. He believes that each of our lives is held together by a chain of desires that never reach their final attainment in this world. The chain is particular to each of us, touching the very core of our being and establishing a unique relationship with God. The things that have delighted us in this life "are not the thing itself; they are only the scent of the flower we have not found, the echo of a tune we have not heard, news from a country we have never yet visited."[58] And this uniqueness lasts into eternity: each of us will know and praise some aspect of the divine Beauty better than any other creature. Although some authors urge us to think of Heaven when we encounter difficulties in life in order to cheer up, Knox suggests that we call it to mind

[56] Lewis, *Weight of Glory*, p. 111.
[57] Knox, *Pastoral Sermons*, p. 472.
[58] Lewis, *Weight of Glory*, p. 31.

at moments of great happiness and remind ourselves that we are destined for something better, fuller, and more lasting than what is presently moving our hearts to joy.

The chain of desire links this world with the world to come in such a way that there is a continuity between earthly and heavenly realities: Lewis likens the relationship to that between a bulb and a flower, or between a piece of coal and a diamond. This brings us to the subject of the risen body. Ever since Saint Paul wrote, "What is sown is perishable, what is raised is imperishable. It is sown in dishonor, it is raised in glory. It is sown in weakness, it is raised in power. It is sown a physical body, it is raised a spiritual body" (1 Cor 15:42–44), Christians have speculated about the qualities of a "spiritual body". Again, earthly imagery fails to capture the sublimity of the glorified body; Lewis asks, "Who wishes to become a kind of living electric light bulb?"[59] Knox points out that, since we cannot form an idea of eternal life, we cannot form a picture of a body adapted to it: whatever it is that expresses itself here on earth in terms of matter will persist, although expressed in quite different terms. My present earthly body is an inadequate symbol of the body I will have in eternity: "A symbol, yes; but we must remind ourselves again, it isn't merely a kind of book token, entitling me to the possession of *a* body in eternity; it is rather a kind of cloak-room ticket, entitling me to the possession of *my* body in eternity."[60] Knox envisions us enjoying unimpeded the exercise of the faculties we possess here on earth, and he suggests swimming as a good image: "I mean a really nice swim; the complete freedom of unlaborious movement, with no consciousness of obstacles. Heaven

[59] Ibid., p. 36.
[60] Knox, *University Sermons*, pp. 299–300.

will not be dull; we shall always be doing the thing we want to do, and doing it perfectly."[61] In order to emphasize the truth that Heaven is more real than earth, Lewis describes the resurrected body as *more* solid than an earthly body.

All of this is beyond our earthly knowledge, and yet we touch the hem of the mystery in Christ's Resurrection. Constrained by a knowledge limited by the lower medium, we cannot know the higher medium of his glorified body; but the testimony of the disciples who met the risen Christ bears witness to both the continuity and the transformation that we ourselves hope to enjoy. It is by our union with Christ that we receive this gift of the risen life, and we do so by following him in self-sacrificing love:

> Submit to death, death of your ambitions and favourite wishes every day and death of your whole body in the end: submit with every fibre of your being, and you will find eternal life. Keep back nothing. Nothing you have not given away will ever be really yours. Nothing in you that has not died will ever be raised from the dead. Look for yourself, and you will find in the long run only hatred, loneliness, despair, rage, ruin and decay. But look for Christ and you will find Him, and with Him everything else will be thrown in.[62]

Lewis examines how everything else is "thrown in", especially in answer to the question "Will we know one another in Heaven?" He suggests that this will depend on the nature of our love for the other on earth. If it was merely a natural love, it will perish along with the natural world. He compares this to meeting in adult life someone who was a friend at school, where the relationship relied simply on common interests and occupations in childhood; if such a person was

[61] Knox, *Retreat for Beginners*, p. 216.
[62] Lewis, *Problem of Pain*, p. 190.

not a kindred soul, he will now be a total stranger. If, on the other hand, our beloved on earth was loved as in some way a reflection of the beauty of God, then when we enter into fuller union with God we will rejoice both because we have moved beyond the portrait to the original and because we now find our beloved in God. Part of the joy of Heaven will be to rejoice in the glory of others. In *The Great Divorce* Lewis describes a magnificent procession of singing and dancing children honoring a radiant woman. The narrator looks at the ineffable beauty of her face and guesses she must be one of the greatest saints, perhaps even the Blessed Virgin Mary herself. In response, his guide says, "Not at all. It's someone ye'll never have heard of. Her name on earth was Sarah Smith and she lived at Golders Green."[63] We would do well, Lewis suggests, to practice contemplating the glory of others here on earth, to recall that there are no *ordinary* people: "It is a serious thing to live in a society of possible gods and goddesses, to remember that the dullest and most uninteresting person you can talk to may one day be a creature which, if you say [*sic*] it now, you would be strongly tempted to worship."[64]

The source of our glory is the source of Christ's glory: his Father's love. To receive glory is to be known by God, just as it is damnation to hear him say, "I do not know you. Depart from me." The desire to be known is the thirst not simply to gaze upon beauty but to bridge the chasm between us and reality. This the Father does when he recognizes us as sons and daughters; and he does so to the extent that we are united to his Son and configured by charity to his Son's resemblance. It is a deeply *personal* knowing; Lewis goes so

---

[63] Lewis, *Great Divorce*, p. 107.
[64] Lewis, *Weight of Glory*, p. 45.

far as to suggest that it is this knowing that makes us persons: "At the beginning I said there were Personalities in God. I will go further now. There are no real personalities anywhere else. Until you have given your self to Him you will not have a real self. . . . How monotonously alike all the great tyrants and conquerors have been: how gloriously different are the saints."[65] Since union with God is the fundamental blessing of Heaven, Knox says, "Everybody will be satisfied in heaven; but everybody will be satisfied in proportion as he has wanted it; and those most of all, who wanted nothing in this world but God, and looked forward to their heaven only because God was there."[66]

In speaking of what we do not know by experience, Lewis found that fantasy could shed some light on reality. At the conclusion of *The Chronicles of Narnia*, he describes the end of Narnia and the beginning of a new and glorious life. Since he believed that "those who attain the glorious resurrection will see the dry bones clothed again with flesh, the fact and the myth remarried, the literal and the metaphorical rushing together",[67] we might consider the end of *The Last Battle*, Lewis' final word on the subject of Heaven:

Then Aslan turned to them and said, "You do not look so happy as I mean you to be."

Lucy said, "We're so afraid of being sent away, Aslan. And you have sent us back into our own world so often."

"No fear of that," said Aslan. "Have you not guessed?"

Their hearts leaped and a wild hope rose within them.

"There *was* a real railway accident," said Aslan softly. "Your father and mother and all of you are—as you used to call it in

[65] Lewis, *Mere Christianity*, p. 190.
[66] Knox, *Retreat for Beginners*, p. 217.
[67] C. S. Lewis, *Miracles* (New York: Macmillan, 1948), p. 192.

the Shadowlands—dead. The term is over: the holidays have begun. The dream is ended: this is the morning."

And as He spoke He no longer looked to them like a lion; but the things that began to happen after that were so great and beautiful that I cannot write them. And for us this is the end of all stories, and we can most truly say that they all lived happily ever after. But for them it was only the beginning of the real story. All their life in this world and all their adventures in Narnia had only been the cover and the title page: now at last they were beginning Chapter One of the Great Story which no one on earth has read: which goes on forever: in which every chapter is better than the one before.[68]

Ronald Knox did not possess Lewis' imaginative gifts, but he shared with him a conviction that Heaven is infinitely more beautiful than anything we can imagine and that it is ultimately *faith* that provides a window into the next world. After all our flights of imagination, it is by the low door of faith that we enter into the mystery:

In such matters, the business of faith is not (surely) to try and force our minds into conceiving of a future life under certain consecrated images which don't, as a matter of fact, appeal to us, gold crowns and harps and glassy seas and the rest of it. The business of faith is to throw all our unsatisfied questionings, like all the rest of our burden, on our Lord, and tell him that we want our heaven to be what he wants it to be, because he knows and we shall know that that is best.[69]

---

[68] C. S. Lewis, *The Last Battle* (New York: HarperCollins, 1956), pp. 227–28.

[69] Knox, *Off the Record*, pp. 173–74.

The Parting of Friends

What we make known is the wisdom of God, his secret, kept hidden till now; so, before the ages, God had decreed, reserving glory for us. (None of the rulers of this world could read his secret, or they would not have crucified him to whom all glory belongs.) So we read of, Things no eye has seen, no ear has heard, no human heart conceived, the welcome God has prepared for those who love him.

— 1 Corinthians 2:7–9 (Knox translation)

We will take leave of C. S. Lewis and Ronald Knox as they contemplate the welcome God has prepared for them. When Ronald Knox resigned from his last position as an Anglican priest, he was inspired by the example of Cardinal Newman to preach on the parting of friends. In that sermon, Knox spoke of how the demands of conscience sometimes call a man to detach himself from loved surroundings and familiar friendships and launch out alone into the deep. Both he and Lewis experienced the "death" that conversion entails, and they knew other bereavements as well. Their profound faith helped them see these experiences as dress-rehearsals for death itself, and they believed that this seemingly final occurrence marked the beginning of new and better chapter. But death also meant saying good-bye to loved surroundings and familiar friendships.

In 1957 Ronald Knox was diagnosed with cancer of the

liver. The disease spread quickly, and he died on August 24, 1957, just two months after delivering the Romanes Lecture, his last public speech at Oxford. Six years later Lewis was invited to give this lecture, but his terminal illness forced him to decline. On November 22, 1963, he died.

Word of Lewis' death was eclipsed by the sensational reports of President Kennedy's assassination. That tragic news overshadowed another significant event as well: on November 22 the bishops of the Catholic Church voted on the first document of the Second Vatican Council, the Constitution on the Sacred Liturgy. This document signaled the beginning of new era both within and beyond the confines of the Catholic Church. November 22, 1963, can serve as an inaugural date for that tumultuous, exhilarating, and violent decade known as "the sixties". And it was on that day that Lewis, self-described dinosaur, closed his eyes on this world. We view him and Knox from the other side of the chasm created by the dramatic changes of the past fifty years. To many they are like the medieval cloisters and dreamy spires of Oxford, quaint relics of a bygone age. Students and professors still enjoy Addison's Walk and Christ Church Meadow, but they are as likely to be chatting with invisible friends on mobile phones as conversing with flesh-and-blood companions. Do C. S. Lewis and Ronald Knox have something more than period charm to offer the world today?

One lesson they teach us is how to argue constructively. Knox was right when he said that we live in "the age of assertion": points of view are proclaimed forcefully, even stridently, but there is little real discussion. People simply assume that their position is self-evidently right and seek like-minded company. When contending parties meet, it is uncommon for the conversation to deal with matters of principle or substantive argumentation—rather, each side seeks to shout the other side down, resorting to ad hominem attacks and acrimonious remarks. It is refreshing to open the books of Lewis and Knox and read authors who are passionately committed to what they perceive to be true, who are able to articulate their positions with clarity and intellectual rigor, and who respect their adversaries. Because they had wrestled with doubts, they were able to sympathize with the doubts of others, and they presented their ideas with a humor that suggests they could see the other person's point of view. What they would not allow was the substitution of assertion for argumentation, and they were frustrated that many opponents would not even deign to argue; they simply presumed that religious belief was intellectually indefensible. Paradoxically, Lewis and Knox would have relished a good argument with one another because they had so much in common. At the end of his published debate with Arnold Lunn, Knox observed: "One advantage at least our discussion has enjoyed: we have had the meeting-ground of a common civilization. The classics, and the tradition of a society now imperilled, and a respect for logic, remained to us, so that we could cross swords."[1] Knox wrote those words in 1932; in 1949 Lunn commented that this common ground was quickly disappearing. Certainly over the past fifty years, many of the shared values necessary for meaningful debate have continued to erode or have disappeared completely.

One of the principal values that can no longer be assumed is respect for logic. Both Lewis and Knox held that truth was objective and that human reason could ascertain it. They certainly understood how it was possible for a person to change

[1] Ronald Knox and Arnold Lunn, *Difficulties* (London: Eyre and Spottiswoode, 1952), p. 241.

his mind about what was true, for they had done so themselves on some of the most fundamental philosophical and religious questions. What they rejected is the idea of relativism in relation to truth. They recognized the wolf of prejudice in the sheep's clothing of "tolerance" or "diversity". What parades as broadmindedness is in reality the bigotry that does not consider an adversary to be worth engaging. Relativism means the death of healthy argument: if truth is not something upon which minds can meet, why discuss anything? It is also intellectually dishonest. When someone says, "That may be true for you . . .", what he really means is that it is not true at all (or he would affirm it) and that if you think it is true there is no point in even discussing the matter. Knox and Lewis realized that if something is true only for some, then it is not true at all. They paid their foes the twofold compliment of believing that they were interested in the truth and that they deserved a reasoned defense of what Lewis and Knox perceived that truth to be. They did not claim a monopoly on the truth, and they were willing to recognize the cogent points in their adversaries' arguments. But they also affirmed a principle that is fundamental to logical thought: contradictory positions demand resolution.

If Lewis and Knox were confident about the ability of human reason to attain the truth, they were also conscious of its limitations. This was particularly the case in the area of *revealed* truth, which is the core of Christian faith. The dogmatic truths of Christianity are not irrational but suprarational and can be known only because they are revealed by God. Our authors believed that human reason could ascertain some of the preambles of this revealed truth. They thought that such fundamental ideas as the existence of God, the reliability of the Scriptures, and the possibility of miracles were matters attainable by reason, and they offered cogent arguments to defend these ideas. They also recognized that the human mind could explore the meaning of truths revealed by God and that theology in this sense was both warranted and necessary. However, they resolutely defended the unique nature of divinely revealed truths in the face of modernist temptations to reduce these to the products of mere human speculation. As far back as *Some Loose Stones*, Knox enunciated his conviction that revealed truths by their very nature are the a priori foundations of the Christian religion, accepted as true not as the hypotheses of human reasoning but because God has revealed them to us in Christ. So, he and Lewis found themselves engaged on two fronts: in response to scientism, which maintained that reality was coterminous with the material world, they argued for the existence of God with evidence that was attainable by human reason; in response to modernism, which attempted to reduce Christian revelation to reason alone, they argued for the acceptance of the fundamental dogmas of the Christian religion by a profession of faith.

Christian dogma has been described as "saving truth", and there must be a way for that teaching, first revealed by Jesus Christ two thousand years ago, to be accessible to men throughout history. One privileged channel of this saving truth is the Bible. From their Evangelical upbringing, both Lewis and Knox had a deep reverence for the Scriptures as the word of God. They devoted their lives to the study of the Bible and followed the work of biblical scholars with great interest. That interest led to apprehension when in their judgment these scholars pursued their research without reference to the dogmatic foundations that should guide Christians in their understanding of the word of God. They tended to be conservative in this matter, but they were certainly not "Fundamentalist" (a label Lewis explicitly rejected). It is clear that Knox consulted the writings of contemporary biblical scholars when he translated the Vulgate Bible. He was troubled when some scholars proposed interpretations that seemed to contradict traditional Christian doctrines, and in his New Testament commentary, he consciously sought to bring that tradition to bear in his biblical interpretation. In this he was admittedly somewhat out of step with much biblical scholarship that throughout the twentieth century was advancing the cause of historical-critical exegesis. A critical approach to the Bible enjoyed a certain prominence in both Protestant and Catholic biblical scholarship in the second half of the twentieth century. In recent years, however, there have been signs that, while historical-critical exegesis continues to enjoy pride of place, there is a growing recognition that written texts have a plurality of meanings. The meaning of Scripture is open to further developments when it is read in the context of the paschal mystery and the faith of the believing community. In their biblical studies, Knox and Lewis combined literary expertise and religious conviction.

As central as the Bible was to both Lewis and Knox, they recognized that it could not be properly understood apart from the living community of the Church. It was this community that wrote the Scriptures, recognized the canon of inspired writings, and interpreted the meaning of Scripture through preaching and worship over the centuries. Both writers realized the importance of the Church, but as we have seen, they articulated different understandings of her nature. For Knox, Jesus had entrusted his mission to the visible community of disciples he had formed, and this visible community has been an organic, identifiable entity ever since the first century. Knox came to the conviction that the Roman Catholic Church uniquely manifested the dis-

tinguishing marks of this community. He also believed that
Christ's teaching was so important that he would not have
left future ages in the dark as to its meaning; an authoritative
interpreter was needed to settle doctrinal disputes, and the
Catholic Church was that interpreter. Lewis, on the other
hand, followed the lead of Richard Hooker and believed
that matters of Church structure were secondary and did
not constitute an element of revealed truth necessary for
salvation. Lewis' normative authority was what he called
"mere Christianity", doctrines that had been professed by
the majority of Christians of all denominations over the past
two thousand years. For Knox, Protestant ecclesiology was
deficient because it possessed no final authority and thus
bred division after division, sect after sect. For Lewis, Catholic ecclesiology was too preoccupied with external structures and needlessly multiplied doctrines that must be accepted—and this, too, was a source of division.

There is much that could be said about our writers' views
on the Church, because there is probably no religious topic
where there has been a greater sea change since their deaths
as in the field of ecclesiology. The Catholic approach to ec-
umenism has shifted dramatically in the second half of the
twentieth century, and Knox, especially in the first years after
his conversion, articulated an understanding of non-Catholic
churches that has been formally abandoned by an ecumenical council and the subsequent teachings of the Popes. But
Lewis would find that the ground had shifted in his Anglican view of the Church, too: the concurrence on basic
issues of doctrine and conduct that Lewis took for granted
when he articulated his idea of "mere Christianity" could
not be presumed today. The viewpoint of both writers could
also be described today as "Eurocentric" (and indeed limited there as well, since they say very little about Eastern

Christianity), whereas much of the growth in Christianity is taking place now in Asia, Africa, and Latin America. Nor did they anticipate the tremendous expansion of Pentecostal religions over the past fifty years. Even Knox, who spent a lifetime studying the kinds of religious experience of which Pentecostalism is an heir, did not address this movement in *Enthusiasm*; and, while he presumed there would always be religious revivals of the sort he examined, he thought they were waning.

Having recognized these limitations, it remains true that Lewis and Knox still can contribute to current discussions because they articulate the issues that continue to be a source of division among Christians. Much of the mutual recrimination and suspicion that have marked relations between different confessions have given way, over the past century, to a greater willingness to dialogue and to learn from one another. To some extent Lewis, Knox, and other writers like them have had a part to play in this welcome change, because in their works, they presented their positions in a positive way and showed an awareness of the difficulties others experienced. But this atmosphere of goodwill has its shadow side as well. For one thing, it must be admitted that the change in climate is due often to indifference, not charity: for many people today, the "Church-dividing" issues are irrelevant because doctrine is irrelevant. This was an attitude our authors anticipated and that they viewed with great concern —because for them the central issue was always truth, and it is not constructive when societies, and especially religious societies, purchase tranquility at the expense of truth. Furthermore, in spite of the welcome advances in ecumenical relations, fundamental problems remain; to find the distinctively Protestant and Catholic positions on several essential

topics presented with clarity, balance, and forthrightness—
as they are by Lewis and Knox—can help identify the theological issues that must be confronted. They did much to
overcome the bad blood that centuries of religious contro-
versy had bequeathed to Christianity, but they would have
been the last to suggest that unity can be achieved by wa-
tering down doctrine to some lowest common denomina-
tor. Indeed, opposition to this approach was a principal in-
centive for their religious writings. Ronald Knox made the
painful decision to leave the Church of England and become
a Catholic; Lewis resolutely remained an Anglican. A study
of the reasons for each man's choice points to the substantive issues that still divide Christians.

As important as such controversial questions are, they represent only a partial view of the Church. While Knox and
Lewis were apologists, they were more fundamentally evangelists who sought to help Christians live a more intense life
of discipleship. Their writings on prayer, on the sacraments,
and on love of God and neighbor are gifts to believers of
all denominations. They did not shy away from controversial topics, but their principal desire was to encourage ordinary people to live more dedicated religious lives. They
were men of robust intellect, and they found in the Christian faith satisfactory answers to the fundamental questions
about the meaning of life. But they understood Christianity
to be far more than a satisfying philosophical system—it was
a romance, because it revealed a deeply personal God who
showed his love to the utmost on Calvary. It would be no
exaggeration to say that Knox and Lewis fell in love with
Christ. They wanted to give themselves completely to the
God who had given himself so completely to them, and they
wanted others to share their joy. It is true that they were

clever and entertaining controversialists, but more importantly they were spiritual guides, and their teachings have a
perennial value.

As dedicated Christians, they urged fellow believers to express their love of God through love of neighbor, and they
taught that the horizon of this love must not be limited to
members of the household of faith. Christ told his followers
to be a leaven in the world, and Lewis and Knox addressed
the challenges of the relationship between Christians and an
increasingly secular world. A principal theme of Knox's *Let
Dons Delight* was the gradual exclusion of religious concerns
from the scholarly world of Oxford, and in this he saw Oxford to be a microcosm of Western society. This secular-
ization has increased dramatically over the past fifty years.
In the first part of the twentieth century, battles about the
Book of Common Prayer were still fought out in Parliament
(Knox's father was one of the principal combatants); by the
end of the century, the combined leadership of all the Christian churches in Great Britain had to make forceful interventions simply to have a cross displayed in England's "Mil-
lennium Dome", and the name of Jesus Christ was not even
mentioned at a royal funeral held in Westminster Abbey. As
dedicated believers Lewis and Knox were understandably
concerned about the impact of this indifference and hostility on their religious communions, but they also worried
about its corrosive effect on society as a whole. They feared
what Lewis called "the abolition of man". To them it was
no coincidence that the century that witnessed the waning
of the Christian faith also witnessed the waxing of totalitarian regimes. They believed that the Christian understanding of the dignity of the human person and the inherently
social dimension of Christianity offered an antidote to the

twin evils of oppressive totalitarianism and solipsistic individualism.

There are many facets to the lives and writings of Ronald
Knox and C. S. Lewis: they were eloquent apologists, in-
cisive commentators on religion and society, imaginative
writers of fiction, sympathetic spiritual guides. Their greatest gift may be the example of integrated Christian life they
offer. They were able to harness their considerable intellectual abilities and artistic gifts and offer them to Christ and
so present to the world a solid and attractive picture of the
Christian faith. Their insightful spiritual teaching is accessible to ordinary readers; they wear their scholarship lightly.
Their sincerity is tangible, their tone conversational. When
they cross swords with their adversaries, their efforts are
marked by good humor and courtesy. More fundamentally,
they know that the inner landscape of the individual human
heart and the outer landscape of human history both tell
the same story, the thrilling romance of God's love for us
—and they recognize the story to be an epic in either case.
Ronald Knox and C. S. Lewis were not friends in this life
(although we can hope they are now), but they befriend
those who read their books. They may be our first friends
who say what we believe, only better; or they may be the
second friends with whom we carry on a running debate in
our minds. But friends they are, and through their writings,
they offer us what only friends can: they challenge us when
we are complacent, entertain us when we are bored, cheer
us up when we are depressed, inspire us when we are irres-
olute. As we imagine each of these figures taking his daily
walk in Oxford, we might think, "Wouldn't it have been
a privilege to walk with him as his friend?" Through their
books, we can.

The Writings of C. S. Lewis and Ronald Knox

Both C. S. Lewis and Ronald Knox wrote in a remarkable variety of literary genres. While readers may be familiar with one type or another, such as Lewis' Narnia stories or Knox's sermons, an overview of all their writings can help us appreciate the breadth of their thought, and it also demonstrates similarities and differences between these two versatile authors. Walter Hooper, in his *C. S. Lewis: A Companion and Guide*, divides his subject's writings into several genres, which will be followed here.

Juvenilia

Students of Lewis' vivid imagination were permitted a glimpse into the early workings of Lewis' mind with the publication of *Boxen: The Imaginary World of the Young C. S. Lewis* in 1985. As small children, Jack and Warnie created a world of anthropomorphic animals—something many youngsters do, but in this case it is of interest in light of the later success of the Narnia stories. Knox's childhood fascination with the animal kingdom was nurtured by one of his favorite books, Wood's *Natural History*; he could still recall it vividly sixty years later when he visited Africa. This book was anthropocentric rather than anthropomorphic: it ranked animals according to their usefulness and declared: "Between man and brutes there is an impassible barrier, over which man can never fall, or beasts hope to climb"—the antithesis of the world of Boxen. Young Ronnie's creativity found expression in Latin plays he wrote for the family "newspaper" published by his brothers.

Poetry

When Knox was a student at Oxford, A. C. Benson advised him: "Go on writing poems; you will find it helps you to write prose."[1] Both Knox and Lewis wrote verse, and their first published works were poetic. While still at Eton, Knox published his first book, *Signa Severa*, a collection of poems in English, Latin, and Greek; this was followed by a collection brought out while he was an undergraduate at Oxford, *Juxta Salices*. Both books were successful at the time (the first went to six editions), but their allusions and charm mean little to us today; they celebrated a waning era. Lewis' first two books were also poetry: *Spirits in Bondage* and *Dymer*, both published under the pen name Clive Hamilton. The first takes an atheistic view of life, and the second reflects Lewis' growing interest in Norse mythology. These efforts were not well received at the time, which came as a great blow to their author. For the rest of his life, Lewis continued to write poems for publication—short ones, not epics like *Dymer*—and most of these were also published under pseudonyms. He wrote long narrative poems for his own enjoyment, and these have been published posthumously. Knox's own poetic endeavors were aimed more at amuse-

[1] Ronald Knox, *Literary Distractions* (New York: Sheed and Ward, 1958), p. 199.

ment than emotional depth; some of these, too, saw the light of day posthumously in a book called *In Three Tongues*.

Autobiography

Ronald Knox hoped that amid the apocalyptic events of the First World War his entrance into the Catholic Church would not attract much attention. But the conversion of such a leading Anglo-Catholic was news, and he felt obligated to describe his religious journey. Inspired by Virgil's epic poem, he called his account *A Spiritual Aeneid*. In the preface, he provided a key to the leitmotif:

> Troy is undisturbed and in a sense unreflective religion; in most lives it is overthrown, either to be rebuilt or to be replaced. The Greeks are the doubts which overthrow it. The "miniature Troy" of Helenus is the effort to reconstruct that religion exactly as it was. Carthage is any false goal that, for a time, seems to claim finality. And Rome is Rome.[2]

More than thirty years later, a publisher approached Knox for permission to produce a new edition. Knox initially balked at the idea, claiming it was a "period piece", and he frankly admitted that he felt sick reading it and could not image anyone having a different reaction. He finally acquiesced but left the work unaltered. In a brief preface entitled "After Thirty-Three Years", he compared *A Spiritual Aeneid* to a notepad by the bedside in which someone furiously scribbled, immediately upon waking, the outlines of last night's dream. Although in the 1950s it was suggested that he pick up the story in 1918 and write an autobiography, nothing came of this.

[2] Ronald Knox, *A Spiritual Aeneid* (London: Longmans, Green and Co., 1918), preface.

In 1933 C.S. Lewis produced his first full-length prose work, an allegorical tale based on his own experience of losing and rediscovering his Christian faith. *The Pilgrim's Regress: An Allegorical Apology for Christianity, Reason and Romanticism* was well received, although many found the symbolism confusing; in a subsequent edition, Lewis provided an explanation for this—and also a categorical statement that it did not tell the tale of his journey to Roman Catholicism, an assumption some readers had made. For years Lewis felt the need to write a direct account of his conversion, a task finally fulfilled in 1955 with the publication of *Surprised by Joy: The Shape of My Early Life*. A few years later, the agonizing experience of his wife's illness and death led him to write *A Grief Observed*. Lewis had not originally intended to publish this account, and when he did so, it was released under the name N.W. Clerk. Some grateful readers sent copies to Lewis, with the hope that he might take consolation from such an insightful book! It was published under his own name only posthumously.

Novels

Hooper presents two related categories for Lewis' works: novels and theological fantasies. The distinction he seems to be making is that Lewis' novels are primarily works of fiction that also involve religious themes, whereas his theological fantasies are books dealing primarily with religious themes in a fictional manner. Thus he includes in the first category Lewis' famous "space trilogy" (*Out of the Silent Planet, Perelandra,* and *That Hideous Strength*), the fragmentary *The Dark Tower,* and *Till We Have Faces*. The trilogy combines many different elements—science fiction, Arthurian legends, the poetic vision of Milton—into a kind of "Christian mythology" that deals with the themes of Providence and redemption in a very imaginative way. The religious themes, especially in the first volume, seemed to elude most reviewers. The trilogy also offered a critique of scientism. *Till We Have Faces* is a modern Christian retelling of the pagan tale of Cupid and Psyche; at the time of publication, it was poorly received but has since been judged by many to be one of Lewis' most profound books.

Throughout the 1920s and 1930s, Ronald Knox produced many fictional works. Some, such as his detective stories, were intended simply to entertain (and pay the bills at the Oxford chaplaincy); others sought to address religious concerns in an informal way. *Other Eyes than Ours* dealt with the fascination for Spiritualism and the occult; it would be interesting to know if Lewis, with his earlier attraction to and later distaste for such phenomena, ever read it. In several books, Knox showed an interest in time travel: *Memories of the Future* (written in 1923 but purporting to be the memoirs of "Opal, Lady Porstock" published in 1988); *Barchester Pilgrimage*, his homage to the novels of Anthony Trollope; and finally, *Let Dons Delight*, considered by many to be one of his most successful efforts (Lewis enjoyed it immensely). In this book, Knox allows us to eavesdrop on conversations in an imaginary Oxford common room at fifty-year intervals from 1588 to 1938. He succeeds in portraying the sweep of English history as it would have been distilled through the informal conversations of academics. He captures not only the issues of the day but the idioms and language of each period. The book is meant to entertain—and it presumes a familiarity with Oxford life that few readers possess today —but its underlying theme is a serious one: the gradual banishment of theology from academic life. Lewis experienced this reality firsthand in the negative reactions of some of his learned colleagues to his religious writings. *Let Dons Delight* was also Knox's valedictory to the Oxford he so loved; soon after its publication, he left the chaplaincy to begin his work of biblical translation. At a farewell celebration, Lewis' friend and fellow Inkling Adam Fox hailed Knox as *fidei antiquae defensor, satirographorum princeps, Academicorum deliciae* (defender of the ancient faith, foremost of satirists, dons' delight).

Theological Fantasies

Hooper places the *Screwtape* books and *The Great Divorce* in this category. Lewis was prompted to write *The Screwtape Letters* after listening to a speech by Hitler on the radio. He was struck by how persuasive evil could be and was inspired to describe evil from the diabolical point of view. It was an immediate success and has remained one of his most popular books; although it is (devilishly?) clever, Lewis claimed that he found it very painful to write, because he had to force himself into such a twisted view of reality. *The Great Divorce* is a Dante-esque tale, with Lewis' friend George MacDonald taking the part of Virgil. Some of the residents of Hell are allowed to take a bus trip to Heaven, but most opt to return whence they came; the story is an extended reflection on Lewis' insight that God does not send anyone to Hell but is bound to respect human free will. In the category of theological fantasy we can also locate Knox's *Sanctions: a Frivolity*, which relates the imaginary conversations at a weekend house party in which the spiritual, intellectual, and moral sanctions for human behavior are debated. Mention might also be made of two short stories: "The Rich Young Man", which identifies that figure in the Gospels with the good thief crucified with Christ; and "The Reprieve", which examines the contradictory horizons of faith and scientism, a theme central to Lewis' space trilogy as well.

Theology

It is in this category that we find the greatest similarities between C. S. Lewis and Ronald Knox. Neither was a professional theologian, but each was well read and wrote to defend and spread the Christian faith on a popular level. From his first apologetical work, *The Problem of Pain*, Lewis sought to express the "common ground" that he discerned among various Christian denominations. This stance was articulated in the title he gave to a book developed from his BBC broadcasts about Christian belief and morality, *Mere Christianity*. He delved more deeply into ethical issues in *The Abolition of Man*, an examination of conflict between natural law and many modern educational philosophies. He also produced a study of a subject that touches many apologetical concerns (including the existence of God, Providence, and the claims of Christ) called *Miracles: A Preliminary Study*. In 1960 Lewis was invited by an Episcopalian studio in the United States to make a series of recordings, and he chose to address the topics subsequently published as *The Four Loves*. Finally, mention should be made of two books of a devotional nature: *Reflections on the Psalms* and *Letters to Malcolm: Chiefly on Prayer*. This handful of books, which present the basic beliefs of Christianity and their impact on our conduct, established Lewis as one of the premier Christian apologists of the twentieth century. Many of these books began life as lectures or radio broadcasts, and their freshness and directness contribute greatly to their appeal.

Although Ronald Knox is remembered primarily as a Catholic apologist, his earliest—and in some ways most significant—religious book was written while he was still an Anglican: *Some Loose Stones*. Its title derives from the work it is critiquing, a manifesto of modern theology called *Foundations*, whose authors were Knox's friends. In *Some Loose Stones*, Knox articulates the fundamental theological vision that he would hold throughout life. It was a vision that led to his conversion and to his subsequent defense of the Christian faith in general and Roman Catholicism in particular. After his conversion, Knox presented his arguments for the claims of Rome in various essays and in his book *The Belief of Catholics*. But many of his apologetical works also dealt with the broader issues of the existence of God and the unique claims of Christ. In a series of letters between him and Arnold Lunn (*Difficulties*), and in engaging the pundits of the 1930s (*Caliban in Grub Street* and *Broadcast Minds*), Knox addressed many of the same issues and adversaries as Lewis. And, just as his fellow apologist reworked radio broadcasts and lectures into books, so Knox offered the fruits of his preaching to a wider audience. Be it by way of conferences to Oxford undergraduates (*In Soft Garments* and *The Hidden Stream*), schoolchildren (*The Mass in Slow Motion*, *The Creed in Slow Motion*, and *The Gospel in Slow Motion*), or newlyweds (*Bridegroom and Bride*), Knox was able to present the truths of the faith with insight, beauty, and humor. Other collections of sermons were produced throughout his lifetime and were posthumously published in two substantial volumes as *Pastoral Sermons of Ronald A. Knox* and *Occasional Sermons of Ronald A. Knox*. Several sets of retreat conferences were brought out during and after his lifetime. Brief reflections published over many years in the *Sunday Times* were assembled in book form as *Stimuli* and *Lightning Meditations*. In conjunction with his work on biblical translation, Knox produced a three-volume commentary on the New Testament. Finally, mention should be made of two extraordinary works: the first, *God and the Atom*, was written in the months immediately following the bombing of Hiroshima. Although Knox generally took his time in writing, this book has a sense of urgency about it and is one of the earliest reflections on the implications of the atomic age for Christian faith. The other work was *Proving God: A New Apologetic*. Here Knox began to revisit the religious questions of his earlier life, and to approach them with renewed vigor and a broader insight. Sadly, he died before making much progress on this enterprise; the fragments were published posthumously by Evelyn Waugh.

Literary Criticism

Although Lewis is associated in the popular mind with his works of fantasy and apologetics, his field of expertise was English literature. In this context he published *A Preface to "Paradise Lost"*, *An Experiment in Criticism*, *The Discarded Image: An Introduction to Medieval and Renaissance Literature*, and what was his magnum opus in this discipline, *English Literature in the Sixteenth Century, Excluding Drama*. This was his contribution to *The Oxford History of English Literature*, to which Lewis enjoyed referring by the abbreviation "O, HEL". He took on the project in the late 1930s, but it was completed only in 1952. Reflecting on the labor involved, Lewis compared himself to a girl agreeing to marry an elderly millionaire: the proposal is most flattering, but then it seems to take forever for the old man to die. Ronald Knox was not a professor of literature, and his interests in this area would be those of a dilettante: he delivered occasional papers on various literary figures, primarily for diversion. (Some of these may be found in *Literary Distractions*.) The work that comes closest to Lewis' contribution to *The Oxford History of English Literature*, in scope at least, is *Enthusiasm: A Chapter in the History of Religion with a Special Reference to the XVII and XVIII Centuries*. As with Lewis, this was a work to which Knox devoted decades of study. But over the years, his views changed: he had set out to produce a warning against the vagaries of "illuminism", but with time, he came to admire some of his subjects. This gave the finished work an uneven quality. Lewis wrote to a friend that it was extraordinary what a bad book it was, but he sympathized with his fellow author, since *Till We Have Faces* was Lewis' own favorite but was generally considered "a complete flop".

Chronicles of Narnia/Translation

As we have seen, there exist several associations among the kinds of books written by Knox and Lewis. There are two exceptions, however: Knox never produced anything like the *Chronicles of Narnia*, and Lewis did not undertake translation work as Knox did. To say that Knox never wrote anything like *Narnia* is no criticism—very few authors ever have. But this does serve to illustrate that, although Knox could be very imaginative in preaching and writing, he had none of the interest in myths and fairy tales that Lewis did;

one imagines that he would be out of his element at a meeting of the Inklings!

An area where Knox did invest his energies was in translation. As a little boy, Jack Lewis created a world of talking animals; Ronnie Knox wrote and translated Latin poems. In adult life, his forays into the world of translation sometimes came in answer to a request: English versions of Latin hymns for the *Westminster Hymnal*; a new translation of the *Manual of Prayers*; a translation of the Holy Week liturgy as a help to the laity; even a translation of Pius XII's encyclical *Humani generis*. Sometimes he translated to assist people's devotion: he had just completed *The Story of a Soul* by Saint Thérèse of Lisieux and was working on *The Imitation of Christ* at the time his final illness befell him. But his greatest effort was his translation of the Vulgate Latin Bible. The project took nine years, and the result was of mixed quality, but it certainly enabled a generation of Catholics to understand and love the Scriptures more deeply.

Index